VL LAWSON

LEARNING TO
BREATHE

LEARNING
TO
BREATHE

Andy Cave

HUTCHINSON
LONDON

First published by Hutchinson in 2005

5 7 9 10 8 6

Hutchinson
The Random House Group Limited
20 Vauxhall Bridge Road, London SW1V 2SA

Random House Australia (Pty) Limited
20 Alfred Street, Milsons Point, Sydney
New South Wales 2061, Australia

Random House New Zealand Limited
18 Poland Road, Glenfield
Auckland 10, New Zealand

Random House (Pty) Limited
Endulini, 5a Jubilee Road
Parktown 2193, South Africa

The Random House Group Limited Reg. No. 954009

www.randomhouse.co.uk

A CIP catalogue record for this book
is available from the British Library

ISBN 0 09 180034 X

Papers used by Random House are natural, recyclable products made from
wood grown in sustainable forests. The manufacturing processes conform to
the environmental regulations of the country of origin

Typeset by Palimpsest Book Production Limited, Polmont, Stirlingshire
Printed and bound in Great Britain by
Clays Ltd, St Ives PLC

For Brigid, Gerry, Kate, Jenny and Arthur

Contents

ASH

Illustrations

Andy during the afternoon storm (© *Brendan Murphy*)
The day after the storm (© *Brendan Murphy*)
Brendan on the fifth day of climbing
Brendan leads the ice tongue during day six
Andy on steep thin ice (© *Brendan Murphy*)
Andy looking jaded on the eighth day
Steve Sustad, Brendan Murphy and Mick Fowler
Andy just below the Shipton Col (© *Mick Fowler*)
Julie-Ann tends to Andy's frostbite (© *Roger Payne/Julie-Ann Clyma*)
Elaine climbing on Fisher Towers, USA
Arthur Cave senior
Andy climbing The Shroud, Ben Nevis (© *John Houlihan*)
Andy on Not To Be Taken Away, Stanage (© *Pete O'Donovan*)

Unless otherwise attributed, all photographs are from the author's collection

Maps

Introduction

From the stygian gloom of a coal mine in South Yorkshire to the sunburst snow-blinding vistas on the summit of a Himalayan peak is quite a journey. Andy Cave made the transition with seemingly effortless ease and has written of the experience with the flair of a born raconteur.

I first met Andy Cave in Islamabad in 1987. A wire-thin man with John Lennon style spectacles, his self-effacing manner and studious air belied the power and determination that had driven him from the pits of Barnsley to play dangerous games on high mountains. I was to discover only later what an extraordinarily talented climber this man was to become. His ready perceptive wit and natural flair as a storyteller quickly endeared him to the rest of the team. Rapidly nicknamed 'Rickets' for his scrawny physique that was daily being ravaged by exploding intestines, he shrugged off the weird and wonderful experience of travelling and eating in Pakistan with nonchalant ease.

We departed for the mountains in a red transit van driven at the speed of Ayrton Senna by a drug-addled Punjabi with the driving skill of a small warthog. Thirty-six hours later, twenty hours overdue, we arrived in Gilgit after one of the most terrifying travelling ordeals I had ever experienced. How we did not die was beyond me. Watching the driver's brother punch him viciously to the ground did little to assuage the frightening memories of the journey up the Karakoram Highway. On the return journey I elected to fly out of Gilgit despite my powerful fear of flying.

It was on the hair-raising journey to Gilgit that Andy told me about the days he had spent working the mines, struggling through the miners' strike and discovering the unalloyed pleasure of fresh air, steep rock and the gymnastic freedom of climbing. Looked upon with frank incomprehension by his friends, he chose to spend many working hours underground reading books in the cramped noisy spaces found beside the rattling mayhem of a coal conveyor belt. I was impressed. It was the sort of gritty life story that film producers would scramble over themselves to acquire. I always thought that they would produce the uneasy nostalgia movies beloved by *Billy Elliot* aficionados and scorned by those who lived such real lives. Andy's descriptions of the miners' strike and work in the pits, told with self-deprecating humour, were far more interesting than the ballet shoes and pickaxe melange served up by film buffs from London.

Andy and John Stevenson went on to make the first ascent of the unclimbed Tupodam and after a wonderful trip bonded by laughing memories Andy set off, penniless as ever, for Nepal and another climbing expedition. His drive and enthusiasm was daunting. I recognised it for the same peculiar illness I had suffered not so many years before. An ailment I embraced passionately, something that defined my life, and something that was eventually to be subdued during some harrowing days in Peru a couple of years earlier. The Tupodam expedition was my first attempt at mountaineering since those days and, despite failing at the high camp owing to a collapsing knee, I had felt the first tremors of excitement about climbing returning to me. I may never again have the passion that coursed through Andy's soul but at least I had not given up on the mountains.

Over the following years, as Andy honed his already formidable climbing skills and amassed an impressive list of extreme ascents, I learned of his attempts to further his education. Applying the same drive and concentration to his studies as he did to his climbing he emerged with a degree and a PhD; not bad for a lad brought up to be groomed for a life in the mining pits of South Yorkshire.

In recent years we had chatted about our life experiences and the subject had come around to writing. Sensing his natural style as a raconteur I felt that Andy should write as soon as possible. He demurred for reasons that I did not question. You cannot be forced to write.

INTRODUCTION

I find it hard to believe how quickly time passes after the death of a friend. I suppose we just get on with life and the years go by swiftly, yet unaccountably in the quiet moments when we recall a lost friend, it always seems as if it had happened yesterday. I remember the shock of seeing Andy after his return from Changabang in 1997. Emaciated and frostbitten, he had the bewildered and glazed look of a man who had spent too much time staring into the abyss. Even in the warmth of a pub in Hathersage, as he quietly explained what had happened I could see that occasional unfocused look drift across his eyes as the telling of the recent tragedy flooded his mind with bitter memories. As always we felt numb, helpless in the face of the stark facts, and irrationally hopeful that maybe we were wrong and the door would crash open and in would stride the smiling tousled-haired man we knew so well. Andy sadly ended that pitiful hope.

There is so much more to Andy than a list of impressive climbs and a stock of hilarious tales to tell. There was always something different in him. He came from a world none of us could imagine yet he lived our lifestyles with casual ease. Somehow he had effortlessly managed to bridge the tough disciplined world of a mining community with the anarchic life of an extreme adventurer. He had the sharp wit and keen intellect that allowed him to see both sides of these disparate worlds and tell tales of each world to his friends on either side of the divide and make them understand where he was coming from and where he intended to go.

When Andy rang to tell me that he was taking the plunge and writing his first book I couldn't have been more delighted and put him in touch with a few contacts who might be able to help him on his way. We talked about his ideas for the book, what he wanted to say and how. I knew at once that he would produce far more than an expedition book recounting one gruelling and ultimately tragic climb. He had stories to weave around that single climb that would tell us so much more than we, his friends, ever knew. Doubtless it will be regarded as the *Billy Elliot* book of mountaineering, but his life and achievements are so much greater than that, and if the association means more people get to read his book then all the better. This is no soft-focused fairy tale of a ballet dancer in a mining town but a delightful, moving and inspiring account of a life lived to the full, embraced for all its contradictions with an exhausting enthusiasm. A tale of split lives fused into one extraordinary story of adventure, laughter, tears and joy.

I had always held Andy in the highest esteem. As the book thumped through the letter box on to the doormat that esteem just notched up even higher. Writing is never easy. Writing well with the clarity of a born storyteller and an unassailable honesty is something few achieve.

Learning to Breathe is, I hope, the first of many superb books to come from Andy Cave's pen, and to my mind as fine an achievement as the many that he has carved out on the rock faces and the mountains of the world. It is a very long way from the dark days crouching beside the coal-laden conveyor belt deep within the pit, reading books by the light of his miners' lamp and dreaming of another bright, clear and beautiful world where he could live his life. Few people have the determination, skill and assured philosophy to make the journey that Andy has embarked upon. This book is another confident stride down the path of life that Andy has chosen to take.

Joe Simpson
March 2005

He drew me up from the desolate pit, out of the miry bog,
And set my feet upon the rock.

Preface

For over 100 years men from my village earned their living from digging coal. In 1982, against the will of my mother, I followed in the footsteps of my father, grandfather and great-grandfather by leaving school and starting work at the Grimethorpe pit, one of the very last recruits in an ever-shrinking national industry. Without realising it, I was one of 'the last of the Mohicans'.

This is the story of a remarkable world, where in return for £25 men spend seven hours and fifteen minutes – often in knee-deep water – in the pitch black, 3,000 feet underground, extracting coal. It is a world full of superstition and ghost stories; a hidden landscape with its own peculiar unchanging lexicon; a world where black humour combats adversity; a world of tall tales. And though it was not an ideal life few other employment opportunities existed locally. So, unsurprisingly, in March 1984 – when the Tory government threatened to close the pits – many miners decided to strike to protect their livelihoods.

The twelve-month strike stretched people – men, women and children – beyond reasonable limits but it also engendered a tremendous feeling of togetherness. What is more, it provided many individuals with time to reflect on their own values and beliefs. Although people had no money, in between picket duty and coal picking on the local spoil heaps, they experienced a certain freedom.

I had started rock climbing the previous year and now, with time on my hands due to the strike, I began climbing obsessively. Ultimately, this passion for climbing led to a more general desire for wanderlust, a desire which conflicted with my sense of being rooted in one place and among a group of people. I often wonder now: without the strike would I have developed such a deep love for the mountains?

This love affair with climbing culminated in an extraordinary expedition to the Himalayas in 1997, attempting to establish one of the hardest climbs ever recorded on one of the steepest and most difficult summits in the world: the North Face of Changabang. I arrived home from this harrowing expedition frostbitten, emotionally fragile and rather less enthusiastic about mountain climbing. I also returned to my studies, having interrupted the first year of my PhD research into language variety and identity among former coalminers to go on this expedition. Aged thirty-one, I now found myself back in the coalmining community I had once been part of. My long absence from the place had given me a fresh perspective on this frail world now in the throes of industrial demise and my own trauma made me see this in a different light. In its turn the dying world of the miner had searching questions about the path I myself had chosen.

Prologue

India, 1 June 1997

Despite the bad visibility, I knew we were approaching the summit of Changabang. For ten days we had battled up this giant shark's tooth of ice and granite, enduring horrific storms and long dark nights as we attempted to sleep suspended from ropes, our buttocks on ledges barely the size of a skateboard. I sensed a lump forming in the back of my throat, slow tears clouding my vision – we were the first people to climb the North Face of one of the most beautiful mountains on earth. 'Don't go any further!' I shouted to Brendan in the mist, framing him in the viewfinder of my tiny camera as he approached the corniced edge of the East Face that fell in one vertiginous swoop 8,000 feet down to the glacier. I joined him and in celebration we hugged each other before kneeling on the snow, totally exhausted, keeping one hand close to an ice axe.

Success on extremely difficult new routes on the steepest Himalayan peaks is never guaranteed. 'I'm really chuffed,' said Brendan in his irritating but loveable understated manner, smiling and showing off his missing front tooth. He passed the water bottle and I took small sips between bouts of breath- lessness: at 23,500 feet the air is thin. We had dreamed of this moment, but thick cloud cruelly denied us a view. 'We could be anywhere; we could be in Scotland,' I commented. 'We could be in the bloody Cairngorms.'

Nanda Devi towered up in front of us as I spoke, the clouds descending beneath our feet, and we stood up respectfully. The sacred mountain, so close I could almost touch her. Next,

Dunagiri rose to the west and, further away still, at the end of the carpet of cloud, sat the bulky pyramid of Kamet. For a moment we hovered, capturing the roof of the world's magnificence. In the back of both our minds was the knowledge that the summit is always only the halfway point; we still had to extricate ourselves from that lofty place.

I had read *The Shining Mountain* twenty years earlier and its incredible story and dramatic images had kept me going while I worked as a coal miner at Grimethorpe Colliery. Brendan probably first read it as a student at Cambridge. Changabang mesmerises all who see it. For over 100 years, the diaries of surveyors and explorers of the Garhwal Indian Himalaya, many of them British, recorded wonderment on first catching sight of the peak. Following the first ascent by Chris Bonington's team in 1974, the mountain became an icon, a stage on which elite mountaineers could test their skill and nerve. Never had I dreamed I would actually be here on the summit. We picked up our axes meaning to start our descent but, for a moment, lingered, suspended in this wonderful kingdom.

Gentle slopes led us down into the gap, known as the 'Horns of Changabang', where two smooth overhanging rock walls curve towards each other. We battled through waist-deep snow to exit via a steep slope before reaching the slightly lower north summit. I peered down the uninviting south-east ridge to our tiny blue tent, perched 2,000 feet below. I felt weary now, unable any longer to suffer the burning hunger pains in the pit of my stomach. Brendan still had a half-eaten breakfast bar stashed away somewhere, I was convinced. Somehow he accepted this lack of food; I, however, was becoming more anxious by the minute. Desperate, I searched the lid of my rucksack and found the last small chocolate biscuit. We shared it, and I let out a groan of ecstasy as I felt every grain melt on my tongue, every morsel of sugar hitting my bloodstream. I made sure no sizeable chunks hid between my teeth. The only food left was in the tent: two small chocolate bars each and one packet of soup with the gas needed to melt snow to boil it, nothing else.

We tied into the ends of the 200-foot rope. I descended first, though going first or second hardly seemed to matter on such a steep, crenellated ridge. One slip and the game was finished.

The unconsolidated nature of the snow made it almost impossible to find a secure place from which to stop and belay. Staring to the left, down the North Face, I felt light-headed. The South Face, although less steep, looked equally menacing, covered as it was in overhanging ice-cliffs and gaping crevasses. If one of us fell, the only plausible solution was for the other instantly to jump down the opposite side of the ridge to create a counter balance, otherwise we would both plummet. The mere thought simply increased the nausea.

Despite having gravity on our side and the occasional footstep remaining from our ascent a few hours earlier, I found the concentration of having to perfectly place each foot mentally exhausting. Our progress was slowing, the long day taking its toll. Place the axes once, then kick the left foot and then the right foot. Axes – left foot, right foot. Axes – left foot, right foot. When the rope came tight, I clawed and stamped my cramponed feet against the mountainside to carve a small platform and then secured myself to a buried ice axe.

'It goes on a bit doesn't it?' said Brendan on arrival.

'Too fucking right,' I muttered through painful, cracked lips.

As he continued down the ridge I leant my forehead against the snow. Suddenly I was jerked from my slumber. A noise? I looked around but nothing, only Brendan climbing steadily down below. Yes, it was definitely voices. I searched the lower part of the ridge. There. I could see something moving! A long way below, a lone figure. So, Mick and Steve had followed us all the way up the North Face after all, despite the atrocious weather.

'Is that you Steve?' I bellowed. 'Steve, is that you?'

'Yes.' Then, after a pause, 'How are you?'

'Good. And you?'

'Fine.'

Overjoyed to see them, I whispered to myself: 'Yes, Yes, Yes.' I knew they had surplus food. Two days ago, I had feared the worst. Brendan had accidentally dislodged two large stones which rocketed 1,000 feet down on to their small bivouac tent as they slept inside it. Miraculously the rocks missed their skulls by inches and they had justifiably hurled up a stream of abuse. I had been convinced that with a badly damaged tent they would have had to retreat. Even with our equipment intact, the continual cascading spindrift had almost destroyed our resolve. Perhaps, like us, they believed that reaching the south-east ridge – although horribly committing – would provide respite from the raging white hell. Unquestionably, Mick and Steve were two of the best, most determined high altitude mountaineers in the world. Maybe they too were hungry for the summit.

Once established in his makeshift bucket seat in the snow, Brendan shouted for me to start down.

'The boys have made it up,' I told him when I arrived, quick of breath.

'Excellent news,' he smiled.

At that moment a curtain of cloud swept in below and blocked our view. Time seemed to slow as we threaded our way down the ridge to the point where I had seen them. But once there, we found only a couple of footprints in the snow. We glanced through the gash in the cornice where they had obviously emerged from the North Face, seeing the trace of their foot-steps on the final slope.

The temperature fell dramatically in the fast fading light and we decided to make our way to the tent, still over an hour away.

Just out of view, over three hundred feet beneath us on the South Face, lay an inseparable frozen heap: our two friends in a tangled and twisted mess of icy ropes, crampons and ice axes.

This passion of mine for climbing upwards – a compulsion for putting one foot in front of the other – had started long ago when, as an inquisitive child, I scrambled up the different sides of the local pit muckstack over and over again. Later, as a teenage coal miner disillusioned with the world of dirt and darkness, I had fallen in love with the game of real mountain climbing. That night, approaching the tent on the knife-edge ridge of Changabang, this love affair with mountain climbing was about to end. The following four days would be the most harrowing of my life.

DUST

'You can become a tramp simply by putting on the right clothes and going to the nearest casual ward, but you can't become a navvy or a coal-miner. You couldn't get a job as a navvy or a coal-miner even if you were equal to the work . . .'

George Orwell, *The Road to Wigan Pier*

1

Sweet sixteen

In the film *Kes*, there is a scene where the employment officer asks Billy Casper what sort of work he wants to do when he leaves school. Billy remains silent and unenthusiastic. Attempting to ignite a spark, the gentleman suggests first office work and then apprenticeships. Billy stares out of the window.

'Well if nothing I've mentioned already appeals to you, and if you can stand a hard day's graft, and you don't mind getting dirty, then there are some good opportunities in mining . . .'

'I'm not goin' down t' pit,' Billy replies abruptly.

'Conditions have improved tremendously,' the man claims.

In a rare moment of self-assuredness Billy silences the employment officer, telling him, 'I wouldn't be seen dead down t' pit.'

In the spring of 1982, aged fifteen, one mile away as the crow flies from where Ken Loach had shot *Kes*, I sat in a careers lesson. Like Billy I had no idea what I wanted to do when I left school. Our short, portly, bespectacled history teacher Mr Taylor (or 'Paddington Bear') addressed the whole class, speaking of how important it was for those pupils not staying on to do 'A' levels to start thinking about their futures beyond the school gates. Periodically pinching his moustache with the thumb and forefinger of his right hand, he explained that, in this final session, he wanted us to choose three occupations in order of preference.

To me, working outdoors in the countryside appealed enormously. During the past few careers lessons I had read about the work of the Forestry Commission. Working in remote parts of Scotland, England and Wales wielding a chain saw, now that would be good fun. The Army had a certain allure too, particularly the Army Air Corps who, I understood, spent a great deal of time flying around in helicopters in exotic over-seas locations. So that was sorted then. Choice number one, 'Forestry Work'. Choice number two, 'The Army Air Corps'. I left choice number three blank until, after some deliberation, I wrote down the word 'Coalmining'.

Unlike Billy Casper I did not baulk at the thought of working down the pit, although mother, sharing Billy's feelings, stated emphatically on a number of occasions: 'No bairn of mine is going down that shit-hole.'

But my mother's hopes for her two sons – my seven-year-old brother Jonathan and me – to have cleaner, saner jobs were held in check by the local economic reality that, in all the villages surrounding Barnsley in South Yorkshire, the pit offered the best money. Despite periodic slumps, this had been the fate of Royston, our village, for over 100 years, and now still almost sixty per cent of local men worked in mining. Our great-grandfather Joe had migrated here from the Black Country in 1902 to start work at the expanding Monckton pit. His two sons Arthur and Albert followed on when school ended, Albert becoming the branch secretary of the NUM. Arthur's son, my father, broke the family tradition of mining by choosing instead to work at the paper mill in Barnsley. But soon enough he succumbed to the money, taking a job as a surface worker at Grimethorpe pit, as the village pit at Monckton had recently closed. In the playground, girls like my thirteen-year-old sister Maria might say that they would never marry a miner because of the dirty, dangerous nature of the job and the unsociable shifts. But the good wages and free coal would make them think again, especially considering their own limited local opportu-nities. Waiting for the careers lesson to end, I chewed my pen and stared out of the second floor window. Beyond the playing fields and the red brick terraces of Strawberry Gardens and Millgate Street stood the skeleton of the old Monckton pit; behind this, out of view, sat the new drift mine. Further still, behind all this and dominating the skyline, was the giant, blue-grey, Monckton muckstack. Our local mountain; the barrier separating us from Ryhill, Cudworth, Shafton and the rest of the world to the south and east.

Later that evening, when my father returned from the

afternoon shift, I told him about the careers lesson. He sat at the table eating his liver and onions which were, as always, surrounded by a ludicrous pile of mashed potatoes. 'Bloody gorgeous that, love,' he shouted to my mother who stood in the kitchen.

I explained that forestry was my first choice, followed by the Army and finally the pit.

'Ar well, just in case nowt else turns up, I've had a word with Frosty and he's put thy name down.'

Mr Frost was the personnel manager at Grimethorpe Colliery, one of the largest coalmines in the area. Having a father who worked at a local pit, who held a good reputation, and who could 'have a word with somebody', was how you got a job in mining. For generations nepotism had ruled supreme and now in April 1982, right in the middle of a national recession, solid family heritage in the industry was at a premium.

Winter slowly turned to spring and as the days grew I waited to hear about job possibilities. I attended an interview for the Army, but was rejected. I believe my school reports put them off: even the 'cannon fodder' infantry appeared reluctant, never mind the elite Army Air Corps. Despite being in the top set at school and occasionally showing potential, apparently I found it 'difficult to concentrate' and could not 'follow simple orders'. No letters arrived from the Forestry Commission either and so when invited by the National Coal Board to attend an interview at Grimethorpe Colliery, I thought it wise to go along. The letter requested that I take along my school reports and so, stuffing them into the pocket of my jacket, I made my first journey down to the pit.

Coal muck got absolutely everywhere in the aptly named village of 'Grimey'. The pavements were covered in a thin layer of damp coal slack so that if you glanced over your shoulder you saw you were leaving a set of tracks, as if walking on wet black sand. And the offices of the personnel manager Mr Frost appeared to be covered by a much finer strain of the same stuff. Every visible item had at least two black thumbprints on it, whether it be a mug, an envelope, a filing cabinet, or an item of clothing.

Mr Frost called me into his office with precious little ceremony.

'What we believe in here, lad, is a fair day's work for a fair day's pay. What do you think of that?'

He had a habit of closing his eyes when speaking to me. As he opened his eyes I replied, 'It sounds alright.'

Slowly shuffling through my school reports, he picked out a couple and began reading. My cheeks burned and my fists tightened. Fidget, fluster. I tried to visualise which particular comments he was reading.

There was one good one:

English
'Andrew possesses a good and lively brain which I intend to extend to the full. Once he exercises some self-discipline he will go far.' Mr R. North

But most were along the lines of the following:

Domestic Science
'Andrew found great difficulty in concentrating at this subject.
    Following quite simple instructions proved out of his range.' Mrs B. Moore

Mathematics
'Andrew has only ever done the minimum amount of work with the minimum amout of effort. He really must make a determined effort to change his attitude, otherwise he will completely waste his ability.' Mr J.P. Lodge

Placing the reports onto the desk in front of him Mr Frost closed his eyes once again and, with his head tilted, to my utter astonishment remarked, 'This is about the right level, this is what we are looking for. Okay, we'll write to you and let you know how you have got on.'

Outside the office, an older man in a nylon suit, holding a flask, stood arguing with the wages staff about his pay note. I walked back up the hill to the bus stop, the winding wheels of number one shaft spinning behind me.

*

At the beginning of the month General Galtieri's troops had raised the Argentinian flag on the Falkland Islands. I had seen something on the news about it, but it seemed far away and unreal. That was until the following Saturday when the manager of the local Co-op supermarket, where I held a part-time job, gave a most peculiar order.

'I want you to check every tin of corned beef and if it's Argentinian get it off the shelf and stack it in the warehouse now.'

As it happened most of the beef was Argentinian. My friend Bill and I stacked it into trolleys before wheeling it out of the shop and into the adjoining warehouse. In there young Mr Jones and his hackney-faced warehouse manager Terry were busy grabbing unopened boxes of corned beef from the shelves and then kicking them repeatedly with such force that the cardboard split, the guilty rhomboid-shaped tins sliding along the concrete floor, clattering finally into the metal, concertina-shaped delivery door.

'You fucking Argie bastards!' the manager called again and again as he struck his toe into yet another box.

This frenzy continued all afternoon, spurred on by reports on the tiny portable radio that British Vulcan bombers were successfully destroying the runway at Port Stanley. Eventually, when each corned beef tin had left the security of its box and had been booted at least once, Mr Jones left the warehouse followed closely by Terry who, over his shoulder, shouted, 'Tidy up all this mess will you!'

Corned beef hash, a local delicacy and a regular weekly meal in our household, all but disappeared. I guess we had somehow to pull together and show our support for the men and women fighting for those islands somewhere down in the South Atlantic.

A few weeks later I came home and found my mother sitting on the edge of the large-winged, red nylon settee, her head in her hands.

'Are you okay, mam?'

'No I'm bloody not.'

'What's up?'

'Read that letter.'

I picked it up thinking it was going to be another letter from the headmaster.

National Coal Board
Barnsley Area
Grimethorpe Colliery

9 APR 1982

Dear Sir,

I am pleased to inform you that subject to you passing the Medical Examination you will be offered employment with the National Coal Board.

You will be informed of the date, time and venue, of the Medical under separate cover.

Yours faithfully,
H H Frost
H.H. Frost
Assistant Manager (Personnel)
Grimethorpe Colliery

'Bastard bleeding pit. After all I've done for you. What a life that's gonna be.'

She sat there, sobbing.

'I nearly threw it on the chuffing fire.'

They were tears of frustration. For almost sixteen years she had nurtured dreams of what I might have been. Like so many other local women she had supported the strikes of 1972 and 1973 and supported all of us, working non-stop in local bars and the sewing factory. She had always vindicated the action of the union and backed the menfolk, proud to be affiliated to the industry. But she also knew that the job was a dead end, dirty and dangerous.

'Why do you think your dad never went down there, eh? Why do you think he works on the pit top?'

When my father came home all he could say, over and over again, was 'I don't know, Jen'. He attempted to console her with, 'I don't know. It's a job, isn't it?'

'It's a job? It's a job? You bloody tell him why you never went down. Go on!'

'Oh for Christ's sake, Jen, give it a rest will you.'

All the small seeds she had planted had failed to germinate: the piano lessons, Latin American and ballroom dancing (four years), the swimming club, the Scouts, singing in the church choir (including the 'Once in Royal David's City' solo at the Midnight Mass). All this and now the pit. But I needed the money. I wanted a motorbike. I wanted to drink. I wanted an adventure and I wanted it now, not tomorrow or the day after.

In the back room of my grandparents' house was a small snooker table and, in friendly rivalry with my dad and granddad, I spent countless evenings on the cloth there that spring after school. The two of them loved telling jokes. My dad brought home fresh material every shift from the pit while my retired granddad Harry retold well polished classics. Now and then my grandma Edith would come and stand at the door, fag in hand, joining in the laughter even though she knew her husband's punch-lines better than he did.

When I told my granddad I had been offered a job at the pit, he said, 'Remember one thing, Andrew love: they give you just enough on a Friday to make sure you swing the hammer on a Monday.' He spoke this in earnest, the furrowed lines on his bald head relaying the seriousness of the proposition. Forty-six years of life down below had ensured that work was never viewed romantically. The little I knew about the underground world of the pit I'd gleaned second hand from my dad or from him directly.

Harry was a gifted story teller with a sharp wit. Despite his love of snooker and horse racing, nothing was more important than 'the fancy'; the breeding and showing of rabbits. That summer he began complaining to my dad that it was becoming too much work and that he didn't know how much longer his legs would carry him up to 'The Warren', as his allotment and shed full of rabbits were known. On one of my visits to The Warren with him that summer we met an old colleague of his opposite the Midland Club, where he had been an active member as well as the secretary of the rabbit club. It appeared he knew everybody, greeting them as we walked. Outside 'The Bush' Working Men's Club we stopped again, my granddad needing to get his breath back. The old pram was stacked high with straw and rabbit feed. We stood in the mid-morning sun and met yet another man. They spoke of jockeys, stables, and the amount of weight being carried by horses. Like so many older local men the man walked very slowly with the aid of a stick. His chest whirred like a dynamo when he breathed. As we departed the man turned away to clear his chest, leaning over his stick. It sounded like something was stuck there, as if this retching might dislodge a painful object embedded deep in his lungs. Locally, people called it dust on the chest.

Over the years The Warren had been repaired and fortified externally with a vast array of materials, including a couple of blue, rusting-tin advertisement plates. I loved this shed. I loved the old clock ticking in the half light. The forty hutches covering the full length of the left wall now began to rustle. Although all the rabbits looked fine to me, apparently some had shoulders that were too narrow, others had pointed ears or fur that was too soft or too woolly. These specimens were denied the long train journeys, the bright lights and podiums of the regional and national Fancy competitions. These second-class citizens might be sold as pets or, very occasionally, in the worst case scenario, given to my mother for stewing (though Harry never ate rabbit himself).

'Right, shall we tidy up a bit, Andrew?'

The acidic stench of the urine-soaked straw and newspaper on the floor of the hutches brought tears to my eyes whilst mucking out. Also, picking up a rabbit by the scruff of the neck as it resolutely guarded its ground still made me nervous. When we had finished we took a minute. I slumped on the sacks of rabbit meal at the very end of the shed. That was the time he told me about the hustler.

Before the introduction of the day wage, miners worked in teams each with a senior figure known as a buttyman. At the end of each week many local men congregated at The Ship Hotel or the Ring O' Bells to share up the money. Often they would use the first shilling to buy a jug of ale for the whole team. Some men used to put the money earned from the first tub of coal cut each week to one side, saving it for Christmas: 'the Christmas tub'. Afterwards, some would go to a 'tossing school', normally the fields by the canal bridge at the bottom of Monckton Hill where tossing coins, heads or tails, a man could double or lose his wage on the way home. In Royston, the police regularly raided these gatherings, trying to disperse the clusters of men. On Friday afternoons after sharing up, my granddad and his cronies preferred to play cards in the privacy of The Warren. One day a stranger from outside the district appeared at The Warren and politely asked if he could join them for a game. 'No problem old boy,' they told him. Playing for pennies the newcomer lost initially. But, as time passed, he began consistently to win.

'Well, do you know, he took every penny off us, Andrew, every single penny. He was a hustling fellow this one, he was like a professional.'

We both started laughing. With hindsight, the hustler's wicked way did not anger him but made him laugh more and more with the passing of each year and a new telling of the tale.

He had more serious stories, though. A story I learnt second hand via my father is etched into my mind. He started work in 'the pick, hammer and shovel days' long before the intro-duction of hydraulic roof supports and high-speed coal cutting machines and, like many others, he moved from pit to pit searching for better wages. For a while he worked at Carlton Long Row Pit, a mile outside Royston in the eighteen-inch Haighmoor seam. With such broad and powerful shoulders I found it hard to imagine how he swung a pick-axe in such a confined space.

One morning like any other he set off for the pit head. Had he seen a woman on the way, he would have turned straight around and gone home – Royston miners believed it was bad luck to meet a woman on your way to start the day shift. Spiritualists, like Little Joey from Meadow Road, could some-times predict disaster. But he had issued no warnings. Men smoked a final cigarette before the ride down the cage.

After taking their tools from the lock-up boxes in the gate at the end of the face, the men got on their haunches and then crawled into their stalls. Often they left some clothes behind in the gate as getting the coal was desperately hot work and it was nice to have some dry clothes to walk out in, otherwise you could catch your death in the draughty pit bottom waiting for the cage at the end of the shift. They carried the normal luxuries: snap (normally bread and jam or bread-and-dripping sandwiches), chewing bacca and a round tin or a quart glass-bottle filled with water, called a 'Dudley', for drinking.

Harry and his team worked steadily away. Hanging behind

them, they had a safety oil lamp, the small blue flame sensitive to changes in the level of methane gas. As one man lay on his side wielding the pick the other rested, crouched down behind where the roof was a little higher, shovelling the coal up into the tub. The air was heavy with moisture and the men sweated profusely.

Wedged tightly against the rock-hard roof, the wooden props began to sing a little. Harry and his men could normally translate every groan muttered by a prop. A man in the adjacent stall listened to the voice of the timber. He scurried around from prop to prop before deciding everything was okay, urging them to carry on working. Some of the men took the opportunity of a quick slurp from their Dudleys. The men now relaxed back into their rhythmic strokes of pick-and-shovel movement. A certain amount of banter followed, signalling relief. But they had misunderstood the noise.

Less than five minutes later a crack ripped down the full length of the face. Immediately the roof lowered down on them. They shouted in blind panic, crawling like frightened mice to the gate end, each man's knees lifting dust so that they crawled through black-velvet air, choking. Before the first man reached the gate the props were driven down into the soft floor, like a giant standing on the candles of a child's birthday cake. Time stood still, a dozen or so men continuing to crawl for their lives. Reaching the end of the gate, Harry could hear bricks and timber being crushed behind him. Next the roof squashed steel tubs, then chewed Dudleys and lamps. Finally, watches and clothes were flattened as the jaws of the roof and the floor locked tight.

Run. Run. Down the gate, crashing through the first set of airdoors, the red and white of their eyes burning terror in the blackness. Then to the cold pit bottom, screaming at the banksman to send down that goddamn cage now! Get us out of this bloody hell hole! Then, one by one, the cage lifted them earthward.

Years later, Granddad would continue to describe that incident to my father as the most terrifying episode of his forty-six years as a coal miner.

As I grew up I learned that this granddad, sitting now with his rabbits and me in the candlelight, was actually a step-granddad.

There had been another. He had died two months before my father entered this world. Perhaps this explained why my father had never worked underground himself. His father had been taken by the pit in a tragic accident.

The following month, just before my sixteenth birthday, I travelled by bus to Manvers Main for the NCB medical examination, the final part of which involved taking an X-ray of my chest to ensure that my lungs were clean, healthy and in good working order.

'I want you to take a deep, deep breath for me, please, then hold it,' the man instructed. I filled my lungs to bursting point, sticking out my chest and holding my cheeks. The radiologist, hiding behind a lead screen, snapped his finger tight on the control button causing the machine to *clunk*. This X-ray was my passport to a new world, a world that no amount of anecdotes could prepare a boy for.

2

Metamorphosis

Risk-taking featured in my everyday life, long before I had been introduced to the game of climbing rocks and mountains. I craved uncertainty, feared predictability and found grown-ups to be far too serious on the whole. Although branded for being childish, my friends and I adored irritating this world, poking fun at its earnestness. Placing stink bombs in busy supermarkets made my friend Nigel and me hurt with laughter, and the joy of jumping over the hedgerows of an entire street at night was simply too exhilarating a sport to quit. Perhaps our *pièce de resistance*, normally only performed on Mischievous Night, was to place a paper bag full of dogshit on to someone's front doorstep, set it on fire, and then knock on the door before running and hiding to watch people – from a safe distance – open the door and start stamping out the flames with their carpet slippers. Despite a number of death threats and countless calls to 'grow up', I found it impossible to let go of play.

My lack of facial hair was why, unlike some of my friends, I was refused alcohol in every nearby pub and club (or so I was convinced). Perhaps it also accounted, along with the immature attitude I had towards life generally, and my diminutive, puny frame, for my distinct lack of attention from any girls. Barring a widespread flu epidemic debilitating the regulars, I rarely represented the school in any sporting events. I never progressed beyond the subs bench in the football team and, even with a poor turn-out, my chances were limited at most to ten-minute bursts towards the end of the match. How could girls take me seriously? To cap it all I possessed neither of the two most potent local symbols of adolescent male identity: the air rifle and the motorcycle.

'I'm not having people knocking on my door telling me you've blinded somebody,' my mother explained when I begged her to buy me a gun.

And what about a motorbike?

'I'm quite happy with you killing yourself, but I'm not living with the guilt. If you want one, buy it yourself.'

Despite constant nagging, tears and lengthy, well planned but frustrated arguments, all such aspirations to street credibility were vetoed by my mother, the final arbitrator in all important social or domestic decisions. Procuring a Black Widow catapult did enhance my reputation temporarily. But unfortunately, ownership of the much-coveted beast ended rather abruptly and, to my dismay, before I had managed to kill any wildlife worthy of my peers' attention – though undoubtedly the local glazier had been kept much busier than normal. Sadly, one Monday morning my mother's keen eye had spotted an article in the *Daily Mirror* which recounted how a young boy up north had committed untold damage to the heads and torsos of innocent people who were out shopping or waiting at bus-stops. After telephoning the police for advice and checking that my machine did indeed match the lethal weapon used by the boy in the tabloid article, she cut it to pieces, battered it with a hammer and then threw it into the dustbin before I arrived home from school.

Being in the Boy Scouts did not help my image either. However, the belief that being in the Scouts meant only conformity, cooking sausages and church day parades was well wide of the mark, certainly in our particular troop. Our leader, whom we occasionally called 'Skip', was a giant man with a gentle, easy-going temperament which one delinquent boy, named Mick, noticed and duly exploited. One of Mick's favourite pastimes involved seeing how much loose change he could insert into the end of his foreskin. During one of the weekly 'Grand Owl' ceremonies, as the Union Jack was being raised and with a totally serious countenance, Mick joined us in the three-fingered salute and chanted the chorus, 'Skip, we will do our best', his above-average-sized member hanging out of his trousers limply, full of copper and silver. What's more, he had managed the fifty pence piece, allegedly the real litmus test of early manhood. Mick's antics bore more resemblance to some ancient African tribal rite of passage than anything Lord Baden-Powell had envisaged.

Perhaps more worrying, though, was the boy's erratic behaviour and his almost pathological hatred of Skip and his authority. This led to Mick once successfully persuading all of us to climb into the attic of the Scout hut in the middle of that frosty, moonlit night, carrying a collection of carving knives from the kitchen. Earlier, we had accomplished a fun, relatively incident-free, twelve-mile midnight-hike to Bretton Hall and back. Skip slept soundly in his sleeping bag in the centre of the lino-floored room, snoring. Mick explained that the object of the exercise was to cut holes in the polystyrene ceiling then, using our torches, locate him (without disturbing him) and triumphantly launch our knives straight down.

'The knife closest to his head is the winner,' Mick clarified.

Suppressing our giggles, we each dropped our knives in turn and they stabbed here and there at various points a few yards from Skip's body. Everybody except Mick.

Suddenly, his behaviour switched towards psychopath mode. He crept along the rafters until convinced he was standing directly above our sleeping leader. After cutting a new hole in the ceiling he shone his torch downward, gazing malignantly. A hushed silence swept through the loft. We held our breaths. He let the kitchen knife fall like an arrow, directly down towards Skip's skull. *Twang.* It struck the lino, but Skip slept on undisturbed, the blade quivering six inches from his right ear.

A couple of weeks after our midnight-hike, bored of tolerating his wild behaviour, Skip banned Mick for life. For a week or two he continued to show up and, seemingly frustrated at being denied access, repeatedly ran up the steps, smashing his powerful shoulders into the locked door whilst screaming insults. Although we missed the fun of witnessing his antics most people, I think, were relieved he had gone.

The fact that I had been a choirboy for many years further undercut any local illusions of my male grandeur. However, perhaps the real nail was placed in my coffin when someone spotted me entering the Tassels Dancing School, and years of weekly clandestine ballroom and Latin American dancing lessons finally became public knowledge. How the hell would a specimen like me survive in the macho world of coal mining? Surely I had something to offer?

On the positive side, I had an acid wit and could dilute, upend or match almost any quip, gibe or other verbal punch; admittedly, learning to restrain my retaliatory banter was something I needed to work on. I also owned a nerve the envy of many, and climbing most of the notable trees in the village soon earned me the proud reputation of being a dare-devil. Indeed, one of my earliest climbing experiences had partly led to the first visit to the house by the police a few months earlier. Whilst I was climbing the electricity pylon down by the scrap yard to check on a kestrels' nest, my neighbour Ado and his accomplices decided to shoot at me with their air rifles. The first few rounds of lead missed the pylon completely, but subsequent shots began ricocheting around, spaghetti-western style, bouncing immediately below my feet and just above my fingers as I climbed higher up the grey, steel frame. Finally, the lead struck and I was instantly airborne, my foot in agony. I landed in the long grass, disgruntled but relatively unhurt, save for a severely bruised and tender foot. A passer-by, witnessing our shenanigans, must have forwarded our names and addresses to the police because later that afternoon they visited the house and reprimanded my parents for failing to take control of their thrill-seeking son. My mother quizzed me once the police had left: why couldn't I behave normally like my sister Maria and my younger brother Jonny?

'You imbecile!' yelled my father, banishing me to my room.

Fortunately, a few weeks before my sixteenth birthday, a breakthrough finally came. Darker-coloured hairs slowly began sprouting along my top lip. An increased trickle of testosterone must have caused this momentous event. With renewed vigour I tried once again to get served alcohol, but without success. My best friends Bill and Swet had been getting served for months by now, and the pressure was on.

'Let's try the Shakespeare,' they suggested one Monday evening as we left Rebecca's, the town's under-eighteens disco.

As we approached the door I hyperventilated, adrenalin surging madly through my veins. By now I had been in enough pubs to know how it worked. Nevertheless, the task loomed larger and larger as, trying to appear cool, I approached the elderly landlord.

'What can I do for you, son?'

'Three pints of bitter please Mister.'

'How old are you?'

'Eighteen.' Internally I chanted my alibi over and over, *the first of May nineteen-sixty-four, first of May nineteen-sixty-four.*

'You don't look eighteen.'

I waited, wanting him to ask me my date of birth, but he didn't. Attempting to fill the awkward silence, I started, 'That's because, you see, I'm the youngest in my class.'

At this point the others, standing directly behind me, began to despair. What the hell was I going on about? Youngest in the class?

'I see,' replied the landlord.

'You know, I think my great-granddad used to come in this pub a lot,' I said, going off on a rescue bid, playing the wild card.

'What's his name, son?'

'Well, he used to sing and that. Everybody knew him as "Non-Stop Walter".'

A smile spread across the old landlord's face and his shoulders dropped, ever so slightly.

'Non-Stop Walter! Well bloody hell. And that's thy granddad?'

'Yes.'

He raised a glass under the tap and started pouring the beer. 'Did you hear that, love? This lad's related to Non-Stop Walter.'

'He used to sell newspapers in the bus station an' all,' I commented in the excitement of the moment.

Leaning against the bar, idly smoking, the landlord's wife looked uninterested; perhaps she was too young to remember the days when my great-grandfather had regularly performed his satirical monologues in the town's pubs. It was with the aid of these aristocratic connections and perhaps the landlord's visual impairment that, during that brief moment in the smoke-filled tap room of the Shakespeare, I went from being a tiny fifteen-year-old to feeling like a grown-up. Certainly it had little to do with my weedy, wispy-haired upper lip.

Clutching the three glasses as if the manoeuvre was old-hat, I carried the drinks over to the table, allowing my chest to swell a little with pride. Bill and Swet, who were already sat down, looked bemused.

'And who the fuck is Non-Stop Walter when he's at home?' Bill whispered, incredulous.

Not too far away, the landlord listened in on my fuller description of the legend's antics. The origin of the nickname had sprung from his days of performing. Allegedly, he worked in return for free alcohol and rumour had it that throughout his career as a showman he never once refused a drink; he literally drank non-stop. After returning from the Great War, he and my great-grandmother, Norah, opened a beer off-shop on Smithies Lane, down below the town hall. Unfortunately, endless lock-in style binges with his pals brought the business to its knees, and inside of three months they were forced to move on. Had Walter still been alive I am sure he would have relished the fact that his reputation had got me my very first pint.

Although riding pillion on my friends' bikes gave me a thrill, I desperately longed for my own machine. The majority of the unhelmeted, off-road tearaways racing up our street to the railway bridge – the gateway to the fields and the stack – sat on mopeds, aka 'plastic pigs', which were revved to screaming pitch. Frequently, a 'pig' was acquired gratis or at a bargain price from an older relative. Very occasionally, a youngster from a wealthy family would show up on a brand new motocross or trials bike, which would make everyone from our estate sycophantic and sick with envy. Perhaps one day, we felt, if my dad will win the pools. As a matter of fact, things were looking up generally for me. By the end of May, I calculated that I had saved up enough money from my job at the Co-op to purchase my first motorcycle from one of the Jones Mafia. Now I was sixteen and a Honda CD175 made its appearance behind our coalhouse, paid for by my own cash.

The final few weeks of school bored me now more than ever, as I longed to get home and ride my bike around the muckstack. My form teacher told me that I would never get a job.

'I've already got a job actually,' I retorted.

Though I showed up, the school exams were a gross inconvenience to me. I was already saving for my next motorbike, doing as many hours as possible at the Co-op and waiting eagerly to start work at the pit. On hearing the bell on the final day of school, I ran out of the place, utterly delighted with my release from internment.

The alarm sounded at 4:30am that late September Monday morning. I crept around the bedroom getting dressed, trying not to disturb my brother Jonathan who slept in the bed opposite. I could not wait to experience the new challenge of work at the pit as well as the financial independence it would bring. I felt anxious, though, about entering a world where I knew virtually no one; my school friends who had gone into mining were working at Royston Drift, Woolley or South Kirby pit. Though I had disliked school, at least I had known everyone and how to conduct myself.

I picked up the towel and snap bag left out for me by my mother and stepped into the dark. The amber street lamps threw halos into the mist and the rotten-egg stench of sulphur from the coking-plant up on the hill hung in the back of my throat. Lone shapes moved in the grey and orange nightlight, hands in jacket pockets, giving monosyllabic acknowledgements or nods as our paths crossed. The change of turning left at the end of the street for the pit bus, instead of right for the school bus, brought a certain novelty, like the start of a tale untold.

At the pit bus-stop, a work colleague of my father's, Joe Silverwood, waited. He was a large-boned man, balding, with round glasses on a round face. Although in his late forties, he still lived with his mother in the Lilacs, a row of terraces down by the canal. He nodded. Then, in a ritual that would continue to puzzle me for some time, he announced: 'She's here', indicating that the pit paddy would be arriving shortly.

I saw and heard nothing. Yet he was right. A minute later the paddy appeared around the corner, its wheels sticking to the tacky glistening road where the fog had condensed. Though I never fathomed the theory in his method, he was always right.

The paddy was warm, unlit and relatively empty, with men choosing to sit at least two rows apart. It was far too early for small talk. I headed towards the back, throwing my snap and towel onto the seat. The windows were filthy on the outside and, on the inside, a few of the men enjoyed a smoke;

a brief pleasure before going down. Apart from when departing on the annual family summer holiday, I had never seen the world at this hour before.

I struggled to keep my eyes open as we passed the old Monckton pit and Royston Drift Mine before journeying towards Featherstone, through Ryhill, Cold Hiendley, and Shafton, travelling over a landscape gentle enough to me but, to other men on the bus, a land riddled with invisible shafts and tunnels, a perpetual geological battleground. This was a country heavy with mining history. Unknown to me, many of these dimly lit villages emerging out of the night had been social and political battlegrounds at some point during the previous 100 years: the soup kitchens in Royston where little Jonny Griffiths sang his song, 'Free breakfast in Royston and nothing to pay', during the 1926 strike; the 'Kinsley Evictions', where men, women and children were literally dragged out of their homes by police under instruction of the colliery owners, and their modest possessions thrown into the streets, during the 1921 lockout; the 'Featherstone massacre', where two innocent striking miners were shot dead and sixteen wounded by government troops in September 1893. These and so many other details never arose in our history lessons at school; they were things you learnt of only if you searched for them, ferreting in the unpublished manuscripts of the local studies section of the library, or if your grandparents remembered to tell you. From Emile Zola to D.H. Lawrence, it was as if the effect of extracting coal in return for one's wages always caused so much more than a mere geological tension. Those with the capital lost touch with the common folk, wrapped, as they often were, in aspirations of a higher domain. That morning, my first day at work, no one perceived that the coal mining community's biggest chapter of political and social struggle was just around the corner.

The bus paused just before the Grimethorpe Hotel and swung right, passing rows of red-bricked terraces that virtually stood in the pit car park. We stopped outside the 'time' office and pit-head baths where reputedly, during the course of a weekday, more than one thousand men would get ready for work and then shower at the end of the shift. Over the top of a wall, made from white concrete slabs, a row of pigeon lofts and allotment sheds curled out of view towards the muckstack. Jets of steam hissed from the rusting joints of iron pipes that ran the length of the baths, creating small, light-coloured clouds in the murky morning light. I took a deep breath and entered the building, feeling awkwardly self-conscious and imagining everyone to be staring at me, the new boy.

Eventually I found my card, clocked on for the first time, and then searched for my locker. Row upon row of tall, two-storey, slender steel wardrobes. I found my aisle, squeezed past a couple of naked middle-aged men, and opened my locker. In the next aisle a voice pierced the morning silence.

'Now then old git, how tha going on?'

'Alright love.'

'Has tha backed any winners?'

'Have I hell as like. Might as well have backed a bloody pit pony.'

I took my time stripping off, hoping that the aisle would clear before I arrived at my underpants, but the man next to me appeared in no rush, methodically placing a single ciga-rette and then a match on the narrow bench that ran the length of the aisle between the top and bottom lockers. The pink head of the match sat vibrantly against the silver-grey steel as he folded up his jeans and jumper. Clutching a towel and bar of soap in his left hand, he picked up the smoking materials in the other and set off through the showers to the 'dirty side'. A minute later I followed. A young man hosing down the showers seemed in danger of spraying a few of us as we passed.

'Shift out of the way you useless twat,' said one man, smiling.

'Does tha want an early bath?' the boy grinned, with the hose in his hand.

'I'll give thee summat if tha doesn't fuck off with that thing.'

The boy turned his hose away, laughing as we passed.

On the dirty side I started to dress, dreadfully embarrassed at the clean, unused look and feel of the work clothing I had been given. Indeed, the only thing I felt comfortable in were my football socks; everything else was NCB issue. The grey, size 'small' cotton Y-fronts were hilarious. I could have pulled them up to my armpits; the matching vest hung around my neck like a bedsheet on a broomhandle. Walking in the baggy, bright orange overalls felt like running the sack-race at a primary school sports day. I rolled up the material that flowed over the top of the spotless, shiny, steel-toe-capped boots, so as not to trip, then picked up my snap bag and made my way to the training officers' building, turning left up a small hill opposite the lamp room.

Essentially I was still a schoolboy and that morning I felt like one, moving awkwardly as if stepping out from the changing room of a fancy dress shop. Approaching the building I took some comfort from the fact that every other boy looked as ridiculous as I did, the bright yellow helmets clearly indicating our status as lowly trainees. I counted eight initially; a few more arrived shortly after six o'clock. Charlie Lyle, the rotund training officer, sat in casual clothing, his fingers interlocked on the desk in front of him. He looked extremely relaxed, breathing long, deep breaths through his nose and sounding like some Indian yoga guru, particularly as he exhaled.

Then, from nowhere, he stared at me and asked, 'And what do they call you?'

'Andy Cave.'

'Andy Cave? What do they call your dad?'

'Arthur, he's a foreman over on t' washer.'

'Oh aye, I know Arthur, yes.'

He continued his questioning of each trainee's kinship ties, as if trying to establish our starting positions in the hierarchical world of mining. His tall, slightly built assistant obviously knew a handful of the Grimey lads, firing off a series of one-liners that had everybody smiling. During the next few weeks I would learn that boys from Grimey, especially those whose fathers worked on the coalface, laid claim to a somewhat hefty status, carrying an air of superiority.

My vocabulary increased dramatically during that first day's work on the stockyard. The main task appeared to be responding to requests for peculiar-sounding materials by teams of men underground. We loaded huge steel tubs by hand with chockblocks, tie-bars or stone dust and flat-bedded trams with split-bars, tin sheets or wooden props. Rings and disc-shearer parts were loaded by two young, pleasantly mad forklift drivers, Tarny and Goughy, or an older, sterner-looking crane driver named Albert. The newness of the clothing soon disappeared with the dirty and strenuous work. The tie-bars were exactly one metre long, made from tubular mild steel, and the boy loading us up developed a ploy of giving us more and more each time we returned from the tub. The same happened with the chockblocks. It was a game, each young man sizing up the other, constantly searching for weaknesses which would lead to teasing.

Once the tubs or mine-cars were loaded, one of the gaffers would chalk a series of letters and numbers on the side, such as RO5s or T11s, which, although it meant nothing to us, indicated the materials' ultimate destinations underground. The exciting part of the job involved pushing the tubs, now weighing more than a ton, down the inclined narrow-gauge rail track towards the shaft. Often, getting them started was hellish. Two or three of us gathered behind a tub and pushed, as if bump-starting a car on the brow of a hill. However, at the bottom of this hill was the entrance to the black-holed shaft that disappeared for 3,000 vertical feet down into the bowels of the earth.

Despite the catches and gates in place to prevent any runaway tubs going over the edge, we had to run alongside them and control their speeds by 'scotching', a technique requiring nerves of steel. A scotch is a piece of wood shaped like a stout wedge of cheese, roughly ten inches high and six inches wide, tilted onto its side with a four-inch handle. The exercise involves placing the thin end of the scotch under the front wheel of the careering, runaway tub and attempting to stop it. It is much easier said than done. Older boys, who had now been working on the yard for almost a year, made life difficult for the new lads by ensuring that tubs had reached maximum velocity before they were scotched. I dreaded attempting the manoeuvre: countless tales of boys losing their hands during scotching mishaps did little for my confidence. I ran alongside the tub, the scotch in my left hand, before I thrust the thing towards the wheel and let go. The front wheel of the tub simply leapt over the scotch, the second wheel repulsing the wooden wedge altogether, and the tub smashed into the lower line of stationary tubs. The onsetter – the man responsible for getting the tubs onto the cage and then down the mine safely – leapt out of his cabin and bellowed at me. This delighted the boys up above on the yard and they jeered relentlessly until my cheeks burned crimson and Tommo ran down, cupping his hands close to my face as if warming them from the glow and laughing devilishly. I quickly realised that the main exercise in life here was to ridicule people and try to break them, work being to a large degree a distraction from the fun.

Midway through the eight-hour shift we retreated to the cabin for our snap. Eating my sandwiches I listened to a boy nicknamed Fox describe the accident recently suffered by one of the pit-top bosses. While he was working on the coalface, a tiny hole had appeared in a nearby chockpipe delivering power to the steel hydraulic roof supports. Apparently the pressure of this fluid is so powerful that if a pipe splits and hits you in the face it can blind you. In fact, the fluid that hit him entered his anus, savaging his intestines to such an extent that he now 'shits in a bag'. I had never heard of anyone shitting in a bag before and my mind ran riot trying to visualise what it meant. Although people like him could no longer work underground, the pit found a role for him; it had a way of looking after its less-able victims. He showed no bitterness towards the world of coal mining, certainly not in public; he just accepted fate and got on with life.

Although the majority of the new starters came from Grimey, a number lived in Lundwood, Shafton and Cudworth. Lundwood, like Grimey, had a reputation, with certain streets or estates being frequently likened to the Bronx in New York or the Gorbals in Glasgow. Whilst this was an exaggeration, as one man explained, 'In Royston you probably have eight or ten people who are really good at knuckling out of say a hundred, but in places like South Kirby, Grimey or Lundwood there are fucking loads of them that are excellent at it.' For me this generalisation gained substantive evidence over the next few weeks, as my work colleagues showed up on Monday mornings with bent, swollen noses and black eyes, boastfully recounting tales of brawling over the weekend at the Brierly disco or The Lundwood Hotel. Amorous tales were regaled too but they were often regarded as a poor alternative to fighting stories – these were the ones people really enjoyed. Even the gentle, mild-mannered Phil from Grimey seemed partial to a little of the Saturday night madness. Although not particularly experienced in fighting and with no desire to get involved in these riotous affairs, I had acquired a taste for alcohol following my recent success in the Shakespeare and accepted the invitation of a night out with my new friends. That Friday evening we finished work at 8 pm, showered, then went straight up to the Grimethorpe Hotel directly opposite the entrance to the pit. Inside I noticed they had a pool table and, fancying a game, I placed some money into the machine. By the end of our first game the pub began to fill up and so I placed a line of ten-pence pieces on the table, securing a few more games. A small, hard-faced man wearing a tight-fitting denim jacket came into the room, glanced at the money on the table and then stared at me intently, his jaws tightening.

'What is it, a fucking family do?'

Clearly unimpressed with my selfish attempts to monopolise the table, the man stood still, glaring, inferring that something quite dramatic was about to occur.

'No I just . . .'

'Don't *just* me, I'm on next.'

As he said this, he turned his index finger towards himself and began stabbing his chest forcefully, just in case I hadn't fully understood his command.

So this is a straight-talking kinda town, I noted mentally.

The Lundwood Hotel was a short bus ride away and by the time we arrived there the disco was already kicking. Four or five pints into the evening I had lost my local companions, John and Gerald. The intimidation I had felt earlier at being on unfamiliar ground, knowing hardly anyone, now subsided as I drifted into an alcoholic haze. I found myself on the dance floor, strutting and spinning to 'Come on Eileen' opposite a pretty girl, her back to the two rows of pulsating, coloured light bulbs.

Three tracks later, still dancing, I became gripped by a wave of fear. A row of stern-faced men gazed fixedly on to the dance-floor and I realised that I was the only male dancing. I panicked and made a swift exit. Staggering through the crowd, I accidentally nudged one man, causing him to spill some of his drink. I apologised profusely and then continued, heading towards the toilets, feeling relieved to have made a break from the main mass of people. Then, without warning, a large powerful hand suddenly gripped my windpipe from behind. I twisted around, staring up at a stranger. He was older and much bigger than me and as he drew on his cigarette the end glowed, brighter and brighter. His eyes sat uncomfortably close together, hawk-like. Well, I guess this is it, I pondered. The man is gunna do me for dancing with the redhead. Bloody marvellous! First night in Lundwood and you're in the thick of it, Cave. How foolish, how regrettably foolish. Without relinquishing the grip of his talons he began slowly exhaling smoke into my face and then made a peculiar request.

'What size shoes have you got on?'

It took me a while to respond, slightly confused. He stared at the shoes and I managed to glance down too despite his vulture-like death grip. The shoes were dark red leather with horizontal stitching. I had bought them from my mother's catalogue just last month, at £1.65 a week for ten weeks. Jesus, I thought, if he wants them he can have them, right now. Just take them if you want.

'I say are tha listening to me?'

I nodded in agreement.

'What size are thy shoes?'

'Nine,' I croaked through closed teeth.

'Speak up will tha it's noisy in here, I can't hear thee.'

'Size nine.'

'Well,' he said, taking one final draw on the cigarette before throwing it to the ground. 'Stamp that fucker out.'

I stamped as hard as I could with my right foot, like the final movement of a chicken having its neck rung. Once I had successfully extinguished the cigarette, the man released his grip and, laughing insanely, disappeared through the crowd towards the bar. I thought it best to escape while the opportunity still remained. I had seen enough of Grimethorpe and Lundwood for one night. In future I would respect regional reputations and drink elsewhere.

As winter shortened the days, the temperatures fell and filling the mine cars left our gloved hands numb. When snow fell at the stockyard we tied hessian sacks around our legs in an attempt to keep warm. We tried to extend our snap-time in the cabin or, better still, up in the canteen, but Clarry – one of the foremen – would come and find us and rollock us. At times like this we longed to be working underground where, allegedly, outside of the pit bottom, temperatures remained high the year round. Someone had heard news, though, that we would not be called underground for at least another four months. The kudos plus the increased pay for underground work meant that most of us relished the thought of it. Many of the older people on the yard worked there because they had either suffered an accident underground that had left them with a serious injury or failed the medical somehow. A few other men I heard of had found the underground environment terrifying. One Grimethorpe man was apparently so trauma-tised by the experience of working just one shift down below that he still suffered anxiety attacks and had been prescribed tranquillisers.

Over the weeks a considerable amount of chit-chat among the local boys attempted to establish who held the much coveted title of 'hardest bloke' currently working on the stockyard. For a good many of them, this was the most important thing in their lives. Until Christmas a small, friendly man named Col – who had just been released from prison after serving a sentence for a number of serious (but undisclosed) crimes – worked with us. For a while the questions about who was indeed the hardest died down. Here, it was whispered, was the genuine article: a man who clearly had nothing to prove. However, being slightly older than the rest of us meant that he began working under-ground sooner, and his departure created a brief instability in the hierarchy of hardness, though my own lowly position remained relatively unaffected. Most argued that Vince, a man who was reputed to be a 'crazy mother-fucker', was the only real contender. The duties that went with wearing the mantle of hardest man of the stockyard always appeared rather fuzzy to me. But soon I was about to learn at first hand. On the afternoon shift we were left to our own devices and generally as long as the work was accomplished Ray, the gaffer, turned a blind eye to us retreating to our cabin for extra tea breaks. There, Vince was hell-bent on us serving him portions of our snap every single day, and this is where the problem arose. No matter how great the threat of violence, the thought of giving this chap even half a sandwich filled me with horror. After failing to deliver four days on the trot, with some trepidation I entered the cabin for my snap. He asked the young men in turn what they had to give him and, to my surprise, cigarettes, cans of pop and sandwiches appeared. I often took a Cornish pasty from Les, our local butcher, as well as my loaf of bread cut into eight chunky sandwiches. He had demanded for the previous two days that I bring him a Cornish pasty too. My robust stubbornness and pride made this impossible.

'Well then, I asked thee to bring me summat didn't I?'

'Yeah.'

'So where is it?'

'Sorry, it's all spoken for.'

'Oh dear. Oh deary, deary me, there's going to be trouble.'

He sat there shaking his head.

The others sniggered as I ate my food in silence. Following snap I expected the worst, but things remained quiet. That was until late in the shift, when we were all packing sacks of stone dust into tubs. I leant over the mine-car, tidying up the sacks, when a terrible blow hit me on the upper back. My stomach slammed against the steel, which winded me. He had launched a full sack of stone dust from two pallets up. After getting my breath back, I carried on working as if nothing had happened. Fortunately over the weeks he got bored and stopped pestering me.

But when Vince left to go underground an altogether different candidate laid claim to the throne. Like his predecessor, Big D. from Kendray demanded a tobacco and food tax from his juniors. Unfortunately, Big D. remembered that I had a liking for Cornish pasties and had refused to share them. My first refusal led to his standing up in disgust and dragging me outside. Here, he screamed at two other lads to pin me down in the damp sludge while he slowly burned his cigarette stub into the flesh of my left cheek. The pain made me feel sick and I lay still for a while after he had left. I began sobbing in the cool, night air, feeling utterly alone. Ashamed at crying I stayed outside and then decided to hide until the end of the shift. If I told the bosses I knew nothing would happen and he would simply seek further revenge. Never before had I experienced hate with such vehemence, such conviction; the feelings soothed and disturbed me simultaneously. At times I felt angry at my own foolish pride. Still, I couldn't part with my snap; I would sooner throw the whole lot down the shaft than give him as much as a crust.

To begin with the long shifts of physical labour had tired me, but now, six months into life at the pit, my body had grown used to it. The work was often dull and repetitive, but the joking and fanciful tales among the lads made it bearable. Everyone seemed to have a nickname; in fact sometimes you didn't know their given names. Fox, The Honey Monster, E.T. Mine was usually Captain Caveman and many of them enjoyed bellowing it out across the yard when they saw me approaching from afar. I didn't mind it; I'd been used to it at school and on the street at home. Perhaps it provided a sense of belonging.

Once a month a large, flat-bed truck arrived piled high with sacks of cement that needed emptying into the storeroom – an opportunity for twenty young men to display their physical strength in competition with each other. When enticed by one of the bigger lads to carry two hundredweight sacks of cement at a time I winced, but to my surprise found that the task was as much a question of balance as it was strength. Though I struggled, I managed it and from then on habitually carried two. In the store, Hoppy accidentally dropped a sack which split, sending clouds of choking grey dust everywhere. Rather than letting it settle, everyone continued to work and Hoppy kicked the pile of cement all over the room thinking it fun. It seemed that among these young men the dirtier, the more physical and the more dangerous the work you performed, the more status you accrued. So I suppose that in a bizarre fashion, choking on cement dust was enhancing our self-esteem. A few of us wore dust masks but in such circumstances they were laughably insufficient.

After snap, Clarry sent Little Jonny, Gez and me down to the lower stockyard behind number two shaft to tidy up, a general term meaning sweeping and shovelling muck off the ground and then hosing it down. It was a glorious spring day, the sun bleaching the corrugated cladding of the gantry that connected the upper level of the shaftside down towards the lamp room. In cracks in the concrete and around the edges of some of the pallets stacked with materials tiny weeds had taken a stance. Once down there it was obvious that there wasn't an enormous amount of work to do, and Clarry had probably sent us down primarily to keep us out of mischief. This was a big mistake. Left to our own devices, relatively unwatched, we arrived at a cunning plan.

'Do you fancy being on the telly?' suggested Little Jonny, grinning cheekily, the sun catching his red hair. We sat on seats we had fashioned out of chockblocks, our helmets off, staring away from the pit and out towards the grey, fractured hillside of the stack. He explained that earlier he had witnessed a television camera crew establishing themselves outside the lamp room in anticipation of the hundreds of men emptying out of the pit just after one o'clock. They wanted to question the Yorkshire miners about the striking miners in Wales.

'Let's go and have a scan,' started Gez, standing up, and we set off, circumnavigating the gantry and jumping over a short wall.

'I told you, ITV it says on that camera.'

'Better get cracking, it's nearly one o'clock now.'

'We'll need to rough ourselves up a bit, to make us look real.'

Jonny was right. We looked pristine compared to men after a shift underground. We sneaked into the conveyor system that carried coal over to the washing plant where my father worked and found a spillage of dry, glittering coal dust.

I grabbed a handful and threw it all over my face; soon we were totally black, our teeth flashing brilliantly as we laughed. Outside, hiding behind the gantry, we practised our poses: chests puffed, arms slightly out to the sides as if carrying rolled-up rugs.

'What the chuff are we gunna say anyhow?' started Gerald.

'I'm with the Taffs, I think it's thin end of wedge these pit closures,' I commented, echoing opinions I had overheard in the baths earlier that morning. At Grimethorpe being militant was nothing radical; this was the bedrock of NUM support and any political stances on issues that might affect the men, women and children of the local villages were taken very seriously. Over time people had learnt to distrust the establishment, to question things which seemed natural and fair because throughout the years they had come to realise that this was the only way to improve things. Positive change never happened by itself: it always required action not apathy.

At a little after one fifteen, the sound of the hydraulic ram pushing towards the shaft signalled the arrival of the first cage, 120 men waiting for the gate to open, then each man thrusting his tiny, numbered, brass check into the box or the hand of the banksman before surging past. The excited noise increased and many of the younger miners began their usual run towards the lamp room.

Showers to be had.

Girls to meet.

Horses to back.

Beer to drink.

My heart beat stronger and faster as scores of feet raced down the inclined gantry. Most of the men had managed to take off their lamps and batteries whilst running, charging towards the lamp room and mostly ignoring the film crew at the entrance. We joined on behind a dozen of the front runners, trying to ape their proud, carefree gait. The news crew did not understand that our yellow helmets meant we were merely trainees, that we carried no lamps and didn't actually work underground.

'Excuse me. Would you mind commenting on what you think to the Welsh miners taking industrial action?'

'I think we should be backing them myself,' shouted one man pushing his way into the lamp room without turning around to answer any more questions.

Then, surprisingly, the microphone arrived under my chin inviting me to put forward my view. 'Well er, I think that if we were in the same predicament we would want them to support us, so maybe we should support them.'

Other men gave their thoughts on the situation as they teemed out of the gallery, those from the Parkgate seam, those from the Newhill and then the Melton Field men. Having established our careers in the world of media we thought it wise to return to the lower stockyard and continue sweeping and shovelling as well as cleaning ourselves up before being spotted. We looked ridiculously filthy, like extras in a B movie.

At home that night the whole Cave clan waited eagerly just on the off chance that the issue might appear on the ten o'clock news. With only five minutes of the programme left we concluded that they had decided to drop the item altogether, but then images of the dayshift men rushing from the shaft towards the lamp room appeared on the screen and I jumped off the settee at once, almost squashing my little brother Jonathan.

'That's us there! That's us with the yellow helmets on.' I pointed at the screen with my index finger and then sat down. My jaw dropped as I appeared on the screen talking.

'Well er, I think that if we were in the same predicament we would want them to support us, so maybe we should support them.'

'Oh bloody hell, film star.'

At work the following morning no one mentioned a thing. That was until just before snap-time when Fox revealed that Danny, one of the stockyard foremen, had seen the news and was apparently hopping mad. I assumed we'd get a ticking-off for having been outside the lamp room with the film crew instead of attending to our allocated task down in the lower stockyard. Hungry, we walked up past Frosty's office to the canteen for a cooked breakfast. While I queued for my food, my back to the room, the glow of his eyes burnt through my jacket. I sat down staring straight at him three tables away; he swivelled his tea mug round and round, avoiding my gaze. There had always been something between us, which I interpreted as regional chauvinism – the fact that I was not a Lundwood or Grimey lad – or that my father had never been a 'big hitter', a term for a well-known underground face worker. I don't think he even knew my father. He wore an outdated miner's helmet that wasn't officially allowed but which reminded him of his glory days as a 'pick, hammer and shovel man' before the war, when he had worked in the 'hand-got' seams prior to mechanisation.

His cheeks crimson with restraint, his tongue having done numerous laps around his mouth, finally he faced me and spoke.

'Who the hell do you think you are?'

I remained silent as he was clearly just warming up. The canteen hushed, cups being placed onto Formica, people in the queue craning their necks around.

'You haven't been at the pit two minutes and you're saying what we should be doing on the telly.'

Then, after a pause, 'What did you say, predic . . . a . . .

ment?' he managed eventually. 'Fucking predicament, who do you think you are coming here and using fancy words? I . . . I bet you don't even know what it bloody means, eh? Do you?'

He sat there, anger quickly flaring to incandescent rage as my own face burned. I ate my sausage and tomato sandwich with shaking hands, trying to appear unruffled.

'Anyroad,' he continued, 'You should never have been up there. Gaffer's given me a bollocking because of you little fuckers, eh?'

Unsure if this was a question, but sure that he was on the edge, I said nothing. Clearly my comments on TV had violated some unwritten law about who the official spokespeople were in such situations and obviously they were not precocious trainees with pretend dirty faces from villages more than two miles away. Until the day I disappeared underground, our relationship remained strained: I despised him and he most definitely hated me.

After snap, down by number two shaft, tidying the yard I saw the men from the dayshift coming back to earth, the circular hole in the earth's crust suddenly plugged with a slow-rising iron cage suspended by a woven, greased metal rope. It stopped right in front of me, gently bouncing and almost coming to a standstill. Men were crammed into each of the three decks, the whites of their eyes and the red of their lips painted onto matt black faces. Some still had their lamps switched on, relieved to see daylight once again following seven hours and fifteen minutes in that gloomy, labyrinthine world. Since the cutting of the first sod here in October 1894, people had descended this vacuous hole in the ground, day and night, selling their labour.

Later in the baths I was stripping off out of my dirty pit rags when two much older men, travelling to work, arrived from the clean side and casually began to dress. The larger of the two glanced at me and then, addressing his friend, began:

'Albert, look at this lad here, he's only a bloody bairn, working at a shit-hole like this. Jesus. What a fucking life, I don't know, what a fucking life. There must be something better than this for t' lad.'

I shut the door of the locker, grabbed my towel and smiled as I passed them heading for the shower.

The strike that many had predicted that year never arrived; the NUM ballot voted against it. Many thought it a shame we had not taken a firmer stance as rumours of pit-closures began travelling like arrows up and down the pit yard, the tunnels and the shafts.

3

Ascension

On the outside the paint had long since gone, which meant that in winter the rainwater penetrated the laminated wood, saturating it and causing it to swell, sag and splinter. Our new kitchen extension, hailed by the local council as modernisation, looked prematurely tired. My mother called our street 'Shanty Town' at every available opportunity. Originally the houses had been built for railway workers and they were, without question, 'the best built houses in Royston' if you listened to my mother paraphrasing Barbara, her own mother. The phrase, which served to distinguish the dwellings from those that had been built for miners, was part of a much broader argument that concerned the superiority of railway work generally. My mother's father and stepfather had both been signal-box men who would never have dreamed of working as coal miners.

On the inside water dripped onto the floor, threatening to dampen the workman's toolbag. Paul (recently retired as Skip from the Scouts) had been sent yet again by the council to try to patch up the kitchen extension. Although clean, his hair was long and unkempt, and the hammer looked small as his hands, particularly his thumbs, were enormous. He had been the crucifer at the church when I had been in the choir and it was there, in the vestry one Sunday, that he had revealed he was in a mountaineering club. I am sure that in private he regretted telling me this as thereafter I nagged him non-stop, pleading for him to take me with him on one of his great adventures. I enjoyed uncertainty and excitement and had tested my nerves by climbing up trees, pylons and old pit buildings, as well as to the top of the church organ during games of hide-and-seek before the Sunday evening Mass. Perhaps I believed that climbing up severely steep cliff-faces where you needed ropes would guarantee a buzz. So why wouldn't he take me?

'You're too young,' he had explained. 'We go in pubs in the evening and you're only thirteen. Wait 'til you're older.'

I had often reminded Paul of my desire to go climbing during my days in the Scouts and he always gave a similar reply. But now, standing there, a little jaded after the morning shift at the pit, I had him cornered.

'I still want to come with you to the mountaineering club, you know.'

'Well . . .'

'You promised, remember?'

'Well, there is a meet next month actually, quite close by. Wharncliffe Crags near Penistone.'

This exchange in the damp corner of the kitchen that grey afternoon was a seismic sentence that would change everything for ever.

In actual fact, I had almost gone rock climbing a few years earlier as part of a week at an outdoor centre with the school but unfortunately, the evening before departure, fate had intervened during my ascent of a sycamore tree outside our house. I could climb all of the twelve trees on the grass in the middle of the street no problem, including the notorious birch down on the corner. The sycamore had a difficult start for which I had a good sequence of moves memorised. This involved wrapping my legs around the trunk and patiently nudging upwards as if scaling a wide, greasy pole. Eventually, the remnant of a once substantial branch came into reach and, with a subtle spring, this could be caught by kids of moderate height; however, as you clasped it, the feet inevitably swung from the main trunk. Familiarity (the downfall of many a risk-taker) breeds contempt and late that Sunday evening, as I reached out and felt my legs swing I was utterly relaxed – even cool to the discerning eyes of the onlookers, many of whom were too timid to try the manoeuvre themselves. Unfortunately, as my full weight (six-and-a-half stone) transferred to the branch it snapped and I plummeted earthwards with my right arm behind me. On impact my arm crumpled into a bent mess. Instantly, a searing pain shot from my wrist to my neck, causing me to scream violently. The onlookers rushed to notify Mrs Cave, who was busy packing clothes for my morning departure. By the time I had risen and begun walking the short distance to the house I met my mother bounding towards me. She slapped me around the face bellowing, 'You stupid chuffing imbecile!'

My tears increased now as embarrassment in front of my peers merged with pain from my throbbing, dislocated elbow and snapped radius and ulna. The knowledge that I would miss the week of outdoor sports only added to my misery.

'Tha's clean enough to wear a white shirt toneet lad, no bother,' said the man, a stranger, as he finished scrubbing my back with a giant car sponge.

'Cheers pal,' I replied, still washing the back of the short, wiry, tattooed man in front. The half-dozen of us had turned around and started cleaning each other's backs with hardly a murmur; it was a polite custom that required extra diligence on a Friday when, later, many men would dress smartly and go out for a drink. My team had been shovelling coal spillage back onto the conveyor belt all afternoon by the side of number two shaft and the mixture of coal dust and sweat had been grafted deep into our skin. Swarfega gel helped clean the hands but to get it out of the rims of my eyelids and lashes would require gentle massage with a tissue and Vaseline at home. Although dust could irritate the eyes, I found this feminine mascara look pleasing, as it marked me out as a miner when in the pubs and clubs, giving the impression to others that I worked underground for a living (which, of course, wasn't strictly true just yet). The excitement I felt tonight though – changing into my clean clothes and dashing out to catch the pit paddy – was not the prospect of going out around town drinking, but my first trip rock climbing with Paul.

We arrived late at the campsite, erected our tents and went straight to sleep. In the morning I paced around desperate for the loo, but not a murmur came from Paul's tent. He was obviously exhausted from another busy week of repairing Royston's council houses. We were camped in a farmer's field with seemingly no facilities, save for a tap. Dave, a copper-headed thin lad who had travelled with us and who had also been an altar boy at Royston church, was already up and about and he pointed me in the direction of 'Alice', as the climbing club's portable toilet tent was affectionately known. As I trod the dew-drenched grass opposite, people sorted out climbing ropes and other pieces of unusual-looking equipment. There could have been no greater contrast with the dull tedium of work the previous week. I had never seen a proper rock-face before and the antic-ipation burned inside me.

Annoyed at Paul's extravagant lie-in, I began circling his tent searching for the entrance.

'It's a tunnel tent,' said Dave, catching my puzzled expres-sion.

Even Houdini might have struggled escaping out of that jungle of canvas, I thought – what an odd design.

'It keeps snow out and that in really bad weather,' he continued. 'He won't be up for hours yet. Listen to him snoring.'

He had a valid point. The sound was familiar. After all, this was Skip who had remained sleeping whilst a multitude of kitchen knives had been thrust into the lino inches from his head just two years earlier. The badges on Paul's faded blue rucksack included something named the Lyke Wake Walk (which he had accomplished twice, apparently), as well as a host of other achievements and this, combined with his hi-tech tent, led me to assume he was a hardcore enthusiast who was going to lead me up precipitous rock walls. Unfortunately, when he did finally arise, he had rather different designs.

'I thought a decent walk would be good, as the weather's not brilliant,' he muttered, still lying in his sleeping bag with his thick, ruffled hair poking out of an exceedingly long tube of canvas.

Walk? My heart sank.

'Will we be able to see the climbers, watch them I mean?'

'We could swing by the cliffs, I suppose.'

Paul was more of a walker than a climber, though occasion-ally he enjoyed tying-on to a rope behind a brave leader. In fact, many people in the club preferred to walk up mountains rather than climb them. Fortunately for me, a little later we found the 'real' climbers down on the crag.

From the top, sheer walls of rock fell to a jumble of sharp, tooth-like boulders before the forested hillside disappeared down to the valley, which housed a handful of large steel-processing plants and a queue of giant electricity pylons.

Later I would learn that coal in our area tilts towards the North Sea and so some of the earliest mining activity began in the west of the Pennines, where the coal seams were visible as outcrops on the surface. As demand for coal grew alongside the concomitant advances in engineering and steam power, owners became more ambitious, moving east of Barnsley to exploit much deeper, hotter and richer seams. It was the combination of an abundance of accessible, good quality coal for smelting and the navigable River Don for transportation that had spurred on the steel producers to set up camp in the Stocksbridge–Deepcar Valley down below. (Allegedly, earlier pioneering rock climbers had found the rocks of Wharncliffe, like much of Barnsley, covered in a black grime; however, by the time I discovered the crags they had returned to a lighter brown colour.) Later that night in the pub, someone said the rock was a 'coal-measure gritstone', not as rough on the skin as some of the other local gritstone edges.

A raw breeze chilled our faces as we scrambled down an easy gully to where the others were gathered. A young man named Pete had almost reached the top of the cliff by way of an open book-shaped corner. A slightly older man, Keith, held his ropes and watched his every move.

'Keep an eye on me here, it's not hard but it's a bit on t' damp side.'

'Don't worry, I'm watching you.'

The leader, Pete, moved slowly and surely. He had broad shoulders for his modest height and gave us a wry grin as if, despite the slightly green, moist surface of the rock and the cold wind, he was actually rather enjoying himself.

'You'll like that, Keith,' he shouted, negotiating the final bulge and standing on top.

When Keith asked if I wanted a go, I couldn't hide my excitement. He put me in a harness and tied me in with a figure-of-eight knot, shouting encouragement as I halted halfway up. I wore my new black Hawkins Kinder walking boots and it took some time before I began to trust them on the slightly damp rock. Exhilarated, I crawled over the top, my forearms swollen and cramped, my hands full of holes; I felt like a real climber now. I rushed back to the base of the cliff, like a small child having just tasted sugar for the very first time, and watched

Dave and Paul perform. They wore odd-looking footwear, 'rock-boots', that you had to buy two sizes smaller than your normal shoes for a tight fit and which had completely smooth rubber soles for maximum friction.

Every climb had a name given by the first ascensionists as well as a grade indicating difficulty that I couldn't really fathom. Apparently an adjective, such as 'Very Difficult', described its seriousness and then a letter and a number indicated the technical difficulty. I watched others climb for a while, noting their individual styles. Keith – perhaps because he was short and found it difficult to reach some of the holds – appeared to be adept with his feet, keeping his weight centred and balancing delicately. Others attacked the rock in a brutish manner, grunting and shaking as if in a backstreet brawl.

'Do you fancy Desolation Angel?' joked Pete, pointing up at a sixty-foot high tower of rock to our right. I craned my neck, marvelling at the utter blankness of it: the underside of a ship's prow, as smooth as steel.

'Fuck me, Betty. Up there? Go on then, you first.' I cleared my throat and spat all over a nearby rock, black and green.

'I'm only kidding thee. There's no protection, it's death on a stick.'

I stared at the rock I had just spat on which sat directly below the climb, a reverse dagger that would rip a falling climber to pieces. It transpired that Don Barr, the son of a nearby pit boss, was the local hero of this cliff. Sadly, Pete explained, he had recently been killed in a freak accident in France. Aged just twenty, Don had been enjoying a prolific season climbing at the Mont Blanc Massif in Chamonix. When conditions of snow and ice in the mountains deteriorated he had travelled south to the Verdon Gorge, a less serious venue, to do some rock climbing. It was here, whilst sat belaying at the top of a climb named *Voie de la Demande* that he was struck by a bolt of lightning and killed instantly.

We did another climb of a similar standard, ate our sandwiches, and then Paul, Dave and I walked leftwards to find the hard men doing battle with a climb named 'Himmelswillen' that was graded Very Severe. It looked preposterous. A vertical wall led up to an enormous ceiling of rock that had a crack on its right-hand side; above sat a featureless smooth tower. The biting March wind now began to deposit a thin layer of sleet on the ground. Staring up, my heart started racing once more. At the base of the climb sharp stones sat in prime position for crushing ankles and splitting limbs; as if it wasn't terrifying enough, for God's sake.

'Tie on. Have a gu, you've nowt to lose,' shouted Pete, spotting my gaze from the top, pulling down the woollen balaclava over his chin and adjusting the hood of his blue-cotton windproof jacket. Paul and Dave refused point blank to tie-on to the rope but reminded me how to do a figure-of-eight knot, knowing I wanted to try. When the rope came tight I kicked my boots against the rock, attempting to clear the damp earth from the soles.

The concentration required in order to puzzle-out the moves of this climb meant that I quickly forgot where I was, as if suddenly alone in a quiet place. I moved my feet up, steadily standing in balance and placing my hands in a horizontal fissure before halting, lost for ideas. 'Lay back up the arête,' Keith advised, gesticulating with his arms. Amazed at how my boots stuck to the rock I made slow but steady progress. At half-height I reached a large, 'Thank God' ledge by scrabbling with my knees and putting small holes into my old school trousers. I peered up at a vicious, thin crack.

'Go for it,' encouraged Pete.

My forearms were already spent from the effort of the first section. I felt the rope tighten from above which brought some comfort, but my breathing remained fast and shallow, adrenalin filling my veins. Although the thought of accepting defeat never occurred for a moment, I knew I was tiring. I battled around the overhang and up the crack to a good flat ledge where snow had settled and hung there, severely lacking ideas of how to progress. Advice floated up and down the cliff as my frozen fingers began to uncurl one by one.

'Mantleshelf it,' someone shouted from the ground.

'Press down on your left hand and reach up with the other,' called Pete, keeping the rope tight.

My face burned, melting wet snowflakes as soon as they landed on my forehead, yet my fingers remained numb. Time was running out. I decided to give it one good shot and sprang up, throwing my chest over the small ledge but finding nothing for my feet. I tried to place the edge of my foot on a small ripple in the rock. Suddenly I was off. I shot down a couple of feet, stretching the rope, then stopped. I tried again and fell. And again. Five times in all.

I hung on the rope, blowing hot air into my hands. 'Next time,' I muttered. 'Next time.'

On the following attempt I adjusted my weight ever so subtly and with the help of a tight rope I crawled upwards, eventually belly-flopping over the top. Pete congratulated me, surprised at my tenacity. My arms had never before experienced such a burning sensation and the blood slowly returning to the ends of my fingers filled me with nausea.

'Bow your head and it will gu,' said Pete, beginning to coil the rope.

It was almost dark and many of the others had already gone to change into dry clothes and to get food.

My exultation lasted all the way to the campsite and beyond into the pub. That move on 'Himmelswillen', the horror of the mantleshelf was now etched onto my mind for ever. The taste of beer simply heightened this feeling of well being, whilst the spellbinding stories that flowed from the climbers appeared to be of another universe. Keith, a particularly distinguished story-teller, created a montage of intrigue and excitement as one anec-dote followed another, mostly concerning his adventures in America. Encouraged by Pete and out of earshot from his new French fiancée, Marie, he painted idyllic scenes: how he had woken at sunrise in California lying next to a beautiful, semi-naked woman cooking breakfast in his tent; when short of money, he and his companion had sold a broken car to a garage by free-wheeling it onto the forecourt, taking the money and then leaving town; how when climbing a 2,000 foot sheer wall of granite in the Yukon in Canada, he and his partner had had to sleep halfway up on a tiny ledge. It all sounded like the adventures of Butch Cassidy and the Sundance Kid. Over the years, I would hear these tales again and again and although the odd detail changed, they were in the main faithful to the originals heard that evening in the pub above Wharncliffe Crags.

Much later I discovered that a surprising number of people in the mountaineering club worked directly or indirectly in coal mining. Pete Swift, who had hauled me up the final climb, was a draughtsman at Qualter Hall in Barnsley, an engineering firm that made hydraulic machinery for the mining industry. A quiet guy named Malc was a ventilation officer based in the head offices at Grimethorpe. A particularly jovial character, Mike, originally from Teesdale, was a mining geologist also based at Grimethorpe. Another man, Barry, was a mining engineer. At the time I made a mental note that they probably didn't see too much of the 'idiot stick' – one of the miner's many idioms for a shovel. However, that night I never once thought of Grimethorpe pit; I was a million miles away.

After numerous ales I could not resist joining in the story-telling myself, desperately trying to keep my dirty pit vocabulary to a minimum.

'Well, in the days, when me, Dave and Paul went to church, the vicar in charge was a hell of guy. Well fifteen minutes before the start of the Midnight Mass, he was nowhere to be seen, so they sent out a search party.

'Now he liked a drink did our vicar and so they looked in the Pack Horse pub, but no he wasn't in there. Of course by now it's ten minutes to midnight. The choir is there. A large congregation has turned up, the organ is going. But still no vicar.

'So anyroad, they go up to the working men's club opposite the vicarage and sure enough he is in there, but he's busy. He's up on the stage sat behind the glass box full of bouncing ping-pong balls calling the bingo numbers, desperate that somebody shouts "full house" . . .'

The sound of beating rain the following morning was such a relief. My temples throbbed incessantly, my leaden arms and shredded hands were incapable of even reaching my water bottle at the bottom of the tent. We decided to go for a walk along the cliff-tops and as I came out of my alcoholic daze I remembered that the night before I had agreed to go to a place called Glencoe in Scotland for a week, over the May Bank Holiday, with Pete, Dave and Paul.

As spring arrived so did news that some of the older lads had been called underground including Big D. The more I observed the man, the more I despised him. He longed for respect and resorted to bullying easy prey in order to get it. The stockyard was so big that I could avoid him and for a long period we worked on alternate shifts and so never met. As the months went by he had grown even larger, yet I had seen weaknesses. Sat in the canteen one morning, drinking tea, he had thrust out his leg purposefully to trip up a young lad as he approached the counter. The men laughed at the tumble until the lad stood up, turned and pounced across the table in a flash. Though short, his upper arms were powerful and he gripped D.'s windpipe with purpose as if squeezing a giant tomato. D.'s eyes bulged, but it was fear that I witnessed, not courage. He remained utterly still. 'Do that again and I'll fucking kill you!' bellowed the lad before letting go and then sauntering up to the counter, politely ordering a breakfast from Josie.

Unfortunately, before D. went underground we ended up working alongside each other, clearing spillage from the conveyor belt that delivered coal from number two shaft. While five of us grafted, resting on our knees and rhythmically shovelling coal up on to the belt he sat there eating and smoking. Six hours into the shift he still hadn't touched a shovel. The excruciating squeak of the conveyor belt wheels, combined with the unavoidable dust from our shovels, was deeply unpleasant and yet I could not imagine sitting there idle. Doing nothing, simply waiting until the end of the shift, was the hardest work of all.

Small coals began to bounce off my helmet. Sat twenty feet away, D. was bored. The stones increased in size but I continued working. Through the dust I saw the white of his face grinning. The pieces of coal stopped coming for a while, then suddenly an almighty blow ripped off my helmet and unsteadied me. In a roaring rage, without knowing what I was doing, I ran and jumped on him. He had not expected it, sitting there smiling, his back leaning against a gently angled pile of coal. I grabbed his throat with one hand and twisted his jaw with the other, forcing his face into the black spoil. 'You useless piece of shit!' I yelled. Then the tables turned. He threw me aside with his enormous hands, pressed his knee into my chest, forcing a palm full of coal over my mouth. I would have called him every name under the sun, had I been able to breathe.

'Don't fuck with me!' he shouted with a mad flash in his eyes. I swung my fist at him, unable to reach his face. It was pointless and I knew it. Eventually he stood up, laughing, as I spat out the coal dirt. Our difference in size meant that no serious threat had ever been posed, yet he understood my feelings clearer than ever. Soon enough he disappeared underground and thankfully we managed on the stockyard without a Godfather figure, I for one never missing the terror.

May 1983

At sunrise we sped along the road that cuts through the vast golden expanse of Rannoch Moor and then glided headlong down towards the entrance of Glencoe where, on the left, stood the most beautiful mountain I had ever seen. It burst through the ground, a citadel of rock, soft-scattered morning light stroking its left side: Buchaille Etive Mhor – The Big Herdsman of the Valley. The journey had taken twelve hours, instead of the anticipated seven, due to the heavy traffic.

Dreamer, nothing but a dreamer sang Supertramp on the stereo as we snaked right beneath the vast grey flanks of the Buchaille's North Face, slivers of snow miraculously glued on up near the summit. Did people climb such things? I wondered, my face pressed against the window, my breath condensing on the glass. We pitched our tents alongside the River Coe at the Red Squirrel campsite, next to a couple of Glaswegians mending a van, and slept until mid-afternoon.

The following day, Pete and I headed towards the mighty Buchaille, stopping for a drink at a small waterfall cascading over a giant rock known as 'the waterslide'. I craned my head skywards, trying to absorb the enormity of the mountain; a complex array of gullies and rock towers. I placed total trust in Pete's judgement as we scrambled towards our climb named Crowberry Ridge. Unlike Pete, I was not from a family of outdoor enthusiasts. His father Horace, a coking plant chemist with the National Coal Board, was a keen hill walker and heavily involved with the local Rambler's Association. Mary, his mother, was even more adventurous, having travelled to the Alps in a converted milk van to climb in the late 1950s. Pete had inherited a deep respect for mountains and was a skilful route finder on the cliffs, always appearing calm as he climbed and establishing solid belay anchors. I was a complete novice but he saw a spark in me: the way I could climb, my steady head, my love of exposure and my desire to learn. That day I mastered the clove hitch and the bowline, learnt Naismith's Rule about estimating time for walking in the mountains, and experienced how to abseil. In the Clachaig Inn later I heard a dozen tales of climbers having epics and the reasons why they had ended up in unfortunate, sometimes tragic circumstances. In the recklessness of youth, I sometimes found Pete too steady, annoyingly logical and sensible, but he was the perfect antidote to the young daredevil from East End Crescent. Climbing was a game, but so very different from tennis, cricket, cross-country running and every other game I had ever tried. Like fire, it was dangerous and yet strangely mesmerising; unquestionably, this was its principal attraction for me. As Pete pointed out, as we soloed down the ridge from the summit of the Buchaille that day, 2,000 feet of air beneath the soles of my boots, my hands holding good but small finger edges: 'If tha slips here tha dies.'

The Gibson family were camped opposite us and Mike, the tall red-headed son, bounded over suggesting that a group of us walk up Ben Nevis the following day. The whole family were wonderfully eccentric. The father, Ken, who was now well past retirement age and had recently discovered marathon running, earned a living doing small-scale building work on people's roofs. He had done a variety of jobs in the past, including being a professional wrestler for a time which was surprising, given his diminutive stature. His wife seemed to spend all day feeding her teenage sons who dashed around non-stop. Pete and I visited their house once in Doncaster where, due to the amount of outdoor equipment in the lounge – including a canoe in front of the fire (that was apparently being repaired) – we had found difficulty finding anywhere to sit down. We were fed half a dozen delicious home-made scones from Mrs Gibson, the chief reason I believe Pete had suggested we visit.

From Glen Nevis we struck up a steep path carrying relatively small packs. I had not yet learnt the art of stopping occasionally to admire the view or to take a drink of water, and was somewhat surprised on reaching the summit to find none of my companions still with me. I waited a while by a peculiar shelter, an old observatory, and then walked back down to look for the others. It was not until almost back at the halfway lochan that I met them and turned around to join them back towards the top.

'You have a lot of energy, young man. Are you a fell-runner or something?' Mike Gibson asked in a serious tone.

'No, I'm not a very good runner.'

'Well you must do something, the speed you shot off up there.'

'Not really, I used to play a bit of football when I was at school, but I was crap.'

'Well you obviously have a talent for going up hills.'

The only explanation was that when I walked I lost myself. Although I had never climbed a mountain before, except Royston muckstack a thousand times, I never found it difficult to put one foot in front of the other and the meditative nature of walking allowed me to forget the dirty, noisy world of Grimethorpe pit. I would go on to earn the nickname 'The Barnsley Whippet' on my first visit to the Himalayas a few years hence; I would take it as a compliment.

The second time on the summit the wind had increased and Paul kindly lent me his Union Jack woolly hat. We posed for photos on top and in an excited fit of madness I dropped my pants, revealing my buttocks to the camera. Etiquette towards fellow mountaineers was something I had yet to discover. I was often told that I swore too much, that I spat too much and that I was a little out of control. Not to worry; at work on Monday the dirty language and spitting would be perfectly acceptable.

Two days later on the first of June – the day after my seven-teenth birthday – Pete and I walked towards the giant North Face of Ben Nevis, which looked formidable, even from the road. Dark clouds sat above the 2,000-foot rock-face and a brisk wind whipped across the Allt a' Mhuilinn, a never-ending plateau of black mud punctuated by islands of peat turf and granite. Attempting to stay clean was pointless as we weaved our own path beneath the emerging sombre walls. At the CIC hut below the main cirque of climbs we stopped for water and food. Our intended climb, Tower Ridge, looked absurd and I explained to Pete that I would be relying on him entirely to lead the way. The ridge rose abruptly out of the ground to the height of 600 feet – the Douglas Boulder – then formed a steep, serrated line of rock over a prominent col before climbing directly up to the summit. By now the mist had descended further, daunting and swirling, but Pete was not to be discouraged. I was swayed by his measured, confident manner. In the short time we had known each other, I had witnessed him deal with adverse conditions and knew he could navigate. When looking at a map I could only tell whether or not a church had a spire or a tower; contours were irritating brown lines that only seemed to confuse things.

Climbing to the top of the Douglas Boulder unroped concentrated the mind, but it would also save time, Pete explained. Some of the rocks were loose and a light drizzle had set in. Once we arrived on the ridge proper we discovered a good deal more snow than we had anticipated. Without axes and crampons, we had to kick steps with the sides of our boots. Finally, with much relief, Pete decided it was time to tie-on to the rope and he led the way slowly but confidently. A few pitches later I paid out the rope, anxious about the weather. I couldn't resist calling to Pete.

'Pete.'

'What now?'

'The clouds are getting worse. It's starting to sleet. What should we do?'

'We haven't got a choice I'm afraid, we've got to keep going now.'

At least the clouds obscured the drop below, which I imagined to be considerable. Climbing down into the impressive col known as Tower Gap, I experienced real climbing commitment for the first time: I had misgivings about continuing but it now seemed easier than retreat, despite heading into uncharted country. I would learn that sometimes a second should offer support to a leader, learn to hide fear and blatantly lie to oneself (yes, honestly, I am really enjoying myself and not frightened at all).

The sleet turned to water as it landed on my paper-thin jacket, penetrating every layer of clothing underneath. At each new belay stance, I shook my head and shoulders – like a dog after a swim – trying to fight the discomfort. Eventually, the technical difficulties eased and we emerged onto a long slope of granular snow where we could move together. I followed Pete's footholes exactly in my squelching boots, leaning my dripping mittens against the snow. The sleet had now turned to rain which bounced hard and fast on my right cheek as we landed on the summit plateau. We took refuge in the observatory shelter, sharing what food we had left, waiting for the rain to subside. After an hour, with darkness almost upon us and the weather unchanged, we took photographs and then started down. Perhaps the mountain Gods had been insulted by my show of buttocks two days earlier: but the weather showed no mercy. Ferocious winds buffeted us as we fought for our balance, sliding on the stones underfoot and searching for the path with our headtorches. It was well after midnight and still hammering with rain when we crawled into the tent.

Despite heavy eyelids, at seven o'clock I woke with a start, realising that my feet had been marinating for some time and my nylon sleeping bag was sitting in two inches of water. Pete jumped out of his bag with a shriek then splashed and paddled his way outside. I joined him, wearing only a pair of saturated nylon underpants. Responding to the deluge, the River Coe had burst its banks and now flowed through the Red Squirrel camp-site. Paul's tunnel tent looked like a damp mass of soggy card-board and the Gibsons had rolled up the side walls of their family tent so as to allow the flowing tide to pass unhindered. Unidentified camping pots and pans, along with a couple of plastic plates, floated comically downstream.

The two Glaswegian fellows sought sanctuary in their yellow Bedford van, the water lapping at the stairwells, the doors ajar. The slightly older, bearded man started first.

'If he comes down here and asks for money ah'm going tae fucking deek him.'

'Deek him? Fuck that shite ah'll kill the cunt ah'm tellin ye. Tight arsed twat,' chimed the younger man, who although more slightly built than his friend looked more menacing. They had spent most of the week repairing the van and now this; they were seething.

When the campsite owner arrived with his small leather collecting purse the younger man began licking his lips. Meanwhile we took down our tent, wrung out our clothing as best we could and then shoved it into the back of the Chevette, keeping a watchful gaze on the campsite owner.

'The weather's supposed to improve now, they are saying, for the weekend,' he announced.

I wondered if this was a cry to rally the campers, most of whom were packing up, to stay a little longer. Not once did he mention payment, which must have frustrated the Glaswegians, desperate for an excuse to release their anger. Fortunately, the owner was polite, although not overly concerned we thought.

'Oh let's fuck off,' growled the bearded Glaswegian, holding the steering wheel and sensing his friend's violent rage. He started the engine.

'See you lads,' he called out of the window as they surged against the flood water and up and out of the field, the engine misfiring and the smaller one still growling at the owner. With everything so damp we headed home too.

The following week life back on the stockyard had changed very little. We loaded chockblock after chockblock into tubs and pushed them down towards the shaftside, waiting for our turn to be called underground. We found the monotony of the work the hardest part, but by refusing to take it seriously we maintained our sanity. The humour was relentless and harsh at times with nothing going unnoticed. 'Fuck me it's Chris Bonington,' was the term of endearment I received regularly now, having spoken to a couple of the lads about my newfound passion.

At the end of the week I received two letters from Charlie Lyle, the colliery training officer. The first explained that I would be commencing my underground training at the local mining college, and the second was confirmation that the National Coal Board were keen to sponsor me to attend the local technical college in Barnsley for one day a week in order to study and become a mining technician, eventually leading to management. I had taken a mechanical and mathematics comprehension exam earlier in the year and had apparently reached the appropriate level. Perhaps I would escape the banality of the stockyard after all.

The summer passed quickly as I began climbing more, even

managing to meet Pete one midweek evening when I was on the dayshift. I had recently begun leading too, a harrowing experience for Pete because, although I could manage the moves of climbs, I had not yet mastered the art of placing protection into the rock, most of it falling out as I struggled on upwards. At the top of my fifth lead, a route named Byne's Crack on Burbage Rocks, Pete curtly remarked, 'Tha'll either get really bloody good, or tha'll die.'

Following a Thursday night drinking session around Barnsley, I tried to explain to Alan and Brian, two of my friends from the street, what all the fuss was about: what is the point of climbing? We had camped out in Coka Woods together count-less times, hopped over people's hedges, run across railway lines as fast trains approached, climbed up inside the old pit-head buildings of Monckton, thrashed motorbikes up and down the muckstack on summer evenings, but now surely we were growing up and moving on: working, taking driving lessons and looking for girls. But it wasn't so simple and they knew it as well as I did. We missed the play element terribly. Was this growing up thing over-rated? Drinking was losing its fun now that we were almost old enough to do it legally and work took up too much of our time. At midnight, standing on the street corner under the stars, Brian – who worked for his father's scaffolding firm – and Alan – the local window cleaner – knew that I'd discov-ered something special, something that was not simply a passing fad. Before we said our goodbyes and headed off to bed, Brian commented: 'You know, Andy, you are so lucky.'

Pete talked of famous people and odd-sounding mountains in the Himalayas that he had discovered in magazines and books. He enthusiastically recommended several books that were avail-able for loan from the library in Barnsley and also lent me one of his own books, *The Shining Mountain* by Peter Boardman.

Two blokes from Manchester had spent numerous nights inside a giant freezer to prepare themselves for the unclimbed West Face of a Himalayan peak named Changabang, which is nearly 7,000 metres high and incredibly steep. They spent four weeks on the mountain hanging in small hammocks and climbing up vertical, ice-covered rocks. It seemed the most ridiculous thing I had ever heard; utterly mad and the pictures looked truly insane.

*

The sixth of September was the day my mother had been dreading – my first day of work underground. The snap she made for me almost filled a carrier bag: pilchards mashed up with plenty of vinegar.

'A lot of stuff doesn't taste right down the pit, you know. Your Uncle Martin never takes tomatoes for his snap, but he loves them at home. You'll be alright with pilchards.'

Apparently 'collier's ham', rhyming slang for bread and jam, was extremely popular as it didn't sweat or go off in the underground heat.

At work I changed and made my way slowly to the lamp room. I picked up my lamp and slid it onto my waist belt along with my self-rescuer: a small metal box that contained a device for use in an emergency which turned deadly carbon monoxide into breathable amounts of carbon dioxide for up to two hours. Outside the lamp room a colliery gardener was raking the soil of a flowerbed with one hand, the other arm lost somewhere underground, I imagined.

I walked up the inclined gallery to the pit bank where Trevor and the boys I was joining stood waiting for the cage. I read the brass badge on the hydraulic rams that pushed forward as the cage rose out of the pit: Qualter Hall Ltd., Barnsley, South Yorkshire, England. I bet Pete helped design those, I mused. We handed our silver identification discs to John the banksman, my friend's father from Lundwood, and kept hold of the brass. Brass can survive extreme heat and therefore serves as a means of identification in the event of an underground explosion.

He quickly ran his hands over our pockets, checking for matches or lighters, then we shuffled on to the middle deck. The rams hissed back and we floated slowly down before pausing briefly. We were suspended at the level of the stockyard now and I could see some of the lads filling tubs with tie-bars in the grey morning light. Then smoothly and quietly we plummeted into complete darkness.

4

Underground

The men remained eerily silent. Laser-thin bright lights pierced my eyes as we flashed past the first upper seam at terrifying speed, the brief drone of machinery existing only for a second before we zipped once more into the black hole. I squeezed the cold steel-mesh door of the cage with both hands. Usually I loved speed, loved to tuck my new Honda around tight bends of tarmac, but flying towards the pit bottom 3,000 feet below at eight metres per second, I was utterly gripped by fear. The sensation of weightlessness, of tumbling uncontrollably, made me feel sick, as if standing in the lift of a skyscraper whose safety rope had just been severed.

A deep void filled my guts as the cage slowed and then stopped halfway down the shaft. The cage bounced then quivered as the steel cables retracted; the whole experience felt like a grim combination of the Big Dipper and the Ghost Train. A slightly built deputy named Judd got out to inspect the disused Barnsley Bed seam. 'Coal from the Barnsley Bed is steam coal,' I remembered my father saying. 'And . . .' He always paused at this point before continuing in a hushed voice, 'I don't know whether it's true or not, but they reckon coal from that seam was used on the Titanic.'

'I shunt gu in there Judd, it's haunted tha knows,' shouted one man.

'Does tha want to take him a sandwich, he'll be hungry,' another joked.

'Ah, you'll not bother me, there's no ghosts here love,' Judd remarked confidently as he stepped onto the bankside, a stick in one hand, an oil lamp in the other.

The banksman dragged the heavy metal-mesh door of the

cage shut and then signalled to the winder man who sat on the surface, controlling the giant drum around which the main cable was wound. We sank a little before rocketing down once more. I shone my light through the mesh on to the curved, wet, redbrick walls of the shaft, certain we were bound for hell.

'Welcome to the Parkgate and Fenton,' a voice uttered in an ironic tone, as if we had just arrived at a seaside resort, the nearing lights signalling that we were approaching the pit bottom.

I followed Trevor and the lads out of the cage, turning left past a giant white electrical transformer that sat in a cave carved out of the rock, and felt the brisk cold air being drawn into the pit via the shaft on my back as two men hurried towards us hoping to ride the cage back out. The older man's eyes watered in the wind, smearing the grey dust on his cheeks, and the tails of his donkey jacket billowed behind. We turned right up towards the base of a one-in-five drift where a man-carrying conveyor belt led up to the Fenton seam proper, thirty metres above. Almost everyone else continued straight ahead towards the Parkgate paddy; a train transporting them, 'inbye', into the interior workings of that seam. Trevor started the conveyor belt and, one by one, we knelt onto it. As we climbed up the drift I stared nervously at the steel supports in the tunnel which somehow prevented 3,000 feet of earth and rock from descending and crushing us alive. I recognised almost all of the materials used in its construction; up on the stockyard we had been packing them into mine-cars and onto trams for the past year.

From the top of the conveyor we turned left into an altogether different world. The pit bottom and the drift had been reasonably well-lit and the apex of the roof had risen to an impressive height, making walking straightforward. Now, with the only light coming from our cap lamps, the roof height sank and the floor undulated erratically. Within minutes I smashed my head against a steel girder and fell to the ground, dropping my carrier bag full of snap into the dust. Tiny silver stars danced in the dark as I opened my eyes. My helmet had been torn off and lay in the dirt, joined to me by the cable of the cap lamp. Immediately, the lads guffawed. 'Watch your head mate,' laughed Taffy

John. When I headbutted the steelwork a second time I took Trevor's advice, holding the cap lamp in my hand and shoving my snap down my jacket. Trevor moved along the gate easily, the lads just behind, their silver beams slicing the darkness. Along this section I failed to keep up, crouching awkwardly and lurching like a drunk, my back bent, head out to the side and my thighs burning from the intense effort. I cursed as I repeatedly tripped, stubbing my toes on the protruding sleepers supporting the haulage rails and every single damn rock in the ground.

Up ahead the others waited at a junction by a set of airdoors which separated 'the intake', the colder clean air being drawn in to the mine, from 'the return', the warmer air being drawn out of the mine by an enormous extraction fan positioned on the surface above the upcast shaft. I followed on into the warm air, leaning hard against the far door and pushing until I stumbled out into cold air once more and a thundering noise. A tongue of rough-hewn, sparkling coal charged towards us, violently transferring from one conveyor belt to another, extinguishing all other sounds. A button man, in charge of the transfer point, sat in a dimly lit corner on a seat made from chockblocks and strips of old conveyor belt; a primitive looking black telephone hung to his right. He nodded as we raised our hands, heading towards the maingate end of a coal face known as RO6s, walking with the belt to our left and the bronze steel haulage rail lines to our right. Power cables and rusting water pipes laced the walls and shelves, suspended from the arched roof, were piled high with white powder.

Soon, at technical college in Barnsley, I would learn that these were 'stone dust barriers', designed to contain a coal dust explosion. Such explosions can quickly develop into rampaging fireballs that race through tunnels, quaffing oxygen and shoving a wall of air in front of them. This wind disturbs coal dust lying on the ground, turning it into a volatile airborne cloud which fuels the fireball; a lethal vicious circle. I saw a film of coal dust explosions at college. The terrifying speed and ferocity of the fireball surging along the testing tunnel and spewing out as an angry, mushrooming, orange mass chilled me to the core.

Our tutor Pete had relayed to us the local Houghton catastrophe in June 1975, which left five men dead and others seriously injured, and which prompted the Energy Minister of the time, Tony Benn, to comment, 'This tragedy has reminded me that there is still a very high price to be paid in human life for the coal we get in this country.'

As we passed a spillage of coal caused by the belt being out of line, I stared at the steel girder legs which had been deformed and partially driven into the earth. The power of the strata to twist and mangle such robust looking steel work disturbed me. It brought my own frailty into sharp focus. We were nothing but ants, I thought, that had burrowed far too deeply beneath the earth's crust. Icy water ran from a corrugated tin sheet in the roof; I ducked but it wet my neck anyhow. This was not how I had imagined it. I had seen underground images on television where politicians and other dignitaries stood in perfectly shaped, large whitewashed tunnels, allegedly 'down in a modern coalmine'. Such pictures now seemed like laughable, pathetic versions of the real thing, for if this was a 'modern coalmine' then God knows what my grandfather had endured. As my friend Tony would say some years later, reflecting on our abandoning education for coalmining: 'We thought we were talking ourselves into some real money, we didn't realise until we got down there we had talked ourselves into hell.' If the devil had a home, I pondered, then surely it was somewhere very close by.

A disc of light swung up and down vertically in the distance, blinding us.

'Haulage is coming, get out o' way!' Trevor yelled over his shoulder, the taut steel rope moving forcefully within the confines of the track and grinding grooves into everything it touched as it towed the creaking, empty mine-cars towards us. Remembering endless tales of hands and feet lost by accidents on the haulage I jumped under the conveyor belt, scrabbling as far away from the tracks as possible. Once they had passed I emerged, accidentally disturbing a pile of silky, dry coal dust with my feet.

'For Christ's sake Caveman lift thy feet up when tha walking, are tha trying to blind me?' Gerald boomed, partly mocking, partly serious.

'Sorry mate.'

'Tha fucking will be if Old Moffa catches thee,' he continued screwing his fists into his eyes.

Old Moffa was a legendary figure who allegedly refused to retire, lying about his age to the authorities. He also had a notorious vicious streak, particularly if anyone farted or created dust upwind of him. One tale told of him yanking one guilty trainee's thumb-nail with a pair of pliers. Another unfortunate soul was rumoured to have had his pubic hairs yanked. From then on I began picking my feet up as well as clenching my buttocks, petrified of discovering Moffa lurking in the darkness.

When we reached the end of the gate, we took a breather, sitting down on wooden chockblocks to save us from the damp ground. In the past miners only began to earn money once they arrived at their place of work. Our approach down the shaft and along the various gates, which had taken at least thirty minutes, would have been unpaid. Sometimes miners had to walk underground for an hour or so in their own time – each way. For us, a standard underground shift was seven and a quarter hours, starting and stopping at the top of the shaft. Only getting changed and going to the lamp room was done in our own time.

Starving, I dragged a sandwich out of my snap bag.

'What we got on snap today then Cavey?' asked Mark.

'Pilchards with vinegar.'

'Pilchards with vinegar? Well I say, aren't we posh.'

Trevor started laughing, forced to remove his water bottle from his mouth and instead holding it out in front of him. Ducket, Selwyn and Gerald took a quick bite of their snap, which looked like bread and jam or dripping.

'You planning on doing a double un?' asked Taffy John on seeing the size of my snap. Beads of sweat ran from his curly mop down his pallid cheeks. 'Trev, I feel shagged today. I can't work.'

'You're a useless drunken twat Taff,' jibed Selwyn.

'I'm badly,' Taff replied.

'How many did thy have last night?' quizzed Trevor.

'Fifteen, that I can remember.'

'Fifteen pints on a Sunday night? You dozey bugger, we're bored of carrying thee, man,' started Ducket, a little glum after a bad weekend backing horses. I had already eaten half my sandwiches when Trevor rose to his feet.

'Right, come on you lot, let's make a start, otherwise gaffa will be bollocking me.'

He hung his waistcoat on the side of a ring girder. We followed reluctantly, hanging up our water bottles and sandwiches out of reach of the mice.

Our job that morning was 'MATS forward', which involved carrying the materials dumped by the haulage lads to the end of the maingate, way beyond the end of the haulage rails where the rippers were busy advancing the gate (ie extending the tunnel). On the surface we had always loaded leg and crown sections of ring girders on to the trams using a small crane or a fork-lift truck; now, in a dark tight place with water above our ankles in places, we carried them by hand. Fortunately I paired up with Selwyn, a sixteen-stone wall of muscle who, when not working down below, played rugby for the Sheffield Tigers. My slender nine stone frame buckled under the strain as I tried desperately not to lose my balance. Finally, we dropped the leg at the rip and returned for more, proud to be helping some of the most respected men in the pit.

Much talk centred on who had the toughest job. Three groups were contenders: face men, shaft men and rippers. Face men operate the shearer machine that cuts the coal, advance the hydraulic roof supports and ensure the gob (the void left by the extraction of coal) closes safely behind as the face moves forward. Although fewer roof falls now occurred on the coal face than in the pre-mechanised era, the giant high-speed cutting machines produced a constant stream of dust and threatened workers' limbs and digits. Trevor had worked on the coalface until a hydraulic chockpipe burst one day, hitting him in the face and permanently damaging one of his eyes; hence his new role of showing us the work. Two of my uncles were also face men: my mother's brother Phil and her brother-in-law Martin. A face man my father knew suffered an accident so terrifying that he lost his nerve and ultimately left the pit. A strained panzer chain snapped unexpectedly and lifted him into the air, throwing him like a cloth doll over the armoured face conveyor and into the direct path of the cutting machine, all its teeth spinning and ripping through coal and rock like candy. He lay there with a mangled arm, his screams silenced by the deafening shearer about to tear him apart. Fortunately his workmate spotted him, shut down the power to the machine and organised first aid and a stretcher.

He made a recovery but the memories filled him with terror. His wife was delighted when he returned to work as they had suffered financially during his convalescence. The man was less enthralled, though, and spent some days walking in the local park, eating his snap and then returning home at the expected time. He had completely lost his nerve. He simply couldn't stomach it any more, but was too embarrassed to admit it: being frightened is not manly in a mining community. Ultimately he found a lower paid but much less risky occupation in town.

Shaft men had respect too. They hung under the cage inspecting and repairing the shaft lining. Few of us could contemplate hanging in the pitch black in a 3,000 foot hole. For most men the regular journey in the cage was challenging enough.

Rippers do one of the most dangerous, physically demanding and dirtiest jobs in a coal mine. Those working in the tailgate of an advancing coal face breathe air that has travelled all around the coalface and is stale, humid and full of dust. Extracting coal is like removing a strip of cream from a gateau. As the cream is slowly excavated the layers of the cake close behind. The rippers construct the two tunnels either side of the extracted strip (like straws between the layers of sponge, running up to the edge of the cream) which are used both as essential supply lines and also to convey the cut coal back to the shaft. On RO6s the left hand tunnel, our gate, consisted of untouched rock and coal on its left side but a supporting wall on the right side known as a 'pack wall', behind which sat the 'gob'. The gob is the area where the roof has collapsed onto the floor once the coalface has advanced. Normally a team of three rippers advance the tailgate tunnel and a different set of three advance the maingate. As Selwyn and I dropped off the final girder we stood and watched for a while, instantly understanding why they had such respect among the men.

Earlier, at the start of the dayshift, the deputy had shot-fired to a horizontal depth of about three metres, leaving a heap of blue-grey mudstone and coal that one man was moving with a small, hydraulic-powered digging machine, tipping it onto the racing conveyor belt. Using just the light of their cap lamps the other two – dressed only in shorts, knee pads and boots – were busy plucking with a pick hammer, swinging in an arc and knocking off any protruding fangs of rock, trying to smooth the side walls and arching roof of the tunnel. Both men had tattoos, the youngest one having immensely powerful shoulders atop a relatively light frame. His mate picked up a hydraulic powered jack-hammer, held it against a defiant tooth of mudstone and tore it off. We started carrying the smaller materials of chockblocks, corrugated tin sheets and tie-bars whilst the rippers started setting the first ring. A clamp known as a 'horsehead bracket' hung from the top of the last erected ring, supporting two jutting steel rails, and the men struggled to get the next arched section, the crown, up on to this rail. They then manhandled the left leg into position, bolting it to the crown with a fishplate before joining on the right leg. Having struggled to carry just four legs twenty metres I sat, awestruck by their skill. To undertake such an operation on the surface with the assistance of cranes and a team of eight in a well-lit area would be impressive enough, but to succeed here in a confined dark hole, slopping about in water, the floor and walls irregular, was remarkable. When I learned that Britain has more miles of underground mining tunnels than the entire nation-wide rail network put together, I held these men in even higher esteem. I believe my father's father, Arthur, had been a ripper.

At snap-time all machinery came to a peaceful standstill. We retreated down the gate to enjoy our food, passing Taffy, who lay on his side asleep under the belt. Ducket couldn't resist tying his laces together and then smacking the top of his helmet with a shovel while the rest of us shone our lights into his eyes. As he leapt up, he hit his head on the belt and then recoiled onto the floor, wriggling.

'Bastards!' he shouted, realising his feet were bound.

He perked up during snap, boasting that he would show us how to do some real work afterwards. This started a lot of barracking. Trevor sat back and listened, enjoying the mock threats between one lad and another. I learned that so much of this humour was aimed at testing relationships rather than destroying them. At times the harshness of the banter disturbed me and in a different context it would have been deeply offensive. But among our gang it served to maintain equilibrium, to emphasise that no individual stood above anyone else; anyone who believed they were superior received the line, 'Who the hell does tha think thy are?'

The slow squeaking of the belts starting up signalled the end of our break and we walked down the gate for 100 metres, searching under the belts for shovels and picks that the team had stashed the week before. Our next task involved shifting the pile of spillage we had earlier scrambled over back onto the conveyor belt. It looked gigantic and was becoming a constant feature of the gate, despite protests from the team to the deputy and under-manager to solve the problem. It seemed they were preoccupied with more serious geological problems on the coal face and, what's more, they were loath to stop the belt in order to realign it for fear of losing productivity. We knelt down as if in prayer and began shovelling coal over our shoulders. The odour of damp coal and the beer in Taffy's sweat stuck in my nostrils. We worked for three solid hours, stopping only to down more water. Slowly, we forgot where we were, settling into our private worlds, each of us lost in his beam of light. Something in the rhythm of the work made the monotony bearable.

By two o'clock we had moved two thirds of the giant heap. We stopped and began our journey back towards the pit bottom. Whilst travelling in the gate, by the airdoors, we met the afternoon shift, 'white faces', coming to work. Trevor knew most of them from his days working on the coal face and, listening to the exchange of greetings, I wondered how much he missed the camaraderie and status of working with the local aristocracy, not to mention the higher wages. One young lad stopped, produced a tin of bacca and offered it around.

'Not for me love, but I'll have a pinch if tha's got one,' replied Trevor.

Nonchalantly, the man pulled a small, square light-blue tin from the inside of his jacket and held it in the palm of his hand, flicking open the lid. As Trevor reached to pinch with the fingers of his left hand he held his right forearm parallel to his chest, spreading out the fingers and thumb creating a hollow for the powder to sit in. He raised his wrist, inhaled sharply through one nostril and then repeated the exercise. I copied him, feeling wonderfully refreshed, if a little light-headed. Inquisitively, I then took a chew of the apple-flavoured bacca also on offer, its pungent aroma piercing the damp air that smelt of musty old socks. Some men believed chewing bacca reduced the amount of dust breathed. Cynics agreed it was nothing but a hit of nicotine for men who normally smoked. Heading towards the cage I wrestled the slippery, foul, brown substance around my mouth, unsure of the correct protocol. Should I eat it?

'The juice is the best bit, swallow plenty of the juice,' advised Selwyn confidently.

'Arghhhhh . . . Jesus. It's hideous. Shit!' I started spitting but it was too late.

'Tha'll be shitting through eye of a needle by time tha gets home Caveman!' Taffy John shouted.

The boys howled and as we reached the pit bottom my stomach was already churning mercilessly. Riding the cage out of the pit the passing bright flicker of each seam startled my heavy eyelids: Dunsil, Barnsley Bed and then the Beamshaw from the blackness. I remembered a night out in Royston a few weeks earlier.

We stood by the bar in the Ace Ballroom disco, listening to my old school friend, Bill, speak enthusiastically about his Royal Marines basic training on the edge of Dartmoor in Devon. He had been running across moors and wading through freezing rivers in such atrocious weather that finally he had ended up in hospital with hypothermia; yet, despite the hardship, I envied the adventures he described. Astounded at how quickly he had adopted a West Country accent we teased him, mimicking his new, higher sounding vowels. Justifiably proud of being a Marine, he began reminding us, 'Without soldiers we'd all be doomed, it's one of the most important jobs there is.' This made Gary – his older and bigger brother – look up attentively, his jet black hair glistening under the light of the bar.

'Remember, down the pit, on that coal face I'm fighting a war every day of the week.'

'But it's not the same . . .' started Bill.

'I'm tellin thee pal, every shift it's war down there. Believe me.' As he said this I stared at his hand, firm around a pint glass, with slight traces of coal dust grafted in the folded skin of his knuckles.

I had not been underground at that time and his words had felt overly dramatic, a macho rhetoric full of self-importance. But what I had seen down there today was an extraordinary display of will power. The working conditions I witnessed would have shocked most people, I am sure. Although they rarely admitted it publicly, I think many miners believed that what they achieved underground was important, something to be proud of.

The cage flashed past the Melton Field seam, its lights briefly illuminating the heads of my mates and then finally, a little before 3:15pm, wonderful sunlight startled us, the sweet smell of fresh air at last. As we rose out of the ground we saw the expectant face of the afternoon shift banksman, waiting to collect our small, round brass checks. I pushed my way off the cage, ran to the lamp room, threw my lamp onto the recharger and then dived into the toilets.

It had been a fantastic day of battling up cracks, deep chimneys and jutting overhangs. A classic gritstone day, one to remember. With the sun already low in the sky Pete negotiated an awkward bulge near the top of Stanage Edge. I had visited the cliff for the first time two months earlier with a gang of coal miners. CISWO, an organisation dedicated to the social welfare of miners 'beyond the colliery gates', had sent a dozen Yorkshire and a dozen Derbyshire miners to an outdoor pursuits centre in Castleton, Derbyshire, for a few days.

On first laying eyes on the Derbyshire miners some of our gang instantly switched into territorial mode, announcing that they were 'going to kick the shit out of them' for no reason other than the fact that they were from Derbyshire. However, they appeared surprisingly friendly and, perhaps more importantly, much more physically imposing. Many of the young men already worked underground and so a day crawling around in mud, down an uninspiring local pothole, proved to be something of a busman's holiday. Most of them loved the climbing on Stanage Edge, however, particularly the abseiling. At the end of the session I announced to the instructor that I wouldn't mind trying something a little more challenging and so he agreed, setting up a top rope on a suitably blank piece of rock. He climbed up first and then lowered down. I didn't own rock-boots and began struggling my way up the climb wearing my old tennis shoes. The lads cheered excitedly. No sooner had I reached the top than they began chanting my name over and over again, claiming that I was a better climber than Richard, the instructor.

'You definitely had quite a tight rope while you were climbing,' I remarked.

This started the boys jeering even more, ever ready for a competition with anything or anyone and particularly a figure of authority. To shut us up, Richard had no alternative but to tie-on once again and attempt the climb with a slack rope. The fact that he succumbed to the bait delighted us, we couldn't care less about the names or grades of the climbs, we simply wanted to get under his skin, to mock his pretensions of high standing. I didn't know the name of the climb we had done that day but I could see it now as I belayed Pete.

At the top Pete declared that he needed a beer, but I wasn't really satisfied.

'For God's sake man the cliff is three miles long. There are six hundred-odd different climbs, tha can't do them all in a day.'

'Okay, just one more. The lucky last,' I replied. Intending to solo climb I took off my harness down below, tossing it next to my rope and rucksack.

The cliff edge unfurled leftwards, sinking then rising towards the horizon like the Great Wall of China. Placing my right foot in a shallow indentation above a tiny pale-coloured pebble, I pulled on to the rock. The lack of paraphernalia dangling from my waist brought a wonderful sense of freedom as I padded my feet up the silken slab. Although comforting and safe, stopping to place protection on the earlier climbs had interrupted the flow of movement over rock, like overhearing a telephone ring whilst watching a beautiful love scene in a film.

My fingers stretched like those of a waiting concert pianist over the rock and found dimples, enough to balance with. Pete turned away disapprovingly, worried. And I preferred it with no one watching. I stood up on to a comfortable large square of detached rock but then I became annoyed at myself for not wanting to leave its sanctuary. Fall thirty feet from here into that jumble of mean sharp rocks and you'll probably never walk again, flashed through my mind. I tried to shut out the void below. Okay relax, I sighed. Finally I committed and the handholds were surprisingly positive, the grains of the rock rough under my fingers, the palms of my hands tender from hours of joy. 'Look at that man,' I heard a small boy shout, but it washed over me; I was lost in concentration, moving up steadily, enjoying the dance.

And it *is* dance, I suddenly thought, as the momentum from one move flowed into the next like the pendulum of a clock, like the spring-turn manoeuvre in a foxtrot. God, how I loved that feeling of bending forward, spinning and then quietly bouncing out, facing the opposite wall of the ballroom clutching Rose, our feet gliding over a well-waxed wooden floor. A gentle wind blew my fringe as I climbed the last part, easier though still dramatic; relaxing yet requiring caution. On the top I stopped a while, breathing in the beauty of the buckled brown moors.

'Erm,' muttered Pete, when our eyes met down at the base of the cliff, as he was packing his rucksack, still disapproving of my desire to solo climbs so close to my limit.

On the walk down to the car I recalled fragments of recent conversations I had had with my granddad Harry.

'Pee on your hands Andrew,' he had suggested to cure the blisters on the palms of my hands caused by all the shovelling underground. A few weeks later when I told him that climbing on gritstone savaged your hands even more than shovelling, showing him the battle scars on my knuckles, he thought for a moment before saying once again, 'Pee on your hands love, that's what we always used to do down pit. It will toughen the skin up.' And so halfway down to the road, I drifted off purposefully into the tall green bracken and, facing the cliff but out of view of other climbers, peed all over my hands.

5

Coal and ice

My brother Jonny burst through the gate, dribbling a football past the front door, his thin pale legs hanging out of an enormous pair of white shorts. The studs of his boots reverberated noisily as he sprinted through the gap between our house and next door's before unleashing a curling right foot shot into the top left-hand corner of the coal house door.

'Ronnie Glavin does it again for Barnsley FC!' he shouted, jumping into the air and applauding the imaginary fans. A look of surprise broke out on his face when he spotted me dangling from the other side of the coal house.

'What you doing Andy?'

'I'm getting tired,' I replied, hanging from my arms, my feet smearing against the shiny red brickwork, two feet off the ground.

'Getting tired, what for?'

'To get stronger.'

'You look daft.'

'Go away Jonny.'

My arms burned but instead of letting go I heaved myself up, pressing down with both wrists, and scrambled over on to the concrete roof.

'Can I come up?'

'No.'

'Why?'

'You might hurt yourself.'

'Oh! You always say that, it's not fair.'

Frustrated, he kicked the ball against the coal house; it rebounded knocking over the empty milk bottles on the back door step. I leapt on to the roof of the kitchen extension opposite, then using the drainpipe reached and grabbed the sill below the bathroom window and pulled up.

'I'm in the wrong job, Jonny, I should have been a burglar.'

I lowered myself down with too much gusto, making a thud as I landed, and jumped back across on to the coal house just as the back door flew open.

'Is he up there again?' My mother spoke quietly but purposefully. 'The bloody kitchen is falling down as it is without you climbing all over it, get down. And keep the noise down you two 'cos if you wake your dad up there'll be bother.'

She retreated into the steam-filled kitchen, preparing our tea. Her latter point was valid of course, for one of the few times I had witnessed my father get angry was when he had been woken unexpectedly following a long nightshift at the pit.

It had been a gorgeous sunny Sunday morning and the local Bethel church had arrived complete with megaphone, Bible and guitars directly opposite our house. They warmed up with a particularly enthusiastic rendition of 'Give me oil in my lamp keep me burning' and had not even completed the first round of the chorus when my father thrust his exasperated, unshaven face out of the front bedroom window as though woken from a terrible dream. His false teeth floated in a glass of water on the windowsill beside him.

'For God's sake will you lot piss off! Some of us have been working all night,' he roared at the youthful, suited and bloused missionaries.

The voices stopped singing, the guitars faded and, after a grovelling apology they moved on, attempting to convert those living at the top of the street.

I climbed down from the coal house and helped Jonny clean out the cage of Thumper, his handsome, dark-beige rabbit donated by Granddad. Later at the dinner table I broached the subject of modifying the side of the house so that I could practise my climbing.

'You must be joking,' my mother replied.

'It won't do any harm, loads of climbers do it to keep fit,' I enthused.

'I don't care love, it's a council house this, we don't own it, we can't start knocking holes in it just anywhere we like.'

'They'd only be little holes otherwise it'd be too easy, in fact smaller the better.'

'Oh not this subject again. It's like listening to a bloody record,' my father snapped, the next fork full of potato arrested in mid-air.

The fact was, I sorely missed the mid-week evening trips to Derbyshire that Pete and I had enjoyed during the summer months. On those afternoons I had run from the shaft to the lamp room, showered at breakneck speed, ripped my rucksack from the locker and caught a bus to Barnsley, from where the two of us would screech off towards the cliffs. But now, sadly, the dark evenings had arrived and we were restricted to climbing at the weekends. Desperate, I did manage to climb a little during the week, locally. The supporting sandstone brick pillar of a former railway viaduct down at Old Royston, next to my granddad Jones' signal-box, provided some interest. Burton Bank above the A61 was another venue, but I had been avoiding it since a recent close shave. Whilst traversing the central section of the damp, crumbling, graffiti-covered quarry wall, a waterfall of rubbish had crashed down from an allotment above. An old child's bicycle, numerous glass bottles, clouds of ash and rotten vegetables had narrowly missed me, high-lighting the potential dangers of climbing in the urban setting.

Thankfully, the prospect of going ice climbing in Scotland during February helped me through the long, dark autumn. The stories of the great alpinists filled me with fire and I simply could not wait to climb in the Alps. But first, Scotland. Steve Benstead from the Mountaineering Club pointed out that moving from rock to snow-and-ice climbing involved a huge leap in terms of the techniques required, and suggested we hire a mountain guide. I agreed and we each sent off fifty-pound deposits to a man named Mal Duff, a guide operating out of Glencoe in the Western Highlands.

After tea my father went off to work and my mother, exhausted after a day of non-stop household chores, collapsed in front of the telly with my sister. My mother was always busy cleaning, washing, cooking or shopping for food. Because my father and I worked on different shifts and my brother and sister were still at school, she prepared snaps and cooked meals perpetually. She also ran the local Cub Scouts on Friday evenings

as well as recently attempting to complete a full-time secretarial course. She dreamed of gaining new skills so that she
could avoid working as a sewing machinist, a job she had done
on and off all her life. However, she quit the secretarial course,
explaining that it was too stressful as 'us lot' did not pull our
weight enough around the house. 'You treat it like a hotel,'
she complained. 'I'll go back to college when you lot have left
home, I'm telling you.'

I went upstairs and lay on my bed. I disliked TV and anyhow
I wanted to finish reading *On The Heights* by the famous
Italian alpinist Walter Bonatti. In the adjacent bed Jonny should
have been sleeping ready for school but instead, like most nights,
he sat reading my old football programmes, carefully digesting
the statistics. It had to be admitted he owned an impressive
memory and could regurgitate football facts to anybody who
displayed the slightest interest. For many years my passion for
Barnsley FC had been unremitting and under the pastoral care
of John, the next-door-but-one neighbour, I had been granted
permission to attend any match I fancied, as long as I paid for
it with the money I earned from my part-time job. We had
visited Grimsby, Watford and Brentford as well as Liverpool
in the 1979 League Cup run, where somehow we held Kenny
Dalglish and friends to a scoreless draw and then got chased
by a pack of scallies down a backstreet. However, I was now
infected by climbing ambitions and, though I would never forget
running onto the pitch to the sound of Gerry and the Pace-
makers when Allan Clarke's men won us promotion to Divi-
sion Three, football had now become second best. Instead of
Mick McCarthy, I idolised the alpinists René Desmaison and
Walter Bonatti, not Ronnie Glavin. Their books conjured up
a fantasy world, a world I found difficult to imagine even
though deep down I urgently desired a taste of it.

Like most people I always believed Europe's highest peak,
Mont Blanc, to be in France. Via Bonatti, I learned that this
is only half-true: in fact, by far the most interesting half of the
mountain lies in Italy. On the steeper, more remote Italian side
sits a 2,000 foot candle of orange granite – the Central Pillar
of Freney. I lay on my bed spellbound by Bonatti's account of
his attempt to make the first ascent of this monolith.

When Bonatti and his three companions arrived in the tiny

bivouac hut on the frontier ridge of Mont Blanc they discovered a party of French climbers, led by Pierre Mazeud, already there with the same ambition. Despite having waited countless years to climb the pillar, Bonatti magnanimously suggested that the French should go ahead and that his team would find another objective to climb. But the French invited them to join forces. Fatefully, Bonatti agreed.

The seven men climbed difficult terrain to within a few hours of the top of the vertical and overhanging tower when it began to snow. By then they were no more than half-a-day from the summit of Mont Blanc, from where Bonatti knew the descent intimately. However, the snow soon turned into a raging blizzard. They sat in primitive bivouac equipment for five long days and nights, enduring vicious winds and terrible cold. Finally, Bonatti decided they must descend at once otherwise they would all perish. Reluctantly, they began retreating. After another night spent sleeping in the open they waded through chest-deep snow, each man utterly exhausted, descending a passage known as the Rochers Gruber. Too weak to continue, Vielle collapsed and died. Eventually, Bonatti and Gallieni staggered into the Gamba mountain hut and raised the alarm. The rescue team rushed out into the night and found Mazeud alive. Tragically Kohlman, Guillame and Bonatti's closest friend, Oggioni, were dead.

Deeply moved by the prose, I lay motionless. I glanced over at Jonny and saw that he had fallen asleep, a football programme still in his hand. I closed my book, set the alarm, then turned off the light.

Every Wednesday I attended the mining technical college where I discovered a long list of tedious facts, such as that 'the mild steel used in mining wire ropes has a tensile strength of about 30 tons per square inch'. I felt frustrated with the cycle of work at the pit followed by the study of subjects in which I had no interest. During lunchtimes I scoured the shelves of the public library behind the college as, undoubtedly, my recent obsession with mountaineering stories had ignited a general desire to read more. I had not particularly enjoyed my time at school but I did remember my English teacher, Mr North. He was a giant of a man who wore thick glasses and roared at any hint of ill-discipline. He had a habit of setting us tasks and offered money for the first to complete them.

'INCREDULITY,' he said one week, chalking the word onto the blackboard. 'The first person to find me tomorrow morning and tell me precisely what that word means will receive ten pence!' Another week the task was to tell him exactly where the island of Tristan Da Cunha was. Mr North was offbeat and slightly mad but I found his company exhilarating. He had lived an interesting life and he spent much of his time recounting extraordinary anecdotes about his experiences in the Korean War. He had a genuine enthusiasm for literature and I fondly remembered our weekly readings from the English set text-book, *Nine Modern Poets*. Perhaps it was Mr North's fault that, at lunchtime on the third Wednesday, I wandered into the general education department, a hundred metres away from the mining college, and sheepishly enquired about courses in English Literature. 'There's a class tonight,' said the lady, encouragingly. 'You can always go along and see how you get on.'

It felt so incredibly indulgent spending two hours reading frivolous poetry, after eight hours of staring blankly at texts such as *The Law Relating to Safety and Health in Mines and Quarries, Parts 1 and 2*. Our literature tutor read out loud wonderful melodic stanzas which I absorbed in giant breaths, feeling my mind come alive. A week later I bought the recommended course book, *The Oxford Book of Narrative Verse*, and instantly fell in love with Tennyson's *Morte d'Arthur*, spellbound by the beautiful lucid imagery:

> There drew he forth the brand Excalibur,
> And o'er him, drawing it, the winter moon,
> Brightening the skirts of a long cloud, ran forth
> And sparkled keen with frost against the hilt:
> For all the haft twinkled with diamond sparks,
> Myriads of topaz-lights, and jacinth work
> Of subtlest jewellery.

At around the same time that I fell in love with poetry I bought a tube of hair dye and behind a locked bathroom door began vigorously massaging the substance into my wet hair. Initially, no discernible difference appeared and so, somewhat annoyed,

I squeezed the rest of the tube onto my head and then went to my bedroom to allow it to dry. When I later removed the towel and looked in the mirror I almost fainted. My hair was bright orange.

I let out a slow, maniacal laugh, not because I thought it amusing but because I simply did not know what to do. I had only wanted subtle red tints. I dragged the small cardboard packet from the bin: 'The dye should wash out in eight to ten shampoos.' Too afraid to leave the bathroom I began shampooing immediately. After four washes it looked exactly the same and so I prepared myself, in the medium term at least, for life with an orange head.

My parents laughed but didn't seem too bothered.

'You've got a lot of red in your hair naturally, no wonder it's gone orange. Anyhow, it'll wash out,' remarked my mother.

In the pit changing rooms on Monday morning I glanced at the tiny mirror on the inside of my locker; at least the combination of the glowing orange NCB overalls and my new matching mop would mean I was easy to find in the dark underground. I hid as much of my hair in my helmet as was possible and strode off towards the lamp room and then to the shaft, stomach tense, bracing myself for an onslaught of abuse. My colleagues spotted the modified hair at once and the jokes arrived in quick succession but, after the initial barracking, the lads got bored and moved the topic on. Mark from Lundwood had permed his hair and a few of us wore earrings. To the older men, my new unplanned hairstyle brought some confusion and seemed to reaffirm their belief that new recruits entering the mine were becoming more and more weird each year.

Walking towards the maingate end of R06 we met the haulage lads, one of whom worked as a part-time tattooist. He placed a piece of mudstone on to the ground, a beautifully etched eagle about to catch its prey.

'I've just done one of them for a lad up Red City.'

'How much we talking for that?' I enquired.

'Eight quid on thee arm, fifteen for a bigger one on thy back.'

One of the young belt men happened to be passing just then and the tattooist requested that he show us his recent acquisition. Without a word the belt man placed his helmet on to the mine car and, slipping his orange overalls from his shoulders, flexed an impressive right bicep. An angry looking British bulldog snarled on the outer part of the arm, sat atop a flowing Union Jack.

'Don't know what I'm going to have done on t' other arm yet,' the lad told us, smiling, obviously delighted with the artwork.

'Tha should have saved money on daft hairdo Caveman and had a tattoo instead,' Gerald suggested.

Sporting a tattoo at the pit was de rigueur, an expression of belonging to the underground clan, a straightforward symbol of masculinity. Somehow men dying hair orange did not rank highly in the local system of social signs.

'How's the yellow monkey fever this week, old boy?' quizzed Ducket, stripping off in preparation for another shift in the swamp.

'Coming on nicely mate, look at this.' I laughed, shining my cap lamp onto the inside of my left thigh where a peculiar fungal rash now extended from my knee almost to my groin. 'How's yours?'

'Not as bad as that. You want to watch it doesn't spread to thy wedding tackle, that would be serious – yellow monkey knob.'

This started us all laughing as, like amphibious troglodytes, we walked up the roadway and then waded into the thick, putrid-smelling sludge covered by four inches of yellow waste water. We were condemned for another week to this water-logged section of the gate, trying to extend the rail road for the haulage up towards the ripping. A pump worked in vain, for as fast as it removed the water more of it oozed from the strata. I wore robust NCB issue wellingtons but in some areas the water was too deep and, whilst holding a rail in place as Selwyn hammered the dog-nails into the supporting timbers, I sank further into the quagmire and felt the inevitable rush of water between my toes. I winced. Only humour could save you.

> 'Oh I do like to be beside the seaside,
> Oh I do like to be beside the sea,
> Tra la la la la . . .'

Andy's grandfather, Harry Round, with one of his prize rabbits. Monckton pit behind where he started work underground in 1925, aged just 14.

Old mining methods

Grimethorpe Colliery

Pickets prevent the bailiffs
seizing the funds of the
NUM, Barnsley, March 1984

Strike canteen, Barnsley

Pete Swift climbing
Desperation on Stanage,
Derbyshire

Ben Nevis in winter

Gasherbrum IV (7980 metres) viewed from Concordia, the route attempted joins
the right skyline at the obvious icefield

The G IV team at base camp:
Brendan Murphy, Kate Philips, Andy Perkins, Chris Flewitt, Andy Cave, Andy Macnae

The North Face
of Changabang,
6864 metres

(*Left*) Brendan Murphy peruses the second hand tooth market in downtown Delhi
(*Right*) Roger Payne receives spiritual healing for his bad back in a temple in Rishikesh

Lower part of face showing climbers in action

I bellowed above the monotonous drawl of the conveyor belt and the pump. At times like this laughter seemed better than crying. Perhaps because it was so bad there was worth in it, pride in the sheer grimness of what we were trying to achieve down there. Maybe laughing helped us to retain self-respect.

Unquestionably, humour was an essential characteristic of the coal miner's behaviour, particularly black humour. My friend Tony, who worked at the nearby South Kirby colliery, often related an accident he witnessed underground.

Tony was working near the ripping when one of the rippers started shouting.

'Pete's lost his hand, he's fucking chopped his hand off with a sheet. Quick!'

'I bet he's lying,' said a big miner named Barry. 'Tell him if I find it I'm going to stamp on his fucking fingers after what he said to me the other day.'

Tony was shocked with this comment as when he met the victim he saw that his hand was quite literally hanging off and he had lost a lot of blood. The men put Pete on to a stretcher and prepared to evacuate him from the mine.

'Hold on a minute, does this mean I don't get my tenner back at the weekend?' joked Barry before searching Pete's pockets, stealing his bacca and snuff.

'They'll not let thee chew that in hospital, tha going to be in there a while.'

Gallows humour extended to the tradition of nicknaming too. I heard of a man accidentally speared by a wooden dowelling through the abdomen who was renamed 'Kebab' when he finally returned to work.

I learnt quickly that a particular brand of humour among miners included exaggeration and the telling of white lies, or 'pillocking'. Spheres of work and social life overlapped in mining communities so that normally private details found themselves in the public domain. On my street, women would know exactly how much a man earned each week, who his family were, and whether they liked a drink or not. Pillocking capitalised on this overlap of worlds. Because I lived outside the Grimethorpe–Lundwood area people had relatively little information concerning my social life, other than what I chose to disclose.

Earlier in the year, in Barnsley, a friend and I had gone back to his girlfriend's parents' house after a night out. We'd sat in the front room drinking, unaware of the time. I had been getting on rather well with Mary's best friend when I heard an alarm clock go off and then the sound of giant footsteps up above.

'What the hell is that?' I whispered.

'That's my dad, getting up for the dayshift. You know he's a deputy at Grimey, down the Fenton.'

'What's his name?'

'Pete.' She smiled as the heavy feet began descending the stairs.

'Jesus, we're off.'

Grabbing our shoes we shot out of the house and hopped down the gravel drive like a pair of startled cats running over hot coals.

I should have known better than to recount this anecdote to Trevor and the boys. Months later we found ourselves working in the district managed by Pete. Remembering the story, Trevor stopped Pete on his first inspection of the tunnel.

'Now then, Pete, this lad Andy here reckons he knows your daughter quite well,' started Trevor, in a tone that hinted at some act of misconduct.

'Who, our Mary? How's that then?'

The huge man shone his beam straight into my eyes.

'Well . . .' I faltered, somewhat taken aback by the pace of the conversation and blinded by the light. 'What Trevor means is that, I . . . I . . . I used to go to school with her, you know, in the same year. Nice girl.'

Trevor relished witnessing me squirm, coolly standing in the background, suppressing his laughter. Gez and the team stopped shovelling, listening in.

'Yes she's a lovely lass.'

'Yes I think so.'

'You don't fancy her do you?'

'No, not at all, not my type, I mean lovely but out of my league, if you see what I mean.'

He fumbled the top of his deputy's stick with one hand, an oil lamp hung from the other. My heart beat harder and faster, terrified that Trevor might reveal that I'd spent until dawn working through his drinks cabinet and larder.

'Good, 'cos she's too good for you,' he answered curtly, then stalked off.

The game had been to land me headlong in trouble and then to watch me cope under pressure. Every man received the same treatment and more if he lost his rag. It brought everyone down to a common level, where no man was better than any other. This could have been destabilising in another setting but underground it galvanised us into a unit.

After laying three lots of haulage rails across the swamp, we changed back into our overalls and donkey jackets. We had missed snap to complete the job and now we had less than half an hour to catch the 3:15pm cage at the pit bottom. To save time we decided to ride the coal conveyor belt to the transfer point. Our system had been honed to perfection. First, one lad spoke a coded message into the tannoy system: 'The eagles are landing'. This warned the haulage lads and the belt men what we were up to and served as a cue for them to watch out for any officials on their way to the coalface. Getting caught riding the coal belts could mean the sack, or at the very least a hefty fine.

Selwyn volunteered to be the front runner. This meant sitting on his knees, checking the route ahead was safe, then dismounting at the end and watching that we all exited safely. If a problem arose he could pull the emergency cable that ran alongside the belt and bring it to a stop.

Though I had ridden countless times before, it still terrified me. Frequently the shape of the roof could change over the weekend and a razor-thin tin sheet might swing down ready to decapitate the unvigilant. I hung from the rusting water pipes with gloved hands, despising the commitment of the initial leap on to the belt as it screamed past. I gave Selwyn twenty yards start, closed my eyes and then jumped. I lay head first on my chest, keeping my head down and hugging the shining black snake of coal. Allegedly, it was only travelling at ten miles per hour, but the utter darkness combined with the narrowness of the tunnel made it feel more like one hundred and ten. If big Selwyn makes it through I should be fine, I told myself. After a few minutes I could make out the lights of the transfer point. Stories of men falling asleep then disappearing down the metal chute and getting limbs caught in the wheels of the belt engine haunted me, increasing my heart rate further still. I crouched up and in a flash lurched to the left, grabbing the water pipe with both hands then throwing my legs clear over the white belt frame. I landed in the dry dirt of the road, my chest pounding with the thrill of it. Selwyn continued to watch out as one by one the lights appeared, briefly dazzling us as each man leapt from the charging belt. 'A miner would rather try and ride a coal shovel out of the pit, before walk', went the saying.

We made the cage, just. In the showers the dye from my hair created a small, bright-red stream that joined the main black one running between the long rows of washing men.

What struck Steve and me the most about these serious mountaineers was their insouciance as soon as they left the mountains. In the corner of the Clachaig pub Mal Duff and Jon Tinker, our guides, spoke about their forthcoming expedition to the unclimbed North-East Ridge of Mount Everest in a surprisingly understated manner, as if going on a family holiday.

'Another pint of seventy shillings lads?' asked Jon.

'That would be great,' I said without consulting Steve, who looked a little alarmed at how much time we were spending in the bar each evening. Steve was an able rock climber and canoeist who was hoping to find a job as an outdoor instructor. He was a great team player.

'It's important to create a decent bivvy layer,' said Mal, pinching his stomach. 'It's the old Don Whillans theory of arriving at base camp with weight to lose. If you arrive too thin you'll be emaciated by the end and not strong enough to tackle the summit.'

Steve nodded at my skinny frame. 'Not much hope for you up there, Andy.'

The ridge they hoped to climb on Mount Everest had claimed the lives of Pete Boardman and Joe Tasker, my heroes from the book *The Shining Mountain*, in the spring of 1982.

'The trick is getting well-acclimatised and this takes time. But also you have the monsoon weather arriving at the end of spring, so it's a fine balance.'

Jon came back with the beers.

'Here's to you guys, you did ever so well today. You'll go a long way.'

'Thanks, Jon, it was absolutely amazing,' said Steve.

'Absolutely brilliant,' I chimed, raising my glass and asking what the plan was for the following day.

'Well there's some weather due in later in the day so I thought we'd go to the Ben and do The Curtain,' suggested Mal.

'What time will we leave?'

'Six thirty, in the van.'

Jon and Mal disappeared over to the bar to chat with Peter, the landlord.

'Jesus I've heard of The Curtain, I think it's quite hard,' began Steve, reaching into his pocket for the guidebook.

The Curtain. 300 feet, grade V ***, 1.5–3 hours
A fine water-ice climb. A large icefall comes down the left hand side of the buttress to give 3 pitches: a long slab, a bulging wall and a rightward ascending traverse.

'These guys are outrageous, it's only our second day in crampons and they're taking us up grade fives.'

'Well you found today alright didn't you?'

'I thought the climbing was fine but what with that hellish walk in and out I feel wasted now,' Steve said honestly. 'These guys are mega-fit, obviously. They are training for Everest.'

I knew what he was saying. We had walked in rather quickly to Stob Coire nan Lochan, a north-facing cliff high above Glencoe. But we had kept up, just. And I wouldn't have wanted it any other way. Jon and Mal knew that we were decent rock-climbers, keen to push ourselves.

'We'll be fine, Steve. I feel knackered but the weather might change after tomorrow and then we'd regret not going for it.'

'Yes that's true. Anyway let's go and get some sleep, it's half past ten.'

I finally caught up with Mal, out of breath.

'Perfect training for Everest, Andy,' he told me before disappearing again into the night gloom. I followed on, trying to find the line of least resistance through the thick mud with the beam of my headtorch, listening for the sound of his ice axes clashing together on the back of his rucksack.

As the sun rose the formidable, ice-streaked shoulders of Ben Nevis pushed upwards, dwarfing us. In the distance I could make out the CIC hut where Pete and I had stopped before embarking on our epic ascent of Tower Ridge eight months earlier.

Mal was sheltering on the leeward side of the hut eating chocolate when I arrived.

'That's The Curtain, our route.'

'Oh great,' I commented confidently, hiding my fear. It looked preposterous. Feeling damp and cold in the breeze, I put on an extra wool jumper and a balaclava. I took out a sandwich and rested it on my pack; a few seconds later a gust covered it in a thin layer of snow.

'Crampons, harness, helmet on here.'

'Okay.'

I had worn crampons for the first time the previous day in Glencoe. Fitting them to the boots correctly seemed a dark art. Long straps had to be threaded in a particular configuration to prevent them falling off.

'Are you ready?' asked Mal.

'Nearly,' I lied, more and more confused by the straps and buckles, my hands deadened by the cold.

Mal bent down and pulled the straps tight.

'Okay let's go.'

Shod in crampons, my leather boots felt heavier than ever. To make matters worse, snow began collecting under the crampons, forming giant snowballs that presented a formidable test of balance.

'You need to tap your foot with the axe if they're balling up,' called Mal into the freshening wind, gesticulating with his axe. I stood on my left foot, raised my right clear of the frozen slope and walloped it with my left axe. I lowered my foot and felt the spikes of the crampons bite. Mal continued, his boots and then his axe stamping the snow slope: dash, dash dot, dash, dash dot. When the angle of the slope reared up he waited.

'The trick is to take small steps, Andy. When you stand up there's a point where the leg is straight and, if you think about it, all the muscles are relaxed at that time – you're getting a rest.'

I watched him as he traversed diagonally right and then emulated his gait. Until then the concept of taking modest steps was anathema to me, I had enjoyed pushing myself. It was a simple piece of advice but it would stay with me forever, becoming the bedrock of my movement in the mountains.

I leant on my axe and craned my head around this magnificent scene. Clouds were descending from the summit now and powder snow thundered down the side of Tower Ridge off to our left.

'Move fast across this next bit; Number Five Gully has a habit of avalanching,' warned Mal, quickening his pace dramatically.

I galloped on behind trying to ignore burning lungs and screaming thighs, joining him on a small ledge below the route.

'We'll rope up.'

'Where does it go?' I asked naïvely.

'What's that?'

'Where does it go?'

'Up to the wee cave there and then out left. It's a classic, you'll like it.'

As Mal sorted out the ropes and clipped me into the belay I gaped up, bewildered. Holy shit. A monster made of blue-green ice crawled towards us, a mass of fangs and tentacles slithering over the red granite rock and then flowing into a wide white smear of ice, perhaps two inches thick. This measly coating of ice swept down directly to where we now stood. Small, pathetic beings.

'Okay, am I on belay?' asked Mal.

'Erm . . . wait a minute . . . The rope's caught on my crampon.'

'We need to get going, there's some weather coming in,' Mal said tersely.

'Right you're on.'

Mal climbed with rehearsed ease, rhythmically swinging his ice tools and, possibly because the ice was too thin, placing no protection whatsoever in the 100-foot long initial rope length, utterly confident in his equipment and his expert ability. We had negotiated some brief steps of pure water-ice the day before, but they had been set within longer, much gentler sections of snow. This entire climb consisted of climbing up pure, hard, water-ice. Before I knew it the ropes tugged at my

85

waist and a muffled cry vaporised in the wind. My time had
come.

I shuffled leftwards until the snow met the ice, so thin at
this point that I could see the speckled granite underneath. I
wielded my Pterodactyl ice axe at the veneer of ice and it
bounced out angrily, narrowly missing my cheekbone. 'Damn
. . .' Just out of reach the ice looked marginally thicker, if
only I could reach it. I swung my left boot, stabbing a strip
of ice the width of a wallet. Half of it shattered and splintered, rolling down the steep slope below. My front-points
screeched down the rock, leaving a scar. I stabbed at the tiny
blob of ice that remained. Miraculously, it stuck this time and
I gingerly transferred my weight on to it. Come on, stay,
please. I knew that with rope stretch I'd tumble a good twenty
feet if I fell. I held my breath, placed my axes in the thicker
ice above, then scampered out on to the vast shield of ice. I
made steady progress but every ten feet or so I was forced to
stop, my calves quivering from the effort of standing on four
points of mild steel stuck just over a centimetre into the
diamond skin of ice.

Just before the small cave where Mal stood I had to stop. I
clung to my axes, listening to my own fast breath, overwhelmed
by nausea. I had the hot aches. 'Bow your head, it will gu,' I
remembered Pete saying. I wanted to sob. 'Bloody . . . hell . . .
Argh . . .' As the blood began to creep back into my hands I
bowed my head. It felt like small shards of broken glass were
being hammered into my finger tips.

Mal ushered me into the cave and then set off confidently
across a much steeper section of ice. It looked horrifying.

'You know how to get ice screws out, yeah?' shouted Mal,
twisting the steel teeth into the ice.

'Yeah, Jon showed us yesterday.'

Whilst I traversed the ice the wind began gusting, unnerving
me. Below my tiny crampon points I felt the space tugging,
forcing me off. I must not fall, I can't fall here. I moved gingerly
to the end of the traverse and started swinging my left axe at
the bulging wall. It shattered, hefty chunks cartwheeling down
into the emptiness. Totally gripped, I let my exhausted arm
dangle, desperate for it to recover. I got angry and then smashed
the axe as hard as I could. Thwack! It held.

I moved on to easier ground above and stopped. The helmet I'd been given by a man in the village was too big and it repeatedly slid forward over my eyes. This led to me developing a sporadic flick to regain my vision; it was a twitch Emperor Claudius would have been proud of.

'I could never imagine leading that, never in a million years,' I told Mal at the end of the pitch.

'The last pitch isn't so bad,' comforted Mal. 'You're doing great.'

Above my head hung a row of small frozen daggers. In the distance, tiny dark figures of climbers beetled up vast sweeps of snow and ice. It was hard to appreciate the scale of the place. Tower Ridge, which I'd climbed with Pete the previous spring, was plastered white and looked treacherous. I couldn't hear Mal in the strengthening wind but I felt the rope tugging three times on my waist, his signal for me to move. I hauled myself up the final rope length, calves aching, knuckles swollen from smashing the ice and a small cut to my cheek from a falling splinter. Yet I was at that moment, I know, the happiest man alive.

At the top Mal held out his snow-covered mitten, winked at me, and then shook hard. In just over three years' time he would telephone and ask me to come and work for him for a few weeks as a mountain guide.

6

Arthur's castle

I saw Gaz, a faceworker from Woolley pit, in the arcade in Barnsley. We had met for the first time in September at the miners' day-release class and we hit it off straight away, often sitting together. He had a great love of music and a deep rolling laugh.

'They're saying bailiffs are coming to NUM offices. Going to seize the union's funds.'

As Gaz spoke his hands tightened, enormous ivory knuckles reaching out from the end of his faded denim jacket.

'They need as many folk up there as possible.'

Then, after a pause, he added, 'I think we should go up.'

'Okay,' I nodded.

At the top of the arcade we turned right along Huddersfield Road. It was a cold March morning, new buds on the trees, a few daffodils starting to unfold outside the town hall. Once past the technical college we could see the crowd gathering by the entrance to 'Arthur's Castle', the NUM headquarters. Every miner paid a weekly subscription to the union and it seemed logical to defend the money, *our money*, donated by our fathers, grandfathers and great-grandfathers too. Groups of men made their way from their homes or direct from picket duty, all walking purposefully towards the pale brick building with its ostentatious turret. As we walked some men gave their opinions on how long they thought the new strike was going to last. Gaz joined in.

'It's going to be a long one Cavey, I'm telling thee.'

'I think you're right.'

The NUM's decision to call an indefinite strike came in response to the government's pit-closure programme, beginning with the announcement of the closure of Cortonwood colliery, followed by a further nineteen pits. The moderate miners of Nottinghamshire and the Midlands were calling for a national ballot and local miners had started picketing these pits in order to persuade them to join the strike.

We squeezed into the bustling wall of two or three hundred men barricading the Victoria Road entrance. There were lads like myself barely out of school, men my father's age and plenty who must have been approaching retirement, dressed in duffel-coats, snorkel parkas and NCB donkey jackets. Here and there a suit. Within an hour the defiant sea of faces had swollen to 500. On the road thirty or so policemen tried to keep the traffic flowing.

We had been on strike now for almost three weeks and it felt good to be in this crowd, to be part of something solid. At home we had spent most of the time trying to work out how we would survive if it continued for much longer. My father had visited the union office, the social security and the council from whom we rented the house. Apparently 55,000 Yorkshire miners were currently on strike, as well as all those in South Wales, Scotland and Kent, but actually witnessing the commitment and feeling the passion firsthand strengthened my resolve to withhold my labour. As a coal miner you had an unwritten obligation to secure the future of the industry so that subsequent local generations had work. It was not the greatest job in the world. It wasn't film star wages either, but with few alternative employment opportunities in the area it had to be protected. And this is chiefly what was at stake. Unlike the strikes in the 1970s, it was not about wanting better conditions or better wages. If the truth be known, many men at Grimethorpe were happy earning a basic take home wage of £78 for a week underground and £115 for a week on the coalface.

A TV cameraman walked down the middle of the road filming us, the soundman following at his side holding a huge furry microphone. A small pocket of men became agitated and told the film crew to go away. Perhaps they were already unimpressed

---

*This is excluding 'bonus'. Bonus depended on the output of coal from a pit – variable due to geological and engineering problems. What job you performed influenced how much bonus you received.

at how the dispute had been represented in some parts of the media. The cameraman picked up on their anger and, balancing the camera on his shoulder, decided to zoom in on them. This was a mistake. The eldest of the men broke out into the road, shouting and gesticulating to the two media men to 'piss off'. The sound recordist thrust the microphone under his chin but he pushed it away and roared at them, clearly annoyed by their impropriety. The crowd drowned out every other sound with a resounding cheer as the two began wrestling in the middle of the road. The film crew attempted to retreat but the miner had hold of the microphone so that, when they stepped back the giant, furry grey sleeve came off in his hand; in frustration he threw it on to the ground and commenced stamping on it. It was joyous, Shakespearean slapstick. Ecstatic, the crowd play-fully surged forward and, intimidated, the two media men fled, clasping their flattened microphone.

By mid-afternoon, with no sign of the supposed bailiffs, many men broke away, heading for a big union meeting in a hall opposite the technical college. I met Gez (Gerald) in the crowd and we decided to go. God knows where Gaz had ended up. We filed into the hall and found free seats towards the back, the excited tones gently hushed and were replaced by applause as Mick MacGahey, the vice-president of the NUM from Scotland, took the stage. The government have declared war on the British miners and the mining industry, he told us. He was a confident, persuasive speaker who believed the government and the media were shocked at our militancy and were now trying to demand that we return to work until a strike ballot had been called. We should not bow to this pressure, he maintained; we were within our rights to defend our jobs. To finish he invited us to come to the front of the hall and become members of the Communist Party. MacGahey received rapturous applause as he left the stage. Without hesitation Gerald went and signed for the CP. I hung back, unsure about it, and having no idea what such a commitment entailed. I left the hall with the majority of the men and caught a bus home.

At home my mother tried to calculate how we were going to manage with both my father and me out of work. My father

returned from Grimethorpe pit declaring that the £15 a week
strike pay that we had each anticipated from the union was
not available. At the end of March the family began receiving
£17.59 in supplementary benefits each week from the Department of Health and Social Security. They maintained that as I
was only a trainee miner I couldn't be on strike legitimately
anyhow, and therefore they paid me nothing. My mother and
father received £21.45, plus £13.70 for my sister Maria and
£9.15 for my brother Jonny. We also received £1.29 towards
our water rates. From the sum of £45.59 they deducted £13,
which my mother received in family allowance, plus £15 for
the strike pay my father was entitled to (though he never got
it). So five of us shared £17.59. That same week Jonny and
Maria were handed a voucher entitling them to free school
dinners, as well as clothes and shoes, when justified, courtesy
of the local Education Department: 'from the 20th of March
1984 for The Duration of Strike' read the letter.

We paid bills until our savings were almost finished, then
we ignored them. The rent for the house was disregarded and
carried forward, week after week. To save bus fares spent travelling to the union office at Grimethorpe, we were told we
could attend Royston Drift Mine area union meetings to keep
abreast of any developments, though we weren't allowed to
vote on any issues. Here they gave us a voucher permitting us
to eat twice a week at the soup kitchen established in the village
civic hall. Les Parkes, the local, red-cheeked butcher, let us have
a certain amount of meat every week. I had worked for him
delivering meat around the village on Saturday mornings as a
thirteen year-old before I found the job at the Co-op and he
had become a friend of the family. 'Pay me when you get back
to work,' he told us.

Bored one night, I went out for a walk. The week spent
winter climbing in Scotland had inspired me, filling my heart
with dreams and desire. I longed to visit the Alps and climb
some of the big peaks I had been reading about. But it looked
like an impossibility now with the strike seemingly having no
end in sight. The government had done their homework:
numerous power stations had been modified to accept oil,
thereby decreasing the reliance on coal; and huge numbers of
police were regularly deployed to intercept flying pickets, tipped

off by bugging the telephones of NUM officials. Most damaging of all, every day Maxwell's media empire was busy undermining the strike in the press. Scargill, our president, simply dug in deeper, delivering more and more militant rhetoric.

I stopped at the top of the street to stare over the darkened wheatfields, past the amber lights of Carlton and beyond the chimneys of the glassworks, towards the inky night horizon, letting my imagination take flight. I saw alpine meadows nestled beneath dramatic blue glaciers. Now rose Mount Kenya in Africa, a beautiful slender ribbon of ice – The Diamond Couloir – falling elegantly from the summit, much more real than the photo in Chouinard's book in the library. I pictured bustling African markets under huge skies and smelt aromatic spices being sold by men and women in brightly coloured silk. So convincing were the visions that when I emerged out of the trance, realising where I was, a shiver travelled down my spine. I felt trapped and confused. Would I ever truly escape this place? On the one hand I belonged here and genuinely believed in the reasons for the strike. But I also had wanderlust in my belly. I went home and packed my rucksack, deciding to go and climb in Derbyshire for a few days.

'Come on children, wakey wakey,' whispered Chris, placing two mugs of coffee onto the carpet. Nigel groaned and turned over. He loathed the idea of any movement whatsoever before lunchtime. I took an arm out of my sleeping bag and reached for a mug, exhausted from our two long days of climbing on Derbyshire gritstone. I had to get up and eat.

'You've been shopping, Chris. Good effort.'

There were eggs, beans, tinned tomatoes, bread and milk.

'My stomach thinks my bloody throat's been cut,' he said with a mock grave look.

Chris Hale, whom I had met out on the crags just a few days earlier, was something of an enigma. He had been brought up in a row of miners' cottages in the notorious village of South Kirby, two miles from Grimethorpe. He had fallen in love with climbing, left home and moved into this flat here in Killarmarsh on the edge of Sheffield. At weekends his flat was awash with random climbers found on the crags. Colour, class, gender or character made no difference to him. You were simply a climber and you stayed. He loved us all, as if we were his family. He was unemployed and watched his money carefully, even managing to run an old white Mini, which he tended to free-wheel as much as possible. Midweek things were generally quieter, but shortly after breakfast a team from Nottingham, Alistair and Danny, charged up the stairs. Alistair and Danny had bombed up the M1 intending to go straight to the cliffs and hurl themselves at some famous gristone jamming cracks, but at the very last minute they'd decided to swing by and visit Chris. The kettle boiled repeatedly and we talked incessantly about the various rock climbs we aspired to.

'I think Froggatt would be good; we could try Cave Crack,' suggested Nigel, who enjoyed doing battle with horrifically strenuous wide cracks.

'You're joking,' said Chris. 'The energy needed for that could light Sheffield for a week. Numerous small boys have been lost in the back of there you know. They've never been found. It would be like doing ten rounds with Joe Bugner.'

This started us laughing. Although Chris had never worked at the pit, his father, Jack, had and he had inherited the sense of humour.

'I fancy Wales,' I chipped in.

'Why not?' enthused Alistair, his smile widening.

'Here we go, the bloody optimists, never satisfied,' began Chris. 'Have you come into some money Andy, or are you planning to rob a bank? Me and Nigel are on the dole, you and Alistair are on strike.'

'You're on strike as well are you?'

'Yes youth.'

'Well . . . There's quite a lot of downhill, you know, we won't need that much petrol,' I joked.

'And what about on the way home, are you pushing?' quizzed Chris.

'I've got a cake me mother baked for me and some tins of rice pudding and some beans, and I think I've got nearly seven quid.'

'Oh well in that case let's go to fucking Yosemite, I've always fancied doing the Nose on El Capitan,' barked Chris, rolling his eyes and looking away for comic effect.

It was raw Kirby humour. 'Anyhow, my Ferrari's in the garage and I don't think we'd get five in the Mini,' he continued.

'We might get five in mine. What do you reckon Danny?'

'Do you think I'm going all the way to Wales in that rust bucket?' said Chris, before Danny could open his mouth. 'How did you get the MOT? Did you find it in a lucky bag?'

'Hey cheeky,' cautioned Alistair.

Nigel couldn't care less what we did. He was a superb and naturally gifted climber but he lacked ambition. He put the kettle back on. He had enjoyed our two days on grit and as far as he was concerned had earned a week off from climbing. Although it wasn't voiced, I felt that the idea of Wales was being approved. We all had famous routes we wanted to try in Wales; what's more, the weather looked set to be fair.

'Right come on, you only live once, let's go to Wales,' said Chris after we'd finished another coffee, and suddenly we were off.

We put five pounds each into a petrol kitty and two pounds for food.

'So which pit do you work at, Alistair?' I started.

I had not met any striking miners from outside Yorkshire and wanted to know what the feelings of people were like elsewhere.

'I'm an underground electrician at Hucknall. Been there seven years. You're at Grimethorpe, Chris says.'

'Yeah I'm still a trainee. I'd only been underground six months when the strike started.'

'I bet everybody's striking at Grimethorpe aren't they?'

'Yeah, as far as I know. What about at your pit?'

'Absolute nightmare. There's only a few of us on strike out of 1,300 union members. I get sworn at for standing on the picket line.'

'What?'

'Exactly, it's a fucked-up world.'

'It's normal to be on strike at Grimey, we're one of the most militant pits in Yorkshire.'

'It's ripping us apart this strike. But the short-sighted buggers don't realise Maggie will shut down the Notts pits along with all the others.'

'I agree.'

'Mind you, I have to be honest, I'm enjoying all this fresh air. It's a chance to clear the lungs out.'

'Absolutely.'

'I've no money Andy, you know, but when I'm climbing I'm so happy.'

We woke to the sound of a gentle, flowing stream and sheep bleating high on the mountainside. The sun swept across Dinas Mot – a vast shield of rock directly in front of us – casting tiny shadows on the blankness and hinting at subtle corners, arêtes and overhangs, features that inspire a climber.

'I've always wanted to do The Diagonal,' started Alistair.

'Alistair, it's the middle of the night,' mumbled Chris.

'Idle buggers.'

'Some of us are trying to sleep. Cavey will go,' Chris sighed.

'Where is it?' I asked.

'Where is it? It's one of the most famous routes here. It's on the right-hand side up that smooth slab. It's supposed to be bold, I don't think you want to fall off.'

I jumped out of my sleeping bag.

'Chris,' I began.

'What?'

'Can I borrow some gear?'

'You really don't own anything do you Cavey? Help yourself.'

We bounded up the short, steep, boulder-strewn slope and climbed quickly up the initial 150 feet to below a smooth-looking wall.

'Wish me luck youth,' mumbled Alistair, having finally run out of excuses.

'You'll be fine, just stay cool. You know you can do it. You cruised the last pitch.'

'Yes but that was seconding, with a rope above my head.'

'I'll buy you a pint if you do it.'

'What with?'

'After the strike I mean.'

He smiled.

'We could be waiting a long time. Okay watch me.'

'I'm watching you.'

Alistair climbed nervously rightwards. I noticed his fingers on the initial holds squeezing more than he needed to. It was a famous route, one that all climbers dreamed of but normally tried to delay ever stepping on to. It was a climb with a nasty

reputation, a landmark route in a climber's career. The combination of being a rising traverse and having very little protection had led some climbers to comment that if you fell in the
wrong place you'd land in Llanberis, five miles down the road.
Trust your feet, I thought as he tried to place some protection,
hanging mainly from his left hand, his calves starting to shake.
He grabbed the rope and clipped it into the karabiner and
looked instantly calm.

'Is that nut any good?'

'Pretty good I think. The handholds are rubbish though.'

'Imagine you're back on gritstone, trust your feet. Hands
just for balance remember.'

'Yeah right,' he sniggered nervously.

'I know you can do this mate, just go for it.'

This was a white lie, of course. We'd never actually climbed
together so how the hell did I know that he could do it? He
moved up into a shallow scoop in the rock, his feet resting
delicately on the sloping grey skin of the wall, his ankles angled
downwards. He stopped, a long way from his last piece of
protection.

'It's too scary Andy.'

'Stick with it. Keep going.'

Although Alistair was the one climbing, I knew what he was
experiencing. A leader's confidence is such a fragile thing, so
easily shattered. He looked lonely now clawing the rock, a
huge sweep of air beneath his feet, ankle-snapping ledges eagerly
awaiting him should he slip. I wanted him to do it.

'Go on Alistair mate, give it some rice, it will be easier than
you think.'

Success after struggle tastes so sweet.

'Okay get ready. I might fall here.'

'Come on, hang on in there.'

He dipped his hand into the chalkbag tied around his waist,
trying to dry the sweat from his finger tips. He breathed in
deeply then moved his foot up on to a tiny edge. He groped
the rock blindly, searching. The rope fell from his waist and
lay on the wall, waiting to be stretched if Alistair fell. I willed
him on but turned away as his feet paddled the slab, frantic
for something to stand on, anything.

'Come on Al, come on,' he shouted to himself.

I glanced at the two small aluminium wedges in the crack supporting my weight. The lower one moved a little if I leaned out too much. Would I get ripped off my stance if he fell, catapulted into the morning sky? I forced myself in to the wall.

'Yes, yes!' he cried. He had done it. He had reached the next belay.

'Well done,' I called across to him, the adrenalin still flowing in my chest. I enjoyed following the pitch, knowing that I had a rope tugging at my waist from above.

'Thanks for believing in me youth. I shit myself,' he said when I arrived.

'Good effort that. I thought you were going to back off at one point.'

'It crossed my mind. That was frightening.'

I led the final, easier pitch to the top of the cliff where we shook hands. At the bottom we grabbed our rucksacks and headed back towards the others, who were attempting to turn the car around.

In the Vaynol pub in Llanberis that evening, Alistair and I had just beaten two local men at pool and were congratulating each other when, clearly annoyed, the smaller man spoke.

'We'll play you again for a pint of beer, if you like?' he suggested tersely.

'I'm not sure we can afford it mate,' I replied, though I felt we stood a good chance of winning. Alistair looked keen even though we would be totally penniless if we lost. Chris, Danny and Nigel encouraged us and so we shook on it.

We won two consecutive matches and drank the beer joyously. It was more than we had drunk for weeks and it had an extraordinary effect. More locals were pushed forward, keen to undermine the usurpers. Interestingly, the more beer we drank the better we seemed to play. We handed some of the beer on to our friends, including Chris who normally never touched alcohol.

Part-way through the evening I started to wonder if the locals had decided to let us win, knowing our plight as coal miners. Local people knew about hardship: until quite recently, many had earned a living from cutting slate in the enormous black quarries directly opposite the pub. Perhaps they understood what it meant to perform a dangerous job and what happens to a community if its main industry is taken away.

Chris drove us back up the Llanberis Pass. We rolled over the wall, crawled into our sleeping bags and, feeling numb, gazed at the starry sky above Snowdon, laughing ourselves to sleep.

My father queued each week in Barnsley for a £20 voucher, as part of a scheme recently initiated by the social services, and my mother exchanged it for food at the Royston Co-op. The soup kitchen at the civic hall was run by a group of energetic, well-organised local women – Royston Women Against Pit Closures. This provided the opportunity to eat two solid meals each week, thereby reducing the burden on families as well as giving people a chance to meet and chat.

We picked coal too from the railway sidings and the site of the former goods yard at the top of the street. It had quickly become a warren of tunnels, trenches and bell pits, and Bob Hutch – normally a face worker – had been trapped temporarily when the roof of one such excavation collapsed. Older miners' knowledge about the different mining sites and spoil heaps led to teams prospecting near Shafton and down at Old Royston.

We had a small riddle and borrowed Granddad Harry's pram to ferry the small coals back home. Most of it was used for our own heating, but small surplus amounts were bartered off to non-mining households who were worried by the shortage of coal. The scene at the top of our street – men, women and children scratching for coal on all fours – became commonplace and yet, to an outsider, it might have seemed to belong to a much earlier age of civilisation. These were the people the Thatcher regime had now branded 'The Enemy Within'.

I heard that a band were playing down at the pub one night, and decided to go along. Funds were non-existent and I managed to make a half of lager last from ten o'clock until midnight. The music took place outside on a makeshift stage surrounded by bales of straw. Thumper, Jonny's rabbit, would love to chew some of that, I thought. I loitered around at the end of the evening until certain I was alone, then threw a bale onto my back and dashed towards Church Hill. Just before the brow of the hill, golden cones of light approached and I quickly threw the bundle of straw into a ginnel on my left. A second later the car screeched to halt and the window wound down. It was a policeman.

'What you up to?'

'Eh?'

'Do you live in a hayloft?'

'Sorry?'

'Why are you covered in straw? You look like a scarecrow.'

I glanced around, noticing a yellow trail running from the base of the hill to the soles of my shoes. I wanted to explain that my brother's rabbit was thin as it was getting neglected, probably because we had bigger concerns just now, what with the strike and everything. But I didn't. Instead I said, 'I took a bale of straw from the pub car park.'

'Well you better put it back son, or there'll be trouble,' he rebuked.

'Okay,' I answered timidly.

He drove off and after a moment's thought I put the straw on my shoulder and jogged home the back way, via the canal.

'If the strike goes on any longer, I'm afraid Thumper's going in the pot Jonny,' I told my brother the following morning, holding a serious countenance. His big blue eyes stared at me in horror then filled with tears before he ran to mother, screaming.

'Ignore him, he's only kidding.'

I went outside and pointed to the straw. Jonny's face beamed and he started punching my legs, unimpressed with my joke.

'We might be eating straw oursens if this strike carries on much longer,' said my mother, only half-joking.

A few days later, shortly before midnight, I heard a knock on my bedroom door. It was my mother, holding a bottle, followed by my father and sister, Maria, who broke into song.

'Happy birthday to you. Happy birthday to you . . .'

Jonny woke up and joined us on the bed. I was flabbergasted. We had no money and yet they had managed to procure a bottle of sparkly wine and a beautiful card with a key on it – 'From Mam, Dad, Jonny, Maz and Rummie (our pet Yorkshire Terrier), with love'. At the end of the bed sat a bulky, black plastic bin-bag.

'It's only cheap booze but it'll taste alright. Anyhow, bugger it, you're only eighteen once.'

'Mam how did you organise all this?'

We never made a huge fuss over birthdays, but we normally received cards and small gifts. I was thrilled with the effort they had made.

'What's in the bag?'

'Open it and see.'

She had been to the charity shop and bought clothes with the modest sum my dad had earned from coal picking.

'Try them on, see if they fit.'

A green checked woollen shirt with only three buttons remaining; a pair of tight-fitting floral shorts; and a multi-coloured sweater with an extravagant Hendrix-style collar and sleeves.

'I hope you like them, love.'

Johnny Dawes shoved the car into third gear, pulled out, and began overtaking the truck in his way. I had seldom driven cars but recognised a blind bend. Pulling level with the truck Dawes stuck his tongue out a little, as if excited, and then glanced at me, wondering if I was enjoying the drive.

'Fucking hell mate, that was a bit radical,' I managed to let out, once I realised we had lived through the manoeuvre, the adrenalin still pumping. Johnny threw the Honda Civic into the gravel, pulled on the handbrake and leapt out.

'Andy that was nothing, believe me. You should see me in a proper car.'

I didn't respond but, the previous day, Chris had explained in a hushed voice that he believed they held the British Ferrari Club meetings at his parents' house.

We walked along the top of Froggatt Edge, and I listened as he talked non-stop about all the absurd ideas he had for new routes on gritstone.

'And they'll all bloody go, that's the frightening thing: these things will get climbed. The problem is that most people have no imagination, limited horizons.'

Johnny was small but powerfully built, with straight brown hair, and when he climbed he stuck his tongue out a lot, as when driving. One thing is certain, I had never seen a climber like this before. I stared incredulously as he stood on non-existent footholds and jumped dynamically for a pathetically small pebble with his fingers. What he possessed more than anyone I had ever met was balance. He really was dancing on rock.

I soloed a couple of slab routes, ones I had done before.

'You think you're good don't you? Well, try this.'

He ran at the slab, attempting to climb it with no hands, and when he failed he jumped into the dirt and ran again, managing to stand on a ledge using just one hand, the other behind his back. This guy should be in the bloody circus, I thought. His enthusiasm and self-belief were gigantic and he seemed intent on unlocking my own potential.

'Have you done Downhill Racer?'

'No. What's that?'

Johnny leant against a bare, impending wall.

'This little beauty,' he said, smiling. 'The holds are much bigger than you might think.'

I stared at the rock, confused by his words. It looked absurd.

'Try it, I'll watch your back. If you jump off, mind that rock.'

I set off, determined to have a good go. After ten feet I realised I'd made an error. I couldn't find any decent finger-holds and I was now directly above a grim, bone-busting rock.

'Stand up on those poor footholds and believe – there are better holds coming up.'

I took a deep breath and pushed on. Now I had passed the point of no return.

'The next move is a rock up, just trust your feet.'

I pulled up tentatively, too gripped to look down.

'Relax. It's easier now, take your time.'

I had never climbed anything so difficult, never mind this high off the ground, without ropes. I felt my chest thumping. I felt my throat turn dry. If I fell from here, I knew I would be going to hospital. I exhaled slowly, puffing my cheeks. Then, trusting my right foot to a vague line in the rock, I stood up, willing the rubber of my shoe to stick. The angle eased now but I could still only ever see one move ahead; the holds were simply too small. Johnny had gone silent. At the top I sat in the grass, feeling giddy. The tiny flowers burned bright, the tune of a sheep bleating, the birds' song gently calling.

'Congratulations,' bellowed Johnny in the tone of an Eton schoolmaster, marching across the moor holding out his hand.

'Ta. What's it called again?'

'Downhill Racer, E4 6a.'

'Wow, really?' I felt pride swelling in my chest.

'Remember that was done seven years ago, plus you're using sticky rubber on your boots. The first ascensionist didn't have that.'

'Oh,' I mumbled apologetically, but pleased nonetheless with my personal achievement.

'I was gripped up there,' I remarked.

'It's good isn't it? I think we should go to the café now and then to Stanage.'

Johnny was full of interesting ideas about economic and social philosophy, such as Adam Smith's 'original hand' as a *laissez-faire* market regulator. He charmed me with his social theories as we padded across the top of Stanage and descended beneath an improbable piece of blank rock. In his guidebook, the line of the unclimbed route had already been sketched in pencil and a tentative grade scribbled below. He tied on and moved up confidently, making peculiar movements and grunting. Towards the top he was slapping his hands up wildly. I was too frightened to try the climb even with the security of a rope from above.

'Okay. There's another new one I spotted further left.'

Johnny decided to inspect the next climb before starting, attempting to clean the lichen from the crucial holds. He lowered down the climb, brushing at almost invisible creases in the rock.

'Oh my word, this looks tasty,' he said melodramatically.

A few minutes later he set off. He placed a small camming device, called a 'friend', in a horizontal break at two-thirds height, and then began tussling with an elephant's arse finish. He groaned and stuck his tongue out, then threw his left heel up high and over the rounded boss of rock: a bionic ape on amphetamines. Then he was off, flying through the air.

'Superb,' he said, still swinging on the end of the rope.

He laughed and I lowered him down. The next time he climbed up, he placed a tiny brass nut into a shallow vertical crack. He began wrestling with the finish once more. Suddenly he was off again. However, this time, the friend ripped from the rock and Johnny came tumbling towards the ground. His head stopped two feet from the floor.

'If I fall again could you run backwards to take in the slack rope? Otherwise I might hit the deck.'

'Erm okay.' I answered nervously, my body rigid with fear.

He reckoned the rock was still filthy with lichen and set about brushing it again. Five minutes later he was back up, grappling with the final moves.

'Come on,' I shouted. He had his foot hooked above and his hands were slapping the rock loudly, as if welcoming a long-lost friend.

This time he made it. He peered over the edge grinning, out of breath.

'Absolutely . . . bloody . . . brilliant.'

I refused point-blank to try it, I was still shaking from witnessing his display.

He dropped me off at the bus-stop and we said our good-byes. Over the next four years he would become one of the most important figures in rock climbing history, raising standards on bold, technical routes to unthinkable levels. Apart from one or two exceptions, it would take the rest of the world a decade to catch up.

I climbed more and more over the next two months. From time to time Phil, the owner of Grindleford Café, gave me free food, knowing my predicament. I helped Keith Brown from the mountaineering club move house in exchange for meals. Another member, Cliff Mathews, and I met at Ravensdale and he brought me an actual sack of food, knowing that I was on strike.

I had given up any hope of visiting the Alps when, unexpectedly, the offer of a free lift arrived. A couple named Phil and Val, friends of Chris Hale's, were planning to drive to Switzerland in early August. Initially I dismissed the idea, but that night I tossed and turned in bed. I could always sell my motorbike.

7

Love in the time of revolution

He had a beard, wore a white coat and held a long drill. He pulled the trigger, filling the room with a high-pitched whine and then, nodding to the others, pushed the drill against something hard, grimacing as bits flew into the air. I lifted my head from the pillow and watched him drill a hole through my ankle, in one side and out the other. I smiled, but nobody else did. A beautiful woman squeezed my right hand, her big almond eyes saying don't worry, everything will be fine. At her feet lay a Whillans harness and a pair of blue pile salopettes splattered in fresh blood, not quite dry. I flopped my head back, smiled at her, closed my eyes, tried to remember . . .

I should have been tired that first night, lying in my sleeping bag by the forest on the edge of Bondo in south-east Switzerland. It had been hectic just before leaving home: selling my motorbike for a pittance; borrowing the necessary equipment; buying sufficient baked beans to last the fortnight trip, not to mention the long car journey. But, on the contrary, I fidgeted with excitement. In the darkness the silhouetted peaks stood silent and threatening, like sharp knives below the crystal-sequinned sky. The skyline of the Bregaglia mountains – dark, foreboding yet intriguing – promising a lifetime of adventures.

The next day we packed our rucksacks then began walking to the hut, my heavy leather boots pacing uphill. The route tracked through woods, along a gushing river and then across a gigantic boulder-field where I spied the hut: a bright square perched on a distant shelf, shining in the midday sun. I leaned into the air, rushing towards the mountains as if possessed by spirits. Their size stole my breath; suddenly Ben Nevis appeared small and Stanage Edge was almost non-existent. Dominating the horizon was the Piz Badile, a 3,000-foot sweep of blank granite tearing out of the glacier. On its left sat the Piz Cengalo, like the arm of an enormous, perfectly-ironed brown shirt.

Phil and Val arrived and we found a spot to spend the night among the giant boulders above the hut. After some lunch I went off climbing alone on the boulders a few minutes walk away.

'Have you got a climbing partner?' asked Bruno, a bald, friendly Swiss man with an earring, who was desperate to climb the north ridge of the Cengalo.

To begin with, I wanted to do a route with Phil and Val as I had travelled with them from Britain.

'After that I'm up for anything,' I explained.

'Good morning, how are you?' whispered the woman who had held my hand the day before, opening the curtains.

'I . . .' my throat was dry. 'Okay thanks.'

A silver steel rod had been driven through my ankle and weights hung from it: a pulverised, pulsing limb; broken biscuits in jelly, like trifle.

'Would you like some water?' she asked.

'Yes,' I replied, then after a pause: 'Will I climb again?'

'Excuse me?'

'Will I walk normal when it's better? I mean . . . will I get better?'

'The doctor will visit you this morning, he will explain everything. Here is your medicine; it will help the pain.'

'Thanks.'

She had a beautiful neck and I guessed her hair to be past her shoulders, when not tied-up. I tried to sit, keen to reach the pills from the table she had just pushed across my chest, but as I did so my leg exploded, searing shock-waves of pain shooting into my waist. I crashed into the bed shrieking, hot tears rolling down my cheeks. I squeezed my eyes tight as she placed the pills on my tongue, one at a time, and I gulped them down with the water.

'Well done Andrew.'

'It's Andy.'

'Sorry?'

'It's okay. What's your name?'

'Ursula,' she said, closing the door behind her.

I had never begun climbing so early before and I felt alive with energy, an electrically charged animal walking towards my very first alpine peak, globules of snow glistening in the beam of the lamp fixed to my helmet. The rocks smell different to the rocks at home, I thought, as we scrambled up the lower, easy part of our route, stopping when the angle steepened and changing into our rock-boots. Mine, which had been worn for months smearing my feet on gritstone, sported holes in the toes. On the advice of a man in the climbing shop, I had cut the rubber from the heels and stuck this over the holes at the front. However, whilst leading on a practice climb in the valley, the rubber had worked itself loose, eventually rolling down the rock over Phil's and Val's heads, and so I was back with my holes.

'You lead the crux pitch Andy, it will be quicker, don't you think, Phil?'

A film of grit crunched under my feet as I pulled up and squeezed my hands into a steep awkward crack in the sharp grey granite. High above the sun burst onto the summit's ridge crest; below the hut had shrunk. This place is phenomenal, I thought, as I shuffled my hands higher in the crack.

'How are you feeling today?'

'Bored.'

'I know, you said. I brought you this book, It's about Bob Marley.'

'Bob Marley, brilliant . . . I mean thanks.'

'You're welcome, I need it back though.'

Immaculate skin. She opened a window slightly. Outside, trees filed down a grand, sharp ridge, backlit by the afternoon sun, and the breeze blew a wisp of hair across her cheek. She took my temperature. *Twenty years old, twenty-two maybe.*

'Do you think he is right?' I asked tentatively.

'Who?'

'The doctor. He said he wasn't sure if I'd climb properly again.'

'I don't know, but he's a very good doctor, he has helped a

lot of skiers and climbers. Maybe they'll know more after the operation.'

'When will that be?'

'When the swelling has reduced, three more days perhaps . . .'

From the top of the final tower we abseiled into a notch. The rocky ridge leading to the descent path looked exposed but relatively easy. Having spent five months soloing and climbing on the gritstone crags at home, I personally felt confident climbing un-roped. To be on the safe side, however, Phil suggested we tie-in to a rope doubled at twelve-metre intervals.

'Tie on in the middle Andy, we can move together.'

I felt uneasy about this unfamiliar technique, Phil climbing first and Val behind. What happens if one of us falls? A small but impressively shaped rock tower loomed ahead. Phil nego-tiated it on the left but, to me, the right side looked much easier and safer. I plucked up courage to comment.

'That rock looks loose Phil. It looks better on the right.'

It was a pale, grey-blue shade, the sign of a recent rockfall. Phil's helmet turned around, staring straight at me, the sun dazzling his black glacier glasses.

'The guidebook says we go left here,' he said firmly.

He faced the rock and began moving. Seconds later a foothold collapsed and his body catapulted into space. I stared in horror at the glacier, thousands of feet below. As he disappeared from view, into the abyss, I watched the slack rope on the ground in front of me uncoiling, mercilessly. No time to react. Power-less. This is where I learn to fly, and Val too. The awful real-isation preceding inevitable tragedy serves only to increase the terror. Dying seconds. Flies flicked from the wall.

I expected my life to pass in front of me during that final precious moment, at least allowing me an instant to reflect on those close to me before I died; isn't that how it goes? But no, time did not wait or slow. I landed upside down. I crashed hard onto granite. Disorientated, I felt pain, gross pain. Alive? Am I alive? Phil was shouting from below and someone from above, Val maybe. So are we all alive? When Phil reached me I had already got myself the right way up; he checked me over, caring.

'Are you okay Val?' he shouted up into the vast lonely sky, his breath quick and shallow.

'Yes, how are you?'

'I'm fine. Andy's hurt his leg though, I think we need a helicopter.'

He helped pass my arms into the jacket, an old jacket he'd given me for the trip, then he handed me two strong painkillers. Just below my knee, bone protruded through the fabric of my salopettes and my foot pointed at a peculiar angle. I turned away feeling sick and dizzy, ebbing into darkness. I began shaking from cold, or was it the shock? Phil put a strong painkiller under my tongue.

'I am a first-aider,' somebody shouted.

It clouded over and then I felt hail pelting my cheeks. Two other British climbers, Mike and Dave, had arrived on the ridge. Dave tied my feet together in a makeshift splint while I winced through clenched teeth. Val and Mike descended towards the hut to raise the alarm. Now time did slow down, and every second of agony became an hour, every minute a day. This is not how I had rehearsed my first-ever climb in the Alps. It serves me right for being so hell bent on coming here this year, despite the circumstances at home. Stupid, selfish idiot! I softly punched the rocks to my right, trying to distract myself from the pain. I began shaking again – was it fear that I might die up here?

Slowly, the distant beat of rotating helicopter blades glided up from the valley, a drum of faith growing in volume. I smiled. Thank God! The sound disappeared and for another moment I felt frightened, alone. Then suddenly, an intense noise shot over the ridge and the red metal bird began circling above, the sharp draught blowing the hood of my jacket and forcing me to close my eyes. A saviour in a red jumpsuit lowered towards me on a steel cable, checked my leg, then clipped the cable into my harness and said something in Swiss-German into a tiny microphone attached to his helmet. I surged into the sky and made an effort to smile at the camera that Phil held, showing the thumbs-up sign as my stupid helmet started sliding over my eyes once again. I gave my (by now habitual) Claudius flick, waving to my friends left down on the dramatically narrow ridge.

*

Sitting beside the hospital bed, racked with guilt, Phil repeatedly told me how sorry he was.

'You did nothing wrong, we were unlucky that's all,' I said.

He pulled a pained expression to which I answered curtly, 'Shit happens.'

I joked about how I had fallen just fifteen feet and yet ended up like this, whereas Phil had fallen over forty feet unscathed. Meanwhile Val had managed to remain on the ridge, fortunately unhurt.

'Thank goodness you fell down the left side of the ridge into Switzerland, I'm not sure how good the hospitals are over in the Italian side,' laughed Val in her mild north-eastern accent.

There was nothing more that Phil and Val could do. I would be flown home once the doctor thought fit, but not for at least a fortnight. They brought my belongings up to the room, including a rucksack full of malt loaves, baked beans, jars of peanut butter and jam. I insisted that I would be fine by myself, and we said our goodbyes.

One of the hospital staff delivered a letter notifying me that it cost £80 per night excluding meals, medication or the major surgery I was to due to undergo at the end of the week. Helicopters were reputedly £50 per minute (presumably you started paying the moment they left the ground). Before leaving home I had wavered over the decision to take out medical and rescue insurance, mainly because I was broke and had received far less than anticipated from the sale of my motorcycle. But, on the advice of Keith Brown, I had written a cheque to the British Mountaineering Council insurance department in Manchester and left it to be posted by my parents. I had cut it very fine and had my letter not arrived before the date of my accident then I would have got myself into a catastrophic financial mess. A male nurse brought me a bedside telephone and I phoned the BMC.

'Hi, I want to know if I am insured.'

After a pause and a check of their records, 'Yes you are. Why?'

'Well that's fortunate,' I said.

'Why?'

'Because I'm sat in a Swiss hospital with a broken leg.'

*

The hospital authorities said they would contact my parents.

'My parents have not got a telephone,' I explained. 'Phone Mrs Ryan at number 1 East End Crescent, Royston, she'll relay the news . . .'

Cath Ryan opened the front door, found my mother in the kitchen and, without attempting to develop a broader context, blurted: 'Your Andrew is in hospital in Switzerland. He's in the middle of a six-hour operation on his leg, but he'll be fine the woman said.'

The words struck my mother like bullets. She collapsed on to the wall and then slithered to the ground. Recovering from the wounds, she lay in bed at night worrying, writing verse as a form of solace. In the daytime she wanted to speak to me, but she couldn't afford to pay to use anyone's phone. Every time she heard the radio play the song 'I Just Called To Say I Love You' by Stevie Wonder she broke down in uncontrollable torrents of tears.

'Good morning. How are you today?' asked Ursula.

'Tired.'

I had woken in a bigger room opposite a young man with jet-black hair, a pot on his wrist and small rods coming out of his leg.

'Yes that was a long operation. Here, you have a new medicine today. You must take one every morning and one in the evening, it's very important that you take it. And you need to carry this blood card with you at all times.'

'What for?'

'You've got a blood clot in your leg, from all the lying down,' she explained and handed me a white T-shirt. 'It's clean, I don't need it.'

'Oh that's brilliant, thanks Ursula, this shirt's getting a bit smelly.'

'You're welcome. Cornelia and the other girls will try and get you out on crutches this afternoon, we need to get you moving, get your circulation going.'

I felt thrilled by the news as I believed I might go insane just lying there, wasting away, and I longed to be able to go to the toilet myself, rather than use the bedpan. That afternoon with the help of two nurses I moved my swollen black limb onto the side of the bed. Shocked at how weak I had become, I had to rest against the wall after just four paces. Gradually I got the gist of using crutches and, satisfied, the nurses left me to my own devices.

Arno, the young man in the opposite bed, explained that he had been knocked off his motorbike and expected to be in hospital for a long time. A local cabinet maker, he feared that he might never work again because of the damage to his wrist. He had been using crutches for a few days now and galloped up and down the ward impressively.

The following evening Arno arranged a clandestine trip to one of the nurses' flats. It felt like a huge adventure just in terms of physically getting there, but also because we weren't supposed to leave the ward. We drank tea, ate chocolate and listened to Bob Marley endlessly. With each track Ursula appeared more and more beautiful, her long dark hair covering her shoulders. After a fortnight confined to a bed, the evening felt truly magical. Life is worth living, I thought, even if I never climb again and spend years dragging my sorry leg around after me.

Arno's next plan to alleviate our boredom involved arranging for his girlfriend to come to the hospital the following evening. After dinner we sneaked out from the ward into the warm evening air, our crutches racing across the garden patio out towards the gate, where Claudia sat waiting on a moped.

'Andy come on friend, let's go,' began Arno enthusiastically, after kissing his girl.

Claudia held his crutches as he clambered onto the moped, balancing on his good foot. I could not resist the opportunity and shuffled on awkwardly behind, left arm on his shoulder, the other on Claudia's arm. As the sun set behind the mountains, we tore around the neighbouring streets of Samedan on the screeching 50cc machine, laughing, the wind in our hair; free at last from incarceration. Back on our crutches we revealed our respective scars to Claudia, like the proud owners of pets. My singular twenty-two-stitch railroad from knee to ankle met with groans of applause.

'Ten bolts in that, and a big steel plate,' I boasted.

'Only ten? I've lost count friend,' joked Arno. The protruding pins from his legs looked particularly menacing.

'Anyhow you should take the thing for a ride yourself.'

I procrastinated then accepted the offer. Though less powerful than the bike I had sold, it was a hell of a buzz after so much inactivity; the problem arose when I tried to stop. My fingers instinctively pulled the left front lever believing it to be the clutch, but the damn thing was an automatic and this was the front brake. Explain this to the doctors, flashed through my mind as the moped skidded slightly then stopped and I fell softly to the ground. I lay still whilst Claudia pulled the moped from me. Luckily I had fallen onto the right side but I felt ashamed by my behaviour, after all the doctors' hard work to help me. A car drove past and I hid my face, fearing that one of the staff might recognise me.

I said goodbye to Cornelia, Ursula and Arno the following week. The doctor was happy with my progress, despite my leg having now frozen into a retracted position of 45 degrees which, from a certain view, made me look like an amputee. The ambulance men waited patiently.

'My boss wouldn't let me cut your hair,' whispered Ursula.

'Why not?'

'Oh I don't know, she's a stupid woman. We have so many rules here in Switzerland.'

'Thanks for the offer anyway, and thanks for looking after me so well.'

My throat tightened with emotion and I turned away, striding towards the ambulance. Before getting in, I turned and waved to the people who had become my family.

Fear, pain, anger, and love. It made my face leaner, harder; the face my mother saw when they carried me from the ambulance.

'You were a boy when you left, but you have returned a man,' she told me.

At home life continued as normal, though normal was a relative term. A neighbour reprimanded my father for speaking to a man at the top of the street.

'He's a scab, Arthur. Didn't you know, cock?'

He was out walking the dog; no he didn't know. He apologized and stopped talking to him. Another man, who lived near the bus-stop and who had gone to school with my father, had also gone back to work, and life became so intolerable for him and his family that he resigned and moved away from the area. At the other end of the village, by the police station, people painted hate slogans on the side of one family's house where the man had returned to work.

I went stir crazy at home, living downstairs initially to avoid the stairs and one day getting so frustrated with my inability to get around, plus the insecurity of not knowing the outcome of my injuries, that I smashed my crutches against the living room door, putting a small hole in it. I felt pathetic now. I had wasted the money from the sale of my motorbike on the trip to the Alps and ended up in a useless state, unable to pick coal and helpless around the house. My mother took the crutches from me and confined me to my room until I learned to show more respect for our home and our fragile situation.

A letter from the technical college arrived demanding that I returned to the day release classes, otherwise they would terminate my study. We would receive no pay for the day and the union were content with the arrangement. Everybody returned but, awkwardly, one boy had broken the strike. Gaz had seen him being shipped past the picket line one morning in a Transit van at Woolley pit. The word got around the class and from then on every time our tutor turned to the blackboard we hissed 'SSSSSSS . . .' like snakes, until the tutor turned around, frustrated by our disruption. When the boy went to the loo he received threats. His father was a manager and perhaps he had been coerced into returning to work by his family. Nevertheless, to most of us it seemed incomprehensible. At home my mother joked, saying that if my father even mentioned returning to work (not that he ever did) she would kick him out on to the street immediately and for good. As Christmas approached we thought, we have come this far, why stop now? Let's see if the winter has an effect, let's hope for a harsh winter where demand for coal is high.

My leg stubbornly refused to bend until one of the large physiotherapists began sitting on it.

'Stop whinging, you're like a baby,' she bellowed. 'We're only trying to help you.'

Once my foot reached the ground again I was told to start

applying light weight to it. With this newfound mobility I visited the Peak District, meeting up with the gang down at Grindleford Café where, having heard about the accident, they welcomed me back to the fold. Out on the cliff at Millstone I became frustrated, watching a few of the team idly chatting and hanging out. Why didn't they climb? For God's sake life is too short! I would have given anything to have been able to move over rock that afternoon. The accident hadn't quenched my thirst but instead dramatically roused it.

Alistair spoke of his odd predicament at work, where he was on strike but his brother-in-law continued to work.

'It's crazy, youth. He hasn't got a car so I drop him off at the pit gates. He goes through the picket line and I stand on the picket line, which means I get shouted at by the pickets and a rollicking from those in our area who have never joined the strike. Fathom that one out.'

'That's bizarre.'

'There are about forty-four of us still on strike out of 1,300 men.'

With winter approaching, the resolve of people in our neighbourhood held steadfast but life was not easy. The soup kitchen helped enormously but there were many hungry hours and normal luxuries were now out of the question. We had never owned a car anyhow, nor a telephone, but now our video recorder was sent back to the hire company, our debts were enormous and our savings non-existent. Farmers' fields surrounded our village and occasionally, in utter desperation, some men picked off the land to provide for their families. My father had never stolen in his life, nor had a day off work, but now he had to swallow his pride. One moonlit night he filled a small plastic bag with a few pounds of potatoes. He was standing beside a group of younger men when suddenly the police arrived with a powerful searchlight and a pack of barking dogs. The crowd rapidly dispersed, clinging to their weekend veg. My father had arthritis from years of pitwork and couldn't run very fast or very far, so he jumped into the bottom of the hedge, his heart pounding with fear. He landed on barbed wire which tore through his trousers, cutting into his backside. Terrified, he lay still as the police ran amok in the field, determined to catch the suspects on behalf of the irate farmer. He lay there for over an hour, motionless, guilty and scared.

We sat at home wondering what on earth had happened to him. When he finally arrived he showed us the wound and told us the tale, but we couldn't help laughing at his misfortune. It would become one of his most personal treasured recollections, the emotional tale of how he did wrong, breaking his impeccable record as a law-abiding citizen, 'just for a few bloody tatties'.

'There's somebody to see you,' said my mother, wearing a silly expression.

Nobody ever knocked to enter our house, and nobody got an introduction before coming into the front room, so I ignored her. I sat listening to Jools Holland on *The Tube*, normally a prelude to going out for a drink, but I had no money. I lounged on the big red settee wearing just my underpants and a T-shirt. During the adverts I admired my scar, almost healed but impressive nonetheless.

'Andy did you hear me? Somebody has come.'

'Who is it? The Queen?' I said, staring at the screen. 'Tell her to come in.'

There was a silence behind me, then a voice I recognised.

'Hello Andy.'

'Ursula, Jesus Christ!'

I hobbled out of the room and then hopped upstairs to put on some trousers.

'What would you like to drink?' I asked her at the Ship Hotel, still in a state of shock. I had enough for two drinks each; not much of a night out.

'Erm, whisky and orange.'

Heads turned at the bar on hearing the unfamiliar accent.

'Whisky and orange please Ernie and a pint o' bitter.'

'Whisky and orange?' He pulled a painful expression. 'Putting orange in whisky is a waste. I'll give you the orange so you can do it yourself, I'm having nothing to do with it,' he said.

'Fine.'

It was early and we sat in the best room, which was empty; a few people stood at the bar in the tap room. I had seldom been out for a drink with a girl, alone, especially locally. I felt overawed and consequently I tried to mentally prepare before speaking. But when I spoke the best I managed was an incoherent mumble.

'Erm . . . there's a disco tonight in the village, erm . . .'

'Sounds nice.'

'Well it's at The er . . . . Bush, where they have the union meetings, and well on a Friday they have a disco like . . .'

'Do you want another drink?'

'I'm alright for the moment thanks.'

I had hardly begun my pint.

Ursula ordered another one and whilst she stood at the bar, the jukebox crackled into life – Lynyrd Skynyrd's 'Freebird' a constant favourite because, as well as being a good solid tune, it went on for an eternity and was considered good value for ten pence.

Ursula had been planning to travel to London and Edinburgh and then on to France but, at the last minute, she had decided to pay me a visit on her journey. Paris, London, Edinburgh, Royston and Barnsley: a certain *je ne sais quoi*, I mused. She explained that the miners' strike was known throughout Europe now, something I had not appreciated.

At The Bush disco, Dave and Dawn, my uncle Martin's sister, came and stood with us.

'Now then mountain man, how's it going?'

Dave had a razor-sharp mind and a wicked sense of humour. He drew on his cigarette between long gulps of beer, firing questions at Ursula: where was she from? had she been to Britain before? Then he threw his smoking cigarette stub onto the edge of the dance floor, saying 'Put that out with thee crutch will tha?' I moved my crutch towards the smoking end, but Dave blocked it with his hand, shouting above the sound of the music, 'Not thee, I meant your lass's crotch, fool!'

I began laughing at his word play, spilling my beer. Despite Ursula speaking six languages fluently, unravelling the meaning of that one-liner above the sound of the disco proved impossible. A conversation thus ensued with me tediously attempting to explain the pun. She either understood the joke or had tired of me and, before I had finished, was striding up to the DJ to request some of her favourite tracks. Somewhat flattered that Friday night at The Bush was now attracting overseas visitors, the DJ played Bob Marley's 'No Woman No Cry', preceded by a long-winded introduction articulating his joy. Outside the last bus to Barnsley approached. Ursula had booked into a hotel in town and refused my invitation of staying with us. We said goodnight, arranging to meet the following day.

I didn't know what to show Ursula in Barnsley and, thinking she might want to see some bigger shops, suggested we go to Sheffield, our grand neighbour. But it turned out to be an unsatisfactory day of aimless wandering, so on the Sunday we caught the bus to Derbyshire. We walked to Grindleford Café, which had become my second home, ate and then walked towards Froggatt Edge.

'Is there anywhere to swim around here Andy?'

Swim! Are you completely bonkers? It's October for God's sake!

'Well there is a river down there,' I suggested sheepishly.

Within minutes of arriving, Ursula stripped naked and dove into a deep brown pool.

'Come on in, it's wonderful,' she gasped.

I leant on my crutches, craning my head around to be certain that no muddy-gaitered ramblers were in view, then tentatively stripped off. I stared in horror at where she had jumped from and chose instead to descend a muddy bank to the right. I stepped on to the slope and began sliding uncontrollably towards the river, balancing on one leg. I thrust my crutches into the damp earth as hard as I could, attempting to brake but, realising the impossibility of the situation, abandoned them before firing headlong into the icy water.

I doggy-paddled with one leg staring up at the cliffs of Frogatt Edge, the temperature of the water stealing my breath.

'Great eh?'

'It's certainly different,' I said trembling.

I swam to the edge of the river and, with the aid of my crutches, traversed up the lethal bank, arriving much filthier than I had wished. We dried ourselves as best we could, then dressed and dashed for the bus back. We ate in Barnsley and took a drink in her hotel. I wanted to tell her that I liked her a lot, maybe even loved her, but somehow I couldn't summon the courage and I left for my bus home, annoyed with myself. Halfway there, I spun round and headed back.

She opened the door to her room, I went in and we hugged. We sat on the edge of the bed – she was naked – I explained my feelings and we hugged again. The problem, she explained, was a guy back home; a complicated situation, plus, she had thought of me as a friend not a lover. I apologised, hoping that I hadn't jeopardised our friendship.

'Don't be silly,' she assured me, lifting my chin. 'Cheer up. Let's meet in the morning.'

The following day was Ursula's last day and I felt sad that she was going; she had been such a big part of my life in Switzerland, itself an important time in my own life.

'I'll come to the soup kitchen with you before I leave,' she said.

It was Cornish pasty with peas, bread and tea, and she ate hers at lightning speed then began slurping her tea.

'I want to make a donation, who do I give it to?'

'Oh Ursula, that's so kind. Speak to the ladies up at the front serving.'

She emptied her wallet and gave the woman £30.

At the train station we kissed like friends and said our farewells.

'I'll be in the Alps again next summer. I'll come to Switzerland and see you, though hopefully not in hospital.'

She smiled. 'You should take care. Those mountains are dangerous, you'll worry your parents sick.'

I watched her, gliding away, disappearing down the platform. I walked away, swinging my leg towards the hospital for my final physiotherapy appointment but stopped opposite the hotel where Ursula had stayed, and on a small green electrical box scratched her name with my house key.

We heard that, over the weekend, there had been riots in Grimethorpe. Men, women and children had been picking coal from the stack on the Friday when 120 riot police arrived and arrested nineteen out of sixty people – many had bad chests and so couldn't run away. On the Monday more young men went on to the stack, which led to 300 police sealing off the village at around 3pm. By 11pm, 600 riot police had arrived to contain a worsening situation. As one local man put it. 'Husbands, brothers and sons have been killed at Grimethorpe colliery. This village has had its share . . . of fatalities; men have paid for coal lying on the coal tips with their blood, and morally the coal is ours.'

At the end of October the orthopaedic surgeon told me to stop using crutches and, to my utter delight, I walked without a limp. It was the most amazing feeling. He told me to swim lots, but the local swimming pool had just been shut due to a shortage of coal to heat it. A fortnight before Christmas, rather worryingly, a bill came from the Swiss Air Rescue for 2,062 Swiss Francs: thirty-eight minutes at forty-nine Francs a minute, payable within thirty days, it read. We had no money for Christmas presents, never mind bills of that magnitude, so I forwarded it to my insurance company.

On Christmas Eve a large package arrived from Switzerland and the whole family gathered around excitedly, intrigued to see what nestled inside. It was beautifully presented, carefully lined with expensive-looking festive paper. On top were two books: *Brave New World* by Aldous Huxley and *Once Upon An Alp*, a collection of humorous anecdotes about Swiss mountain people. My mother's face lit up when we discovered a small bottle of perfume and Maria and Jonny were delighted to find a big bar of chocolate and a jar of honey. There was real, fresh coffee, which we had never tasted even when at work, and biscuits.

'To the Cave family. Hope you are well this Christmas. Thinking of you, love Ursula,' read the note.

'Absolutely amazing,' sighed my father.

'It's gorgeous, smell it,' started my mother, thrusting her wrist under each of our noses.

'Can we have some chocolate Mam?' asked Maria.

'Let's save it for tomorrow love,' she said.

Christmas hit the striking mothers and fathers the hardest as they had to explain to their children why Santa didn't have much on his sledge, and why we were eating less food this year. Much harder to take were jibes from the police on some picket lines where they taunted men with incredible lines, such as, 'Your kids aren't going to be getting much are they?' They made fun of a Grimethorpe man in this manner and, infuriated, he decked the officer responsible and got himself arrested. I came across this 'below the belt' stuff away from the picket line too. At Grindleford Café one weekend I overheard a climber I knew to be a policeman boasting, loud enough for me to hear, about how much money he was making out of the strike.

The longer the strike lasted, the more bitter it became, and we all knew that relations with the coal board management and the police could never be the same again. The manager of Royston Drift sent out letters begging the men to come back to work, giving them a confidential number they could phone. However, pickets remained in force, and on one ocasion a huge battle ensued between police and the men, culminating in pickets fleeing the police batons, with some running through our garden and into the allotments. Meanwhile, Jonny told me about a new game he and his friends had initiated in his primary school playground called 'cops and pickets'.

'We split into two groups, those whose dads are on strike versus the rest – they are the cops. They line up and hold arms, and then we charge and batter each other.'

One evening my leg began to swell, feeling like fire. My mother brought the doctor to the house, who claimed it was probably my tissue reacting with the metal plate and bolts. I had just begun walking again, and now this. Eventually it settled down and a couple of weeks later I agreed to join Pete Swift and some others on a two-day walk over Kinder Scout above Edale. It felt wonderful just to be out in the wilderness again.

As we crossed the stream of Grindsbrook heading back towards Edale, we met Alistair and a friend of his from Nottingham.

'You look knackered youth, what you been doing?'

'Oh we bivvied out at the Downfall, it was a long night. What you up to anyhow?'

'Going for a walk. We'll be down for a pint in the Nag's Head later though.'

'We'll be in later as well, try and dry our stuff out.'

'Some bad news I'm afraid, Andy,' said Alistair.

'What's that?' I said, looking straight at him.

'I've gone back to work.'

I walked on past him a little and lowered my head. 'Wanker,' I said.

'Well fuck you,' he replied.

That night in the pub, Alistair was clearly upset and desperately tried to make me see the decision from his point of view.

'It killed me to cross that picket line, I'm telling you. But I kept promising Dee I'd go back by Christmas if it hadn't been sorted. She's put a deposit down on a house and if I don't get some money together soon we're going to lose that money.'

'But . . .'

'Andy we're engaged to be married, she won't wait for ever.'

'But I can't understand it, we've come this far, why go back now?'

'I don't want to lose her, can't you understand?' he explained, his eyes filling with tears.

I felt uncomfortable, torn inside. All the others who had returned to work were unknown to me, making it easier to deal with, easier for me to despise them. But this was Alistair, one of the lads. I recalled our weekend in Wales before my accident. It had been such a memorable couple of days away from the reality of the strike. I had enjoyed climbing The Diagonal with him and would always remember our victorious evening on the Padarn pool table.

'Look Andy, I've already lost enough friends because of this fucking strike.'

I could feel myself withdrawing from him, my skin hardening. I would have to avoid him now; there was no choice.

'Come on, let's go,' I said to the others, and we left.

8

Into the light

It was 11pm when the door of the cell slammed shut. I sat in the corner, smirking; they had made a big mistake, but they would realise soon enough and, what the hell, this would make a great story. I stood up, flapping my arms around and cursing the fact that I'd not put on a jacket before going out for a pint. So this is what prison is like. I paced around glancing at the graffiti, surprised by the number of 'NUM' letters scratched into the pale green paint. Twelve months on strike and what had we achieved? I had been sat at home when I heard it had been called off and I'd felt a lump swell in my throat. Thatcher's government had swayed public opinion against us via the media; they had also converted many power stations to oil and given the police new powers to block flying-pickets. In early March, though, despite the defeat the men, women and children had walked back to work with heads held high. I remained off sick with my leg.

Just after midnight, officers scuffled past dragging a man in a drunken rage.

'Filthy fucking scum!' he shouted, long after the door had been locked tight.

At 2am, an officer led me to an interview room where two detectives sat, both wearing suits.

'Where's Steve? Is he okay?' I asked, sitting in the small chair.

'Your friend is fine, now tell me, where do you work?' said the slightly older, friendlier looking man.

'I'm a miner.'

'Which pit do you work at?'

'Grimethorpe.'

'Well that's it, you're guilty,' he laughed.

The other detective spoke next.

'You told the officers who arrested you that you were a climber, how many climbs have you done?'

'Well, I don't really know. Erm . . . last year during the strike sometimes I climbed four days a week, ten routes a day, that's forty routes a week.'

'Look, son, don't get cocky with us.'

He looked stressed, the skin drawn tightly across his cheek-bones. Probably a smoker.

'But they're only small climbs, fifty feet high or so.'

'Do you think it is normal behaviour to climb up a doctor's surgery at night?' he continued.

'We climb all over the place in Sheffield.'

'Look you can carry on telling us this cock-and-bull story about being a rock climber or you can admit you were going up that drainpipe to get into that surgery.'

I began to think about the crowbar that they reckoned they had found below where we were climbing.

'It's your first offence, you'll probably get off lightly,' said the older man.

'But we weren't breaking in and we weren't going up the drainpipe, that would be too easy. We were climbing the arête on its right-hand side, honest.'

I showed them the scar on my leg, told them the whole Switzerland episode.

'That's why I'm still off work, until next month,' I said.

Back in the cell the temperature had fallen and I called to the man on watch who gave me a coarse, musty-smelling blanket. I lay on the floor shivering, beginning to doubt whether this suffering was worth a good pub yarn, when the door burst open and an older guy staggered in. Once orientated, he lay down beside me. He was foul-smelling, farted and had a serious bronchial complaint. To make matters worse he then began muttering nonsense, incessantly. I lay absolutely still, feigning sleep and clinging to the blanket, dreading the thought that he might suggest we share it. Fortunately, it appeared he was too intoxicated to notice my selfishness.

I woke to the sound of banging on the metal door and the other detainees sliding open their hatches. A hand shoved a fried-egg sandwich on a plastic plate into the cell. I ate it in four mouthfuls. The tramp guy had vanished. I stuck my face out of the hatch and saw the eyes and noses of a dozen or so people stretching along to the right.

'What you in for, pal?' asked a guy in a cell opposite.

'Suspicion of attempted burglary.'

'First offence?'

'Yes.'

'No worries pal, admit it and you'll probably get less than three months, might only be a month.'

Three months. Did he mean prison, was he insane?

'I say does tha want to play a game?' bellowed a different man directly opposite.

'What game's that?' I queried, intrigued how we could play anything, being locked up in separate cells ten feet apart.

'I try and spit into tha cell hole and tha tries and spits into mine, right I'll go first.'

Before I had appreciated what on earth he meant he had begun clearing his throat and promptly delivered a mouthful of spit through the hatch. I jumped, but not before my ear had been covered in the revolting damp gunk. Furious, I fired a mouthful back but he ducked.

'Hey good shot, that's one all,' he called. 'It's a good game, isn't it?'

I slammed the hatch shut and sat down, ignoring the cries of the deranged delinquent. Is this how I will spend my days inside? God help me.

Meanwhile the forensic scientists were leaning from ladders, brushing powder onto the edge of the surgery and attempting to ascertain whether or not we had only climbed up the arête, or instead (as they hoped) up the drainpipe, as any normal, rational burglar would have done. At the same time the two detectives visited the home of Keith and Marie Brown, where I had intended to spend the night.

'Is a man named Andrew Cave residing with you at the moment?'

'Don't tell me, you've arrested him for climbing on the side of the library building,' she said in her Marseilles accent.

'No actually, we found him and his friend on the side of a doctor's surgery.'

Marie started laughing, 'Yes I knew something must have happened when he didn't come back last night.'

It was almost three in the afternoon when Steve and I were led into the chief's office for a final ticking off. Steve looked distraught; he had missed work and his mother would be wondering where the hell he was. I winked at him. Evidently, the forensic team were satisfied that we had not used the drain-pipe; nevertheless the chief constable remained unimpressed.

'Look lads, we have a lot of break-ins in that area of Doncaster. Drug users love to get their hands on GPs' prescrip-tion pads. But come on, imagine yourself laid in bed with your wife at midnight. Picture it, you hear weird noises outside so you decide to take a look – opening the bedroom window – and lo and behold you spot two men climbing up your house and they shout up: "Oh don't worry mate, we're rock climbers, we're just practising." Now think about it lads, it's not on is it?'

We both shook our heads like guilty school boys before being escorted out into the fresh air.

Satisfied that my leg could withstand all the kneeling at work, the doctor signed me off sick and so, one fine June morning, I joined Trevor and the boys at the shaftside and shuffled on to the middle deck of the cage. Near the centre stood a strike-breaker. Uttering the word 'scab' had been made a sacking offence, so the men hissed. An extraordinary eeriness beset the cage as we cut through the darkness to the harmony of 'SSSSSSSS . . .' – the man like a small, terrified dog surrounded by a seething wall of cobras. The cage doors had been left open, and I wondered if he might actually wriggle from this pit of hate and jump into the void, unassisted, unable to bear the persecution any longer.

We headed towards a development tunnel that was under construction in the Fenton seam, in order to carry materials forward to the rippers. En route they listened to the story of the helicopter rescue in Switzerland, pronouncing me 'moun-tain man' – partly a gesture of respect, partly mocking. The heat and intense humidity made us all strip down to our under-pants as soon as we arrived, and within minutes of starting to carry forward we were lathered in an oily mixture of coal dust and sweat. I had grown in height and weight, and the climbing and then the crutches had given my hands a solid grip. Other than my leg, which would take a while to settle down, I felt physically stronger than during my previous stint underground, despite not having worked for fifteen months. I found it easier to switch off from the monotonous and filthy work too. A small pool of water quickly turned to a quagmire as we walked back and forth, dampening our feet, but I simply ignored it. Gerald loaded me up with chockblocks and I didn't care whether it was four, five or six – the tougher the work the more I thought about the mountains. As we toiled, I visualised the North Face of the Eiger and the Walker Spur on the North Face of the Grandes Jorasses, preposterous objectives given my total lack of alpine experience (save for a ride in a helicopter).

After eating snap I finished my water and then, still thirsty, got back to it. One of the golden rules underground was never to drink another man's water, no matter how desperate you were – unless he offered you some. We had been given dust masks to wear but in this humidity they were unbearable, even when standing still, let alone when working at a furious pace – you simply could not get enough air into the lungs and felt dizzy. What's more, the increased sweating turned my skin bright red and sore. Unexpectedly, the under-manager arrived and began chatting with Trevor. He could be a hard man, not someone to get on the wrong side of.

'Look at these lads Trevor, what a shit hole, what a fucking shit hole,' he started.

I leaned on the brattice cloth taking a breather, intrigued by his tone and careful not to blind him with my lamp.

'It's rough down here, boss.'

'Rough? Look at it. I never wanted this you know Trevor lad.' Tiny beads of sweat glistened on his forehead.

'What do you mean?'

'Well, when I was a little lad all I dreamed of was flying aeroplanes, up in the big blue yonder,' he said. Then, after a pause, '. . . But I ended up here. It's no life for anybody this Trev lad, no life at all.'

Over the next few weeks the work was more varied than I had remembered; however, in the long term I knew in my heart that I wanted to leave. The strike had given me the chance to prove myself climbing, which had in turn bred confidence and I now believed that one day I could go on and climb some of the highest mountains in the world, including the Himalayas. But it was something I could never achieve with the standard fortnight summer-holiday policy at the pit. This year I planned to return to the Alps, to Chamonix.

The strike had changed many things at work too, in particular the relations between us and the bosses. We had retained our self respect but the bosses were being heavy handed. It was as if they wanted to remind us of the fact that we had been defeated and we now had to bow to their increased status and power.

That filthy, wet afternoon in the corner of the crowded Bar National in Chamonix, John McKeever's thigh bounced up and down as if operating an outdated sewing machine. He was bored. Hero and legend Phil Thornhill was recounting another recent epic he had just survived in the mountains, and the usual disciples had gathered around waiting for the didactic point; Phil's stories always had a point, a lesson to be learned by amateur alpinists like John and me. Today's advice was always to disconnect the power supply to your battery when not using your headtorch. Phil had learned the hard way. With no light, he'd been forced to bivouac in the open at the top of the Super Couloir the previous winter and, as a result, had suffered frostbite. Maurice, the eternally forgiving patron, leant on the bar and listened in while his cross-eyed teenage daughter swept the floor, trying to maintain a modicum of order. I had made half a lager last almost three hours, had washed and shaved in the tiny sink downstairs and had made and eaten my own sandwiches. But Maurice didn't mind. It seemed he had a soft spot for British alpinists, for these obsessive lost children who returned to the mountains year after year.

The following day the sun appeared, prompting John and me to pack our rucksacks and set off walking towards the Argentiere Glacier, intent on climbing the Swiss route on the North Face of Les Courtes – a much bigger climb than either of us had ever previously undertaken. Water dripped from my forehead onto my pumping thighs as I battled to keep up with John's furious pace. When we reached the enormous flat glacier basin, a cool breeze forced us to stop and put on a fleece. I gazed around, seeing the gigantic kilometre-high

wall of vertical rock and ice stretch for almost two kilometres: Aiguille Verte, Les Droites, Les Courtes, Le Triolet.
It was the most dramatic mountain scenery I had ever set
eyes on.

'Looks good, hey Andy?'

I failed to reply immediately, my head full of questions. Will
the weather hold? Where's the descent? Is John the right man
to be climbing with? We hardly know each other. Are we up
to this? Am *I* up to this for God's sake?

'Looks scary and big if you ask me,' I said, fumbling the zip
on my fleece.

'It's always worse looking straight on. Let's go and find
somewhere to bivvy.'

We slept on the crest of a lateral moraine down below the
Argentiere refuge, directly opposite our route. We couldn't
afford to stay in the refuge, plus we intended to leave at one
o'clock in the morning.

After our meal of pasta and sausage we forced down one
last mug of tea. I felt bilious, but I had read that it was important to drink four litres a day when at high altitude. John kept
the conversation light-hearted, reassuring me that we would
cruise the route, then he lay down and, rather annoyingly,
began snoring at once. As the sky darkened to steel blue, I
stared up at the 3,000-foot North Face. Our route didn't look
technically desperate but it was so much longer than anything
I had done before, my first '*Grande Course*' – the French term
for a major alpine climb. I tightened the draw cord of my
sleeping bag and closed my eyes. I tried hard to regulate my
breathing – long, slow inhalations; long, slow exhalations –
trying to remain calm, but I didn't sleep a wink.

By dawn we had reached the upper icefield, the section of
the climb we had anticipated would pose no difficulty, but we
began to tire. My calves felt as if they had doubled in size and
grown knots on the side as I wearily kicked my crampons into
the brittle ice, my throat desperate for liquid. I hammered an
ice screw into the slope, cracks appearing like the legs of a
giant spider.

'Okay John, climb when you're ready.'

As John climbed I heard the faint sound of a helicopter.
Instantly a shiver danced across my shoulder-blades, the

association of that noise and hideous pain still fresh from my encounter the previous year.

The sun sat high in the sky by the time we reached the summit ridge. We shook gloved hands and then headed east towards the Col des Cristeaux, wet snow collecting under our feet and forcing us to balance on one foot and tap the other with the ice axe. Just before the col, John demanded a rest and sat down in the snow, curling into a foetal position and then falling asleep. Worried about the descent route and our slow progress, I sat on my sack feeling anxious. After fifteen minutes, stressed by our inactivity, I nudged him and we descended into the Col des Cristeaux. I stared down the vast steep slope, gulped, and then turned away; I was out of my depth and I knew it. Though less steep than the way we had ascended, the snow was soft and our feet sank into it, sometimes up to our knees; above us hung a line of heavy cornices, the midday sun shining through their necks. Our feet continued to perforate the rotten snow as we moved on, two unimportant fleas hopping down the 3,000-foot white slope. Moments before we reached a tiny island of rock a terrific boom sounded – avalanche! Oh my God!

Initially I couldn't decide whether to stand still or make a dash for the rock, then instinct took control and I ran, galloping, my lungs burning.

John made it to the rock first then I crawled on, gibbering with fear as tons of wet snow rushed violently towards us – an avalanche started by the collapse of the cornice in the heat. It sounded soft as it glided by; strangely quiet, like sand emptying out of a giant hourglass. When it finally stopped we stared at each other; we had no choice but to run as fast as we could and get the hell out of there.

We negotiated the Bergschrund by way of a fan of snow and ice that led out on to the glacier. I felt sick as we crawled back up to our bivouac site, and by the time we arrived the sun had disappeared. We made one drink and collapsed into our sleeping bags. The following morning, munching salami and cheese, we gazed up at what we had climbed the previous day. It looked so huge now and I remembered the events like a film. I was delighted by what we had achieved but also sad, as at the end of a dream, that something so recently an idea, an ambition, had already transformed into memories.

'I can't wait to get back to Edinburgh and write it up in the Mountaineering Club book,' said John.

It sounded odd to me, but then I wasn't part of a close-knit climbing scene. At the pit no one cared or understood what this strange pursuit meant, and most of my regular climbing friends stuck to rock, having very little interest in such big mountain routes.

Most of us wanted to work on the coalface, partly because of the increase in wages, partly for the challenge, and partly for the perceived status it brought among one's colleagues. However, a plethora of older men were accepting early retirement, meaning that their jobs needed filling. Many of these were 'button men' jobs, which entailed manning strategic points of the numerous coal-carrying conveyor belts out of the mine. That autumn, the training officer ordered me to the remote gate between Ro4s and the new South Side Drift as a button man. The camaraderie I'd had with Trevor and the gang vanished now and, apart from the deputy and the haulage lads gliding past twice a shift, I was alone. If I switched off my lamp I experienced tiny, sharp, purple stars fading to larger fuzzy stars and then pure, black, noth-ingness; the ultimate darkness, as if I had been buried alive in a pit of clay. A gentle breeze carried the smell of burnt tar and when the belt stopped for some reason, an extraordinary quiet fell about the place, save for the occasional settling of the roof. It was an easy place to get frightened, a place where you needed to control your imagination.

On the night shift I frequently worked twelve hours, as I wanted to save as much money as possible before quitting the job. I built a seat out of chockblocks and pieces of old conveyor belt, between the haulage rails and the tunnel wall, which gave me a clear view up and down the gate so that I could see advancing officials or the haulage gang. One night I fell asleep in the middle of the shift and woke to find the belts stood still and a peculiar rustling sound in the darkness. Semi-comatose, I scoured the pitch black with the beam of my cap lamp then jerked back to life on seeing a silver figure perhaps a hundred metres away. I froze stiff. I turned my lamp off and waited for a few seconds then turned it back on to check that I wasn't hallucinating. The figure advanced slowly towards me.

The palms of my hands became clammy, despite the cool breeze. I heard my chest thumping in the stillness. The figure stopped in the dust of the roadway, waiting. Behind me sat a tannoy system; should I call Bill, the nearest button man to me? Instead I gently grasped the shovel with my right hand and stood up. I took small, gentle steps, trying not to disturb the dust, my throat dry. After just five paces I dropped the shovel and began laughing – it was a huge clear plastic bag, some sort of packaging, that had been blown down the gate on the breeze. I cursed myself for being so gullible, yet the stories of ghosts were ever present when working down here.

When my father worked the night shift, his work mate Les often gave him a lift. Les is a natural comedian with incredible stories and the whole of our family would gather round and listen to him in the kitchen before he and my father disappeared off to the pit. He knew of a pit pony that loved to chew tobacco, a one armed miner who snorted six tins of snuff a day and countless other tall tales. But he also had serious stories concerning his experiences of the strike, like being on the picket line the day David Jones was killed at Ollerton. When he heard that I was working as a button man, he told us about a ghost his brother had seen underground at Grimethorpe.

'Watch out for ghosts down there, Andy lad.'

I remembered the men joking with the deputy, Judd, about a ghost in the Barnsley Bed seam but that was hundreds of feet above me.

'Ghosts, are you sure?'

'Ask my brother Johnny. He used to work the twilight shift in the Parkgate seam, six at night 'til six in the morning. One particular shift the over-man put him on the haulage, driving the engine. During the shift, a man by the name of Clarke arrived; apparently he had been sent to clean up. He wore a black jacket and an old-style helmet. At the end of the shift when our Johnny told the boss, he got annoyed, explaining that there was nobody else down there.'

'Straight up?'

'Honest to God. When he got out of the pit he went straight to the time office, and apparently nobody by that name should have been down the pit. In fact the only person that had ever worked at Grimethorpe by that name had been killed in a terrible accident years ago.'

After further investigation Les and his brother found that this man Clarke had been related to their stepfather. From then on whenever Johnny entered a local disco, the song 'There's a Ghost in My House' was played – an acknowledgement of his supernatural experience.

Ashley Scully, a mechanical underground fitter at Barrow colliery in Barnsley, and the father of a climbing friend, had also witnessed something odd underground. Whilst in a small tunnel between two shafts, repairing a pump, he had decided to strip off down to his underpants because of the heat and humidity, before wading through about a foot of water to get to the machine.

'I was working away when,' he snapped his fingers crisply, 'Something happened. I can only describe it as somebody opening the doors of a giant freezer. It dried the sweat on me, cold. It spooked me, the hairs on my back stood up and I thought, "What's happening?" There was only my light bouncing off the small lake, and the water was still 'cos nobody had walked in it. I was stood on a small plinth and I just happened to look behind me and there was this figure of a man, the shape of a man, his face, well he hadn't really got a face, but he was wearing a flat cap and a white muffler. And he just faded into the rings, into the steelwork, just went. I picked up my tool bag and splashed out across the water to the pit bottom. No overalls on – I'd left them – just my underpants and my vest. I mean, well, when I got in the pit bottom, the onsetter says, "What the bloody hell's up with thee?" And I says, "I feel badly, I've got to go out." And he says, "Tha badly?" He says, "Tha looks bloody badly tha going to get pneumonia." I says, "I've got to get out, rap that chair!" And I went out and I sort of thought, well, it's just panic with being on your own in a lonely place. You always hear and see things in pit.'

However, to his astonishment, Ashley found that quite a few people had seen the same thing in that vicinity. Apparently, it was the ghost of a stableman who used to look after the pit ponies – reputedly a nasty, cantankerous old man who rarely spoke to anyone and who led a very solitary life.

*

As winter approached I thought about the mountains every day. On the dayshift I saw virtually no sunlight, descending at six in the morning and emerging only an hour before darkness. Some mornings I ran to work, and I continued weight-training twice a week; underground I discovered a piece of suspended scaffolding bar where I could do pull-ups – tough when wearing steel toe-capped boots, plus a battery pack and a self-rescuer.

Bill introduced me to a small, illicit, underground library: a dozen or so dog-eared, black-thumb-printed paperbacks living behind a vertical steel girder in a hidden channel, along with a couple of well-used pornographic magazines. Bill had enthusiastically recommended *Papillon* by a Frenchman named Henri Charrière, by far the thickest book there. It was an account of Charrière's wrongful conviction for murder and his subsequent years spent in penal colonies in Central America; I became deaf to the coal screaming past, absorbed in Charrière's picaresque adventures.

One shift, still riveted by the tale, I was blinded by an unexpected light at close range. I jerked, looking up.

'Tha was miles away there young un,' spoke a bear of a man, his teeth hidden behind shards of dark-brown chewing tobacco.

'Who are you?'

'Leon. I'm from Amco, one o' lads that's building this bunker. Tha might know me brother, Mark Radtke, he goes climbing.'

He tucked his thumbs into a leather belt straining around an impressive girth.

'Yes I've heard of him, I've seen in him in the magazines.'

'Rait then, see you later, and watch thy ear holes we might make a bit of noise later on.'

As soon as he left I fell under the spell of the book once more, even reading whilst eating my snap. Suddenly, a terrifying boom ripped the mine apart, the roof moving around me, and I bounced to my feet not knowing where to run, the steel rings shaking, the walls jumping. My first thought was of an earthquake. When it stopped there was total silence, as if nothing had happened; only the pungent smell of carbide from the explosives drifted by, and a general hum continued in my ears. When the flow of adrenalin slowed, I realised that had been Leon's idea of 'a bit of noise'. I envied his job constructing the bunker, it sounded exciting; instead I sat like a dumb animal staring at the conveyor belts.

That weekend a climber named Ian, a scientist living in the Peak District, offered me a one-way lift up to Scotland the following Friday afternoon; apparently conditions were superb. This presented a dilemma: I was working the nightshift that week and wouldn't finish until five o'clock on the Saturday morning; also, the following week I was due to start on the dayshift at six o'clock Monday morning and, with no lift back south, I would be chancing it. Another complication involved a pretty seventeen-year-old girl named Rachel from the Barnsley Mountaineering Club. We had started going out together and I had promised I would go walking with her for the weekend in North Yorkshire. I spent the week twisting and turning. I could financially handle taking a shift off by working twelve hours on the four preceding shifts and then using a self-certification sickness leave slip, but I'd used these too often recently. Relax, there will be countless other chances to go to Scotland. I rationalised all Wednesday night, sat staring at the noisy spine of coal rocketing by. However, on Thursday morning I woke with one clear thought. Damn it, I'm off to Scotland tomorrow. I phoned Rachel; she was already growing weary of being in a relationship with an obsessed climber.

'Just go,' she said.

This is the life, I thought, my inch-long crampon points stabbing the ice of Ben Nevis's 'Zero Gully' that now dropped away for over 1,000 feet. I had decided to climb alone as I wanted to see how I would cope on a big, classic ice route; plus I had to be at work for six the next morning and would be hitchhiking. Interestingly, it had been the approach to the climb that worried me the most; it scared me stupid, in fact, as the striking white line of ice suddenly came into view, rearing up. Once established on steeper ground, my worries eased. Now it was simply a test of self-belief, of keeping cool, of being methodical, knowing that every placement of the ice axe and every kick of the crampon had to be perfect – never 'so so' or 'it will do', but simply: 'Yes, that will keep me from falling a thousand feet to my death'.

On the final, gentler slope leading to the summit I stopped, allowing the fire in my calves to subside. The wind had sculpted the slope into a crusty, rippled white sea and up above tiny sapphire tongues reached over the rim, their tips stuck to the slope of the gully. I craned my head around under the big, frozen blue sky. This is the life, this is living. 'Yeah, yeah, yeah,' I sang to myself, punching the slope with my ice axe and setting off towards the top.

Almost there, I could see the hand of sunlight stroking the summit's plateau. I arced the right axe into the firm table of snow-ice above, pushed the palm of my hand on the lower ice tool and danced my feet up. I stood on the plateau mesmerised, the Isle of Skye in the distance, hanging just below the horizon. To the south sat the shapely hills of Glencoe and to the north-east the flat summit of Creag Meagaidh. In a moment everything had changed, from concentrated anxiety to relaxed contemplation; from the vertical world to the gently inclined. I glanced at my watch, twelve o'clock, and smiled smugly. After all the worry, I had climbed it in just over an hour and a half. I sat on my rucksack and chewed some malt loaf then sipped at my water bottle, which had begun to freeze around the neck. Walkers strode towards the summit cairn and another climber appeared at the top of the adjacent route and sat down, feeding the rope around his waist, belaying his partner. He waved and I waved back. I put one of my ice axes away and then I set off, descending down the Red Burn, floating, not a care in the world, with the ice on my green cotton anorak turning damp and then steaming in the sun.

I hitchhiked from Glen Nevis to Fort William and then as far as the road by the King's House Hotel, where I stood for a good while. At Carlisle I stepped out of a truck into the night, snowflakes like tiny curled feathers gliding down the black frozen motorway slip-road; there, scratched onto the back of a road sign, I read the words 'welcome to the hitchhiker's graveyard'. This amused me for a short while but by midnight, stood in an inch of snow, I had long lost my sense of humour. I had no sleeping-bag, traffic had all but vanished, and I worried about explaining my inevitable absence from work yet again. The euphoria I'd been cradling from the summit of Ben Nevis seeped away.

Struggling to stand, with my eyelids almost sealed, I thought of a miraculous plan to minimise the inevitable discomfort of the long, cold night ahead. Just below me stood a long line of road cones. If I lay them horizontally, alternating the points one to the left and one to the right, I had a makeshift bed. I set about the task, brushing snow from a dozen orange bollards, and then spread out my thin green bivvy bag. Leaving on every item of clothing, as well as my boots, I crawled into the highway version of a futon bed and shivered until dawn.

People stared at me as I landed in Barnsley bus station at noon the next day: surely an alien from another planet?

'Andrew, are you still in the Boy Scouts?' asked Mrs Teal annoyingly, giving me a curious glance at the end of our street.

Definitely not.

'I'm a mountaineer,' I said, proud and cocksure.

'Well you be careful,' she said. 'Your mam worries sick.'

'What the hell for?' my mother's mother asked when I voiced my decision to leave the pit. 'It's a job for life. There are local lads crying out for work at the pit.'

Extraordinary, I thought, as she'd always led me to believe that she considered coal mining a poor alternative to work on 'The Railway'. Anyhow, my mind would not be changed.

My parents were more sympathetic, especially when I explained that I intended to move to Sheffield and study 'A' level English. My father knew how strong willed I was and my mother had never wanted me to work underground in the first place. I think most of my friends at work and from the street appreciated the calling I had from the mountains.

Pete Swift had been made redundant from Qualter Halls, and was studying an engineering degree at Sheffield; a shrinking mining industry meant shrinking mining-engineering firms. I began spending weekends there at his rented house with Rachel (who had finally forgiven me for my disruptive last-minute decision to disappear to Ben Nevis rather than walk with her on the North York Moors). There were many benefits to student life in Sheffield it seemed: more free time;

proximity to the cliffs; good social scene; no shiftwork. To me, currently spending twelve hours a day down a dark, damp tunnel thousands of feet underground, Pete appeared to be having the time of his life. When the college offered me a firm place to study and Ian, from the Peak District, offered me a room to rent in his house my mind was made up: I would quit in June.

I climbed myself delirious at weekends and in the week I continued to run. My leg felt strong now. At work the under-manager found me asleep, my makeshift seat by the conveyor resembling a bed now as my departure date approached. He stood over me, waving his beam of light, burning my eyes. I recoiled, startled by the brightness.

'I've a good mind to send you out of the pit,' he barked, his face full of anger.

I wanted to remind him of his story about wanting to fly aeroplanes as a child and how he thought the pit was a shit-hole, but it didn't seem appropriate.

'Sorry boss.'

'You will be lad. One more time and you'll be coming for your cards and going up that road,' he said. 'Do you under-stand?'

Is he bitter? I wondered. He had wanted to fly among the clouds, a boyhood dream still alive in his heart; an ideal, still, despite the passing of years. Instead, he was down here.

'Okay,' I said.

'Are you listening?' His hand clenched his stick, the flame of his oil lamp flickering.

'Yes,' I mumbled, thinking how he resembled Dickens' tyran-nical headmaster, Creakle.

'Good,' he remarked, and then walked off down the gate, shaking his head.

I continued working twelve-hour shifts, trying to save as much money as possible. Between shifts I read my alpine guide-books voraciously, memorising the descriptions of some of the more famous climbs, such as the North Face of the Eiger and Central Pillar of Freney on Mont Blanc. One evening, in the middle of the week, I confused a couple of local men out walking their dogs. I attached a rope to the top of a poplar tree down by the muckstack, abseiled down and then prussicked back up, believing I needed this technique in case for some reason I fell into a crevasse in the Alps.

When I finally entered Mr Frost's office to offer my resignation, he asked what my plans were.

'All the best son,' he said. 'See John through there. He'll give you a form you need to fill in.'

On Wednesday of the final week, Bill and I walked up the drift together. At the top, where he turned left and I right, he turned and asked in a serious tone, 'So are you really leaving to go off mountain climbing, or is it just a dream, an idea like?'

'Look, Bill mate, I can tell you straight, after Friday you will not see me down here again.'

'Well,' he faltered, 'Good lad. If I didn't have the kids I'd come with you. All the best.'

He held out his hand, an intense blue in his eyes.

'It's one thing talking about it, but it takes guts to do it.'

'Thanks,' I said, and then we parted, walking into our separate tunnels.

The following morning I lay in bed, contemplating my two final shifts at the pit, a wall of sunlight pressing heavily on the curtains, forcing a golden stripe across the floor and over my arm. That afternoon I would spend twelve hours sitting by the conveyor belt, watching coal sail out to the surface via the drift, where it would be cleaned and sorted by my father and his gang and then sent off to power stations, steelworks or peoples' homes.

'Are you up yet Andy? You're going to miss the pit bus,' my mother hollered up the stairs.

I pictured the blooming bracken below the rocks of Stanage; the song of the skylark, its darting flight across the heather. I could eat my snap up in Robin Hood's Cave, quietly surveying the greens and browns; solo a classic easy climb or two. I let my eyes close, enjoying the warmth of the sun on my arm.

'You're snap's done,' drifted up from the kitchen.

At work my pit boots, donkey jacket and overalls sat in the grey, steel locker, smelling hot, sweaty and dusty. In the time office hung my brass and silver checks, my lamp charging by the shaft.

'Andy love,' coerced my mother.

'I'm not going to work. I've done.'

AIR

'As one ascends through the atmosphere, barometric pressure decreases (though the air still contains 21% oxygen) and every breath contains fewer and fewer molecules of oxygen. One must work harder to obtain oxygen, primarily by breathing faster. This is particularly noticeable with exertion, such as walking uphill . . . As the amount of oxygen in the lungs decreases, the blood becomes less and less efficient at acquiring and transporting oxygen. This means that no matter how fast one breathes, attaining normal blood levels of oxygen is not possible at high altitude.'

Thomas E. Dietz, *Emergency & Wilderness Medicine*

9

Divine Providence, 1991

High above Snell's Field, beyond the trees, the last rays of the sinking sun suffused the Chamonix Aiguilles. I hadn't been here for four or five years but the campsite had lost none of its verve. The evening air was full of excitement. Alpinists from all over the world, but mainly Britain, had come once again to fulfil their dreams. They sat on the grass and on makeshift seats drinking cheap red wine and beer, out of large brown bottles, while pans of pasta boiled. A few were still organising their equipment, ready for an early start. The sound of Deep Purple boomed from the back of a Spanish climber's van, ricocheting from tent to tent.

'Damn it. Let's set off tomorrow,' I'd said earlier in the day. The weather forecast was excellent and we felt fit after three weeks of non-stop climbing. Paul had agreed and we'd spent the afternoon paring down our equipment until we could squeeze it into two relatively small rucksacks. Looking at the rucksacks now outside our tent, you wouldn't have guessed that we were about to try the most difficult route in the Alps.

Divine Providence is on the remote Grand Pilier d'Angle face of Mont Blanc, a place notorious for its long, serious approach. The most technically difficult section of the climb centres on a 350-metre high, vertical and overhanging shield of rock. But to reach this, 'the Red Tower' – a long section of dubious rock – has to be negotiated. From the top of the tower the route joins the long and highly exposed Peuterey Ridge up to the summit of Mont Blanc. Two local mountain guides, Patrick Gabarrou and François Marsigny, both famous for their vision, made the first ascent in 1984. However, the climb came to prominence the previous summer when two other hotshot alpinists, Thierry Renault and Alain Ghersen (also local mountain guides), free climbed* the majority of the route in superb lightweight style. Andy Parkin, an expat Brit living in Chamonix, had arranged for Paul and me to go and meet Alain and Thierry to find out more specific information about the climb.

We threw our rucksacks into the tent and set off towards the centre of Chamonix.

Before this year, Paul Jenkinson and I had never climbed together. Paul had done less climbing in the high mountains than me, but he was a gifted and extremely bold rock climber. He was also a superb fell-runner. Paul had finished his degree in Sheffield and was now teaching science in Staffordshire. During the spring he'd spent most evenings climbing alone at the Roaches, soloing many hard routes, including an E7. One weekend he went to visit his parents, who lived on a small farm in North Wales, and decided to enter the Carneddau championship fell race, a gruelling ten-mile circuit with over 4,000 feet of ascent. He finished second. Among other climbers, Paul was known for three things. Firstly, he was extremely thrifty with his money; reputedly no one had ever witnessed him buying a drink for a friend. He was also fixated on his diet, which comprised chiefly vegetables and beans, and which led to him farting incessantly wherever he was. Finally, Paul spoke with a peculiar rolling 'r', particularly in words like 'groove'. This sound was so characteristic of his speech that many climbers nicknamed him 'The Grrroove'.

'In actual fact,' he had explained during the ferry crossing the channel, 'the "r" is something I picked up from my mum. She's French, from Amiens, close to the Somme; it's a feature of the Picardy region.'

Despite his musical backside, I found Paul to be excellent company. Like many of the people I had climbed with successfully in the mountains, Paul had a healthy balance of ambition and good judgement combined with honesty.

*

* Free climbing: meaning to ascend without standing or pulling on anything other than the natural terrain encountered. Ropes and protection devices are used at discretion, to safeguard the climbers and for establishing belays, but not as direct aids to ascent – this is 'aid climbing'.

I felt a little overawed when we finally met Thierry and Alain; after all, we were two lads in our early twenties who spent most of our time climbing on the relatively small cliffs of Derbyshire. We were now going to attempt the hardest climb in the Alps.

Thierry handed us each a glass of red wine and began talking straight away about their remarkable ascent.

'We climbed the lower part of the route late in the morning and slept on a small ledge at the base of the red tower, below the most difficult section of the route.'

'Did that work well?'

'Yes, it was okay. We had the morning sun on the initial hard pitches. The problem was that by the time we arrived at the final roof, the snow above had melted and the rock was wet through, which meant we had to use aid to escape.'

We explained the routes we had climbed over the previous three weeks. We had free climbed the Brandler Hasse on the North Face of the Cima Grande, as well as The Fish on the South Face of the Marmolada. We had also soloed the Cassin route on the Piz Badile (Paul's idea of a rest day). This had been my first visit to the Bregaglia since breaking my leg there and it had felt good to leave with positive memories. We had descended from the west face of the Dru only yesterday after making a rare repeat of the Harlin–Robbins *direttissima*.

'Wow. You guys must be fit. I think if you leave the hut very early you could free Divine in one day.'

'But if not, is there anywhere to spend the night?' asked Paul.

'There is the place we slept at the base of the Red Tower, and up on the tower itself there is one ledge. Probably big enough to sit on. It's above the hard groove pitch.'

This was the 7b+ pitch that Thierry had climbed without falling and which had captured the attention of the climbing world. I stared over at Ghersen's forearms; they looked almost as wide as my thighs.

'What sort of protection do we need?' quizzed Paul.

'A set of camming devices, a set of wires, plus some tiny wires and some quickdraws of course. Nothing unusual. There are quite a few pitons already in place on the groove pitch, left by the aid climbers.'

'Well thanks for your help,' I said, standing up. 'We're going to take the Midi lift in the morning and get round to the hut before the sun softens the snow too much.'

'Good idea.'

'Hey, do you know why the route is called Divine Providence?' asked Thierry.

'No,' I answered for both of us.

'During the first ascent, in 1984, Patrick fell whilst seconding and the protection above him ripped out of the crack. François was belaying out on the left, on the ledge I said you could bivouac on.'

'Yes.'

'Well, it is very steep just there and Patrick swung out into space, and the rope ripped across a very sharp edge of granite. Only a few threads of the rope remained uncut.'

Thierry lit a cigarette.

'Jesus.'

'Patrick told me he thought it was only because Divine Providence intervened that the rope didn't shear completely. This is why he lived.'

Thierry held his hands up as if affirming the intervention of God and then started to laugh.

'Mmm . . .' we sighed in unison as we shook their hands. '*Bonne chance.*'

From the window of the *téléphérique* the stone and tarmac of Chamonix spread widely and then receded, the emerald square of the swimming pool briefly glinting. Now the metal cabin swayed as it picked up momentum, causing the tourists to release a spontaneous chorus of 'Whoa . . .', as if to comfort each other. The seasoned alpinists smiled knowingly. Some of the newcomers looked around nervous.

I stared at the speed gauge mounted next to the door of the car, we were travelling at eight metres per second, precisely the speed the cage at Grimethorpe had whisked us up and down the shaft. It was just five years since I had left the pit, but it seemed like another life altogether. I could never have imagined then that I would end up studying a degree in English. My relationship with education had always been so tenuous: at school because of disaffection and during my 'A' levels because of my continued obsession with climbing.

On the day I had to attend the interview at Sheffield Hallam University, I was working with a demolition gang just half-a-mile away from the campus. The foreman agreed to let me off site for an hour and I cycled furiously over to the department, utterly black from knocking down chimney breasts all morning. I took my place, sitting in a semi-circle of smartly dressed teenage girls who averted their gaze from the filthy oddball dressed in rags.

Though I had grown to relish the challenge of learning, educational settings and most of their staff still unnerved me, dissolving any self-confidence I may have gained through my climbing achievements. The longer I sat there waiting for my name to be called, the more nauseous I became. Perhaps it was a fear of failure combined with self-consciousness about my regional accent and my class origins. Subject to my 'A' level tutors providing satisfactory references I had a place, I was told. I cycled back to work whistling all the way.

During the previous term, before leaving for the Alps, I had met Paul Tarn, one of the fork-lift truck drivers from the pit stockyard in a corridor by the lecture theatres. He had quit the pit, too, and was now training to be a science teacher. He had felt precisely the same as me on first arriving at university, despite his superb 'A' level results. The fear was irrational, but real enough to us. It was impossible for me to imagine, sat there that morning dressed in dirty demolition garb, that I would go on to complete a PhD and return to that same room, working as a lecturer.

Now, two years into the course, university life allowed me to pursue my climbing ambitions passionately, chiefly because of the free time available. During my final year underground I had worked twelve-hour shifts; now I had just twelve hours of lectures a week. During each term we also had a week-long break, officially known as a 'reading week', which I used to earn extra cash. In my first year I was invited to Ireland in the autumn and then Sweden in the spring on lecture tours, talking about my exploits in the mountains. I read the university set texts as I travelled from one place to the next. In February of this year, just a few months before coming to the Alps with Paul, I had worked for my old friend and mentor, Mal Duff, as a mountain guide in Glencoe. I took a free lift from Sheffield to Edinburgh in the back of a Transit van, managing to write an essay on 'The representation of eighteenth-century rural England in the poetry of George Crabbe' along the way and leaving it with Mal's wife, Liz, to post to the university. At 3am Mal and I drove to Glencoe, met our clients for breakfast and then walked on up into a blizzard. I got a 2:1 for the essay.

Paul and I shuffled out of the *téléphérique* cabin at 3,850 metres, stepped over the fence aimed at securing the tourists, put on our crampons and climbed down the sharp arête to the glacier below. Overshadowed by a cirque of towering peaks, we roped up under a metal-blue sky. It felt good to get going at last; we had been dreaming of this climb all year.

We contoured below narrow, white seams of ice that split red, granite pillars, heading towards the frontier ridge where the Fourche bivouac hut nestled. To save weight we'd brought just one ice hammer each, which meant we had to take special care with our footwork on the long steep slope that led up to the hut.

We planned to leave at midnight in order to cross under the notoriously dangerous hanging ice-cliffs of the Brenva Face at the coldest and safest point of the night. We spent the afternoon hydrating and resting, delighted that we had the place to ourselves – most other climbers had chosen to stay in the lower and more easily accessible Ghiglione refuge.

I tried to sleep but it was futile, my mind racing around all the potential catastrophes ahead. I had climbed on this side of the mountain three times before and each time I felt the same pressure. What if the weather turns on us? What if one of us fell? Did we have enough food? Were our rucksacks too heavy? The list was endless. The first time I climbed Mont Blanc was via the Jori Bardill *direttissima* on the Freney Pillar, a few weeks after leaving my job at the pit. Throughout the entire route Bonatti's epic tale of his companions dying stuck in my mind, even though we enjoyed perfect weather. However, a few weeks later I climbed Mont Blanc again, via the Brenva Spur, with Pete Swift and a violent wind struck up just before we reached the summit. It turned into a stern test of will power and skill to get over the summit and safely back down to the valley. That incident only seemed to make Bonatti's story even more tangible. This side of Mont Blanc is notorious for unpredictable violent storms. If caught in a prolonged storm, as Bonatti and co. were, escape is difficult as numerous avalanche-prone slopes must be crossed, not to mention the sheer distance that has to be covered in order to reach the safety of a hut.

The alarm bell sounded and I switched on my headtorch and jumped out of bed, relieved that we could get on with the job in hand. I opened the hut door; the weather had turned.

'I can't believe this.'

I was greeted by a sky full of snow rapidly falling on a brisk breeze.

Incredulous, Paul came and peered out.

'We're not going anywhere in this lot,' he proclaimed.

Back in bed, in the darkness, I felt angry with the weather forecast. We reset the alarm for 2am and turned off our lights. I knew about the reputation for unpredictable weather here, but still I fumed. We wanted to try this climb more than anything. We had spent three weeks preparing in the Dolomites and the Bregaglia and then on the Dru. Now this. I felt my fists tighten under the blankets.

At 2am the snow fell even thicker and faster.

'Thank God we're not up on the route now. We wouldn't last long with the kit we've brought.'

'Don't remind me.'

We had come super lightweight, determined to try to free climb the entire route in one day. We had a litre of liquid each plus one minute gas canister, which would melt enough snow for two or three litres of water if we were lucky. We had just a small amount of macaroni, one packet of mushroom soup, a bit of muesli for breakfast and a few cereal bars each. Essentially, there was enough for two days' climbing at a push. By day two we had to be over the other side of the mountain and heading back to the valley. We had no sleeping bags; instead, we each had a lightweight down duvet and a double plastic bag to bivvy in, if necessary. Our theory was that we were fit and could move quickly over rock. A serious storm like this, though, could be fatal.

At 4am the weather remained unchanged. It was getting too late to leave now, for by the time we reached the technical climbing it would be well after midday and we would never make it to the summit before darkness.

After such a fitful night of checking the weather we both finally fell into a deep sleep. When we woke we had a cereal bar with a cup of tea. Outside the snow had stopped but the refuge was still shrouded in thick cloud.

'If we had brought more food we could perhaps have spent the day here waiting for it to clear,' I started.

'I know.'

'I think we'll have to go back to the valley.'

I could feel myself becoming negative, or perhaps realistic.

'Whatever you think.'

I began packing my rucksack, swearing out loud, cursing the weather man. We put on all the clothes we had and then left. Paul started down the slope first, the new snow over the old, rotten ice making it much more awkward than it should have been. Less than a hundred feet from the glacier a swirl of blue sky above us hinted at a clearing. I stopped still.

'Do you think somebody is up there torturing us?' I shouted down to Paul, one hand raised into the air.

'Are we doing the right thing, descending?'

'I don't know Paul, I'm torn. I really am.'

'We've hardly any food left though.'

I knew he was right. As we stood there more blue sky appeared, only tormenting us further.

'Let's climb back up to the hut, just in case,' I gambled.

By the time we arrived at the refuge the clouds had lifted so that only the very summit of Mont Blanc itself was obscured. Without too much discussion we set off towards the climb; we could always spend the night out where Thierry and Alain had, we reassured each other, and from there we'd make the top, surely.

We descended steeply down onto the Brenva glacier and then dragged our feet through the fresh snow, struggling for breath as we headed towards Col Moore. For the first time we were about to enter into a blatantly dangerous section. Up to our right the enormous ice-cliffs of the Brenva Face flashed in the midday sun. Terrifying. As we paused there, I recalled my friend

Trevor's theory for crossing potentially lethal avalanche zones. 'Split the whole area into thirds', he had suggested. 'Walk the first third at normal pace so that if something peels off towards you, you have enough energy to scamper back out of the danger. In the middle third, run like hell. Then, if things are still calm, catch your breath in the final third.' I had liked the theory at the time but now, a little older and wiser, I felt sceptical.

Before committing ourselves we stopped for a drink and a cereal bar. The sun was beating down now. It was surprisingly warm, considering the altitude.

Paul passed his water bottle.

'Thanks. I'm not sure about this plan any more, Paul.'

'I know what you mean, it's getting late; it's not the best time to be crossing under this lot.'

I felt relieved he felt the same way. If truth be known, I was also exhausted. I hadn't really slept much and the uncertainty of the whole enterprise had drained my motivation.

'It's only a climb for God's sake, there are lots more. We could do a route on the Grand Capucin, it's great rock on there,' Paul commented, a wonderful rolling 'r' resonating out of the 'grand'.

'It might be safer,' I added.

We lounged in the sun for fifteen minutes then put on our sunglasses and smeared sun cream across our faces. Suddenly the huge burden – the pressure that had been crushing us for days – vanished. We turned around disappointed but relieved; finally our attempt was over. We climbed towards the Ghiglione refuge that was slightly lower on the ridge than the Fourche and looked to have an easier-angled approach. We had moved just a few hundred metres when an almighty roar filled the sky: one of the Brenva ice-cliffs had collapsed. It took almost thirty seconds before the debris crashed on to the glacier, the place we would have almost certainly been moving across had we not changed our minds. I felt a shiver down my spine. Paul was open-mouthed – he had spent less time in the high moun-tains than I had and I don't think he had ever witnessed anything quite so formidable, an event so utterly destructive. Our mood improved now as we congratulated each other on our decision to retreat.

The Ghiglione hut was a monstrous metal structure that had

been abandoned by the Italian Alpine Club because of its unstable nature. It looked like a rusting trawler riding the back of a steep wave. Although it was officially closed, there were four or more teams inside. In its heyday it had been able to accommodate thirty or so climbers, but now its floor was tilted at twenty degrees and twisted.

By late afternoon we were plagued by a frustrating, cloudless sky; perfect weather and not enough provisions to make another attempt on Divine. I couldn't bear to watch the other alpinists chatting excitedly about their plans for the following day so I went and lay down on one of the creaking, steel-sprung beds, annoyed that we had not carried extra food.

'Hey, Andy,' grinned Paul.

'What?'

'Things are looking up.'

He held up half of an onion.

'Look what I found in the bin.'

'What the hell are we going to do with that?' I sulked.

'Well, an Israeli guy in there, Yousaf, has offered us some couscous. He reckons he's got spare gas too.'

My psyche had been up and down so many times in the last twenty-four hours I didn't know what to think. Paul looked delighted; I knew that in his mind this constituted a perfectly good meal. Outside there wasn't a breath of wind. I knew we might not get another opportunity this season.

'I suppose we have no excuse,' I heard myself say, incredulous that our decision to mount another assault on the most difficult mountain climb in Europe had been taken on the strength of half a small and rather dishevelled onion, retrieved from a dustbin.

We left the shipwrecked hut at midnight and made our way down on to the glacier. Now we had three small muesli bars each, the packet of mushroom soup and the macaroni, plus tea bags. We also had a full litre of water each. Less than 100 metres below the hut Paul stopped and knelt down on the slope, shining his light towards his feet.

'My crampon's broken.'

'You are joking?' I said, now convinced that a higher being was toying with us and our plans.

'The nut holding the front points has snapped off.'

We hadn't any tools or spares; we couldn't afford the extra weight.

'I've got an idea,' said Paul, turning around and limping back up the slope towards the hut. I followed on.

He remembered that a repair job had been done on the underside of the bunk-bed above where he'd slept. Miraculously he found some bolt croppers and disappeared into the dormitory. Painstakingly he snipped at the wire, trying not to disturb the large, snoring, German climber above.

'Sorted,' proclaimed Paul outside the hut, strapping on the repaired crampon.

'Divine Providence ascent, sponsored by Ghiglione bed-wire,' I joked.

The outing was rapidly developing into a Monty Python sketch.

At one o'clock we set off again towards Col Moore, the humour allowing us to relax a little as we crossed under the Brenva ice-cliffs. I suggested we use the rule of thirds and in the central section we jogged, our feet weaving a line around the huge blocks of debris deposited by the collapse of the ice-cliff the previous day.

To our right, four tiny lights snaked up towards the Brenva Spur. Now, joined together by seventy feet of rope, we climbed up a sixty degree, perfectly frozen slope, the squeak of our crampons and our breathing the only sound in the still night. After an hour of effort the slope became steep, brittle and pock-marked with small grey rocks, like the bonnet of a car attacked by machine-gun fire.

'Shall I go first?'

'If you like,' said Paul. 'Pass me a sling, I'll belay on this rock spike.'

We changed into our rock-shoes, stuffing the heavy, double-plastic boots into one rucksack to be hauled or to be carried by the second, depending on the angle. The other pack contained the stove, food and water, and it clawed at my shoulders as I grappled with the awkward, friable first pitch, my headtorch desperately searching out decent footholds on the smooth granite.

At dawn we emerged on to a much steeper shield of grey

rock that guarded the entrance to the base of the red tower. It was impossible to tell where the correct route went. I followed a series of grooves and cracks up disturbingly freshly cleaved granite, the two nylon nine-millimetre ropes falling from my waist down towards Paul, a hundred feet below. A thousand feet beneath him, down on the glacier, the morning sun illuminated a sea of gaping crevasses. I tried to block out the frightening story Thierry had recounted about Gabarrou and Marsigny. That bit of the climb is much higher anyhow, I tried to reassure myself.

The next pitch proved harder still, and Paul managed a strenuous and bold lead to deliver us on to the small ledges at the base of the red tower.

'Good work Paul. That was hideous,' I congratulated, once I stood on the ledge. 'This must be where Thierry and Alain slept.'

'Yes, I think so.'

The whole route took on a different character now. The rock was a vivid rust colour, much steeper but wonderfully solid-looking. Paul committed to an impending wall with appalling protection: just a couple of tiny brass wires and a thin knife-blade piton beaten into a crack. He inched his way up, his fingers squeezing tiny matchbox edges of rock, his lungs working hard in the rarefied air. He gave me a flash of his eyes, saying: this is hard and scary, get ready to hold the rope. I held the rope firmly, but had to look away briefly. I knew that a fall here would be disastrous. I felt a tension in my stomach. We had no means of communication, no radio or telephone, and there were was nobody to shout to. We were alone.

'Okay safe,' he called finally.

I followed, inspired by his courageous display.

We understood the next section to be more difficult still, but I felt invigorated by what Paul had managed.

'Hold on, before you go I'll put my duvet on.'

The sun had long gone now, and it was cold for the person left on the belay stance.

I climbed out leftwards in a very exposed position, the first joint of my fingers wedged behind a series of small, creaking, damp flakes. I arranged some chocks in a small crack and then launched up the wall, aiming to reach easier ground before my arms noticed. There was little evidence of previous ascents; the climb had minimal fixed protection and not a single expansion bolt, and this contributed to a great feeling of adventure. This place is truly outrageous, I thought, taking a hanging stance and craning my head back. I shouted to Paul to start up. Above us was the famous groove pitch. For the first time, a few pegs and *in situ* chocks led the way. Sadly, the left wall of the groove was running with water which, at some points, had turned into a veneer of ice. The earlier sun had obviously created meltwater somewhere above us.

'What time is it?' asked Paul when he arrived.

'Wow, it's seven o'clock already.'

'There's no way we'll make the top of this tower before dark, never mind the summit.'

'Isn't the bivvy ledge they talked about at the top of this groove?'

'I bloody hope so.'

Paul set off in a determined manner, but straight away his feet were skidding on the water and the ice. I could hear the effort he was putting in, clipping the rope into a chock and throwing his hands up into the next part of the crack. Water streamed from the rock along his forearms and off on to my helmet. I struggled with freezing hands to feed the rope through the belay device – ice was now forming on the rope.

He had no choice but to take three rests on the rope. It was wet, almost dark, and we couldn't possibly spend a night suspended in our harnesses here – not in these temperatures. It was seventeen hours since we had left the Ghiglione refuge and we hadn't stopped once. We had eaten just two cereal bars each all day; the liquid was long since finished.

By the time I joined Paul on the ledge it was pitch-black. We crawled into the plastic bag, wedging the stove against the wall behind us, and began melting snow for the pasta. Although in a sitting position, I fell into a deep sleep as soon as we'd eaten.

I woke with a start, shivering, snowflakes sliding down my cheeks. I switched on my headtorch as snow, like tissues, tumbled quietly and smothered the folds of our plastic bag. I wanted to tell Paul but he was sound asleep.

I knew how easy it was for the imagination to run wild, especially in the loneliness of night. But still I was scared. My brain short-circuited once more to the Bonatti epic just around the corner on the Central Pillar of Freney; how could anyone ever forget that story. Our situation was serious. We had virtually no food; not enough for one day really, and we wouldn't last long sitting in this plastic bag. We would have to battle to the top and then seek shelter in the Vallot refuge.

Dawn seemed to arrive later than normal, the sun piercing through a curtain of cloud draped over the red tower and allowing us to view the summits of the Gran Paradiso peaks to the right and the Combin massif. The Matterhorn hovered on the horizon, small but unmistakable. Immediately I realised that the snow in the night had simply been a localised storm. It had frozen our limbs and fingers but had now passed. I had over-reacted.

'I'm not sure which was worse last night, Jenkinson – the snowstorm or the smell coming from your backside.'

He took great pride in maintaining his reputation and my comment started him laughing. He spilt a little of the tea.

'Hey, don't spill that, there's no more until we get down over the other side of this beast.'

After our meagre breakfast there was no reason to sit there any longer; our arms and fingers were rigid. We both agreed that the sooner we got moving the better. I had contemplated suggesting that we abseil back down the groove and try to climb it again without the rests. But it still looked wet. What was more, if we reached the final big roof in time, perhaps that would be dry. I swung my arms around and then thrust my fingers between my neck and the collar of my fleece jacket to warm them. It would be excellent to try and free climb that, I told myself.

I set off, squeezing up into a chimney system above the ledge. Minute by minute the rock felt warmer as the sun rose into the sky. My hands were swollen from all the climbing the day before and from severe dehydration. The granite had bitten into my fingers, leaving dozens of small but deep incisions. Belaying on a small ledge I struggled to see where the route went next; all natural lines had disappeared into a seamless, golden wall.

'It goes out right across that face,' Paul said confidently. 'There's a crack system over there. It should lead us towards the big roof.'

He rubbed the sole of each rock-shoe on the inside of his calf, clearing away any bits of dirt and fragments of rock, then proceeded to tiptoe horizontally across an orange wall that looked as if it had been ironed flat.

'Just like being back at the Roaches. There are little chicken-heads to pull on,' he called, apparently resting both feet on nothing.

'Alright, climb when you're ready,' Paul shouted. Once in the crack and securely tied off he was ready to belay.

I found shallow dishes for my feet. For the hands there were protuberances, though 'chicken-heads' seemed too optimistic a term. Sparrows' beaks perhaps. It was an exhilarating test of balance, which deflected my gaze from the 2,000-foot drop to the glacier.

By early afternoon we were resting beneath the final roof which, to our surprise, looked dry. I felt nervous, the fear of failure rising right into my throat. I organised the protection on the gear loops along the side of my harness, taking longer than normal, trying to find a positive focus. A granite roof like this would test any climber's skill and fitness at sea level, never mind at 4,500 metres with an empty stomach; God only knew what it was like up there.

I climbed the lower wall and fiddled a large camming device into a slot on the underside of the roof, then clipped in the rope. On the lip of the overhang I discovered a tiny edge with the fingers of my right hand. I brought up my other hand just as my feet swung into space. The adrenalin was pumping wildly now.

I threw my left heel over the roof, which took some of the weight off my arms, allowing me to scan the wall above for something to pull on in order to gain a standing position.

'Go on Andy, give it some hammer,' encouraged Paul, hanging sixty feet below.

I had climbed roofs similar to this on the gritstone edges of Derbyshire and, though my arms were rapidly tiring, the famil-iarity spurred me on. My lungs ached with the effort, my chest heaving like an aging smoker.

'Come on, don't fall now,' I muttered to myself.

'Go on Andy,' hurled Paul.

Somehow, I managed to claw my way over the lip. I could see better handholds a few feet above me.

'Yes!' I cried. I was stood on the lip of the overhang. My right leg trembled a little as adrenalin rushed through my body. I pushed down firmly through my big toe, trying to minimise the shake.

In every direction the view was stupendous: to the right, the gigantic sweep of the Brenva Face; out left, the base of the Central Pillar of Freney; and below that, the Aiguille Blanche de Peuterey. I climbed the next thirty feet elated; we might have failed to free climb the groove late last night but we had freed the roof. I made a secure belay, pulled up the rucksack and then signalled for Paul to start.

'Yee ha!' I shouted into the sky.

It was already late afternoon by the time we had changed into our big boots and crampons to tackle the Peuterey ridge. We followed easy-angled rocks smeared with ice and then climbed up on to the narrow ridge itself. Here we decided to climb unroped to speed things up. Under the snow sat a layer of brick-hard blue ice. As the sun sank, the wind increased, buffeting us, and I decided to stop and put on my down jacket. I balanced on my crampon points, tugging at the sleeve to pull it over my mitten; and as I did so the fabric tore and a plume of feathers shot into the air like a jet of steam.

'How's the bed-wire Paul?' I called down.

'The bed-wire's brilliant, but check this out.'

Paul held up his ice hammer. The blade had lost its fixing pins, rendering it virtually useless. We only had one ice tool each, but Paul seemed happy to jab the spike at the base of his hammer into the slope instead.

'Do you need a rope?'

'I'll be fine.'

'You want to treat yourself to some decent kit when you get home, you tight-arse,' I laughed.

It was 9.30pm when we made the final steps up on to the summit of Mont Blanc. I felt a tingle run through my veins – after everything that had happened to us over the last few days, we had cracked it.

'*Berg heil*,' said Paul, his lips hidden by his balaclava.

'What does that mean?' I asked.

'Praise the mountain,' he said, holding out his gloved hand.

Despite the thirst and the hunger as we set off down towards the distant, dazzling lights of Chamonix, I sensed my boots lighten. I felt like a man on the moon.

10

Gasherbrum IV

3rd July 1993

Andy Perkins stopped and bent over his ski poles, trying to ease
the weight of the rucksack from his shoulders and gasping, his
lungs sucking at the meagre air. For almost two hours, using
our headtorches, we had weaved a path from base camp up
through a jumble of glacier ice, leaving tiny crampon marks
along narrow snow bridges that dissected the endless huge
crevasses. Fathomless, petrifying holes. I waited for Andy's call
to follow on: we had to keep the rope tight between us so that,
should one of us tumble in, the other could at least attempt to
arrest the fall.

Initially, the neighbouring American team on Gasherbrum II
had been climbing through this chaotic maze of ice unroped
and in the middle of the day, when snow bridges are softer and
more unpredictable. They dubbed us the 'night riders', insinu-
ating that we were being over cautious but, after a week of
fearful teetering, they too began setting their alarms early and
tying into ropes. Yasushi Yamano, a solo Japanese mountaineer
– like ourselves, attempting Gasherbrum IV – had obviously
heard about the treacherous icefall. He had brought a fifteen-
foot, robust-looking piece of bamboo that he slotted under the
lid of his rucksack. The theory was that if he fell into a crevasse,
the pole would jam on the lip, preventing him from plummeting
to his death. The difficulty, of course, was predicting how the
crevasses (often lurking under the snow) were oriented. This
was the cause of countless derisory jokes among our team
members. If he had really thought about it, we mused, he would
have three poles in a star configuration, thereby covering every

eventuality – save for holes larger than the circumference of the bamboo umbrella!

Suddenly a beautiful emerald flame arced eastwards across the sky.

'Wow, did you see that shooting star?' I yelled up to Andy. 'That was amazing.'

'Sure it wasn't the Pakistanis and the Indians, bombing each other again?' he asked.

'Jesus, yeah, I forgot about that lot. I thought it looked a peculiar colour.'

'Some of the team reckoned they saw some action the other morning. Okay Andy, let's get out of this place before the sun arrives and fries us.'

He had a point. Brendan Murphy had become delirious from severe sunstroke descending the icefall at just 10am the previous day and was still in base camp recovering.

Slowly, subtly, the mauve shades of dawn began to light the earth's white giants; silent, big beyond comprehension. Once past the icefall, a more gently-angled, curling snowfield led to our advance base camp at 6,000 metres, two hours away. We removed the rope here and took small paces, counting one hundred at a time, until our chests burned with the effort and we had to stop. Sometimes it felt as if my lungs were two large pink balloons of bubble gum, about to pop. Free from the concentration demanded by the icefall, I relaxed a little and began thinking about the nine Pakistani soldiers who had traipsed below our base camp just two days earlier, waving, with wide grins; proud to have been chosen to man the 4,500 metre Conway Saddle for a couple of months. Our Liaison Officer, the Captain, waved back – his chest swollen, a proud look about him – shouting words of good luck that shimmered in the afternoon heat. The six of us waved too, bemused and concerned by their pathetically inadequate clothing and equipment, as well as their outdated rifles – things our great-grandparents might have used in the First World War.

Eight years before, the Indians had moved up into the Siachen Glacier and established military positions, staking their claim on this disputed, inhospitable, beautiful frontier. The Pakistani Army swept in to oppose them, creating a stalemate. A battle of low intensity followed, but one with major psychological and political symbolism of the continuing tension between the two nations. Reputedly, during the 1990s the war cost the Indians half a million dollars a day, mainly on helicopter fuel. The Pakistani government refused to release a figure.

Not wishing to upset the Captain, we had kept our thoughts to ourselves as the soldiers disappeared up the glacier. So young and frail, they were not local mountain people but slender, suburban-looking youths, probably from Karachi, Quetta or Lahore: enthusiastic, hopeful and probably relatively ignorant of cerebral and pulmonary oedema, hypothermia and frostbite.

At the two tents pitched below the Gasherbrum cirque, I threw my pack into the snow and sat down, feeling light-headed. Andy filled the pan with snow and then sparked the stove into life. Half an hour later our team-mates, Kate Phillips, Chris Flewitt and Andy Macnae, came into view carrying heavy loads; their faces strained like champion sprinters, yet they walked at a snail's pace, as if wearing lead boots.

'Ah Mr Cave, Doctor Perkins, good morning gentlemen,' greeted Macnae, arriving first, as he normally did.

Andy had a predisposition for adapting to high altitude relatively easily, which annoyed some of his climbing partners, for back home he did no training whatsoever and spent a great deal of time in the pub. I knew this as we had worked together for a few weeks before leaving the UK, painting and decorating at Nicky and Mick Fowler's house, and a considerable amount of beer was consumed every evening. Officially, Mac, (as we called him) was the leader of our expedition, but he assumed more of an ambassadorial role, utilising his diplomatic skills to soothe ruffled feathers. In truth, we all believed Perkins to be the real mover and shaker, the one who genuinely relished responsibility and logistical hurdles.

A few minutes later, Kate and Chris appeared.

'How was Murphy when you left?' quizzed Andy, pouring tea into the various coloured-plastic mugs.

'Oh alright,' answered Kate, trying to regulate her breathing. 'He's frustrated, but he needs a couple of days rest, needs to drink a lot.'

Kate had met Brendan at the Cambridge University climbing club, where his unassuming attitude, Celtic good looks and genuine talent for climbing had become legendary. The pair had begun going out together in 1990, during a successful expedition to Ama Dablam in the Khumbu valley of Nepal. Andy had climbed with Brendan on Cerro Kishtwar in India two years earlier and had spoken to me about his phenomenal tenacity and drive, but he had worried about the dynamics of having 'a couple' along on this particular trip. One evening Andy interrogated Kate during a pre-expedition get-together at a curry house in Manchester. As Kate had explained, she found it easier being here climbing than sitting at home worrying about Brendan. We would soon discover that Kate's commitment and strength when climbing in the Himalayas were commensurate with that of anyone else in our group.

'Here, stop gassing you lot,' started Chris, unquestionably the most eccentric member of our trip. 'I want to get down for my egg butty and *The Archers*.'

This made us chortle. Chris had spent hours unfurling a giant aerial over the moraine and ice slopes around base camp in order to catch up with the activities of Eddie Grundy and Linda Snell back in Ambridge.

'Yes, better get going, otherwise we'll get burned to death,' started Kate.

The snow under their feet was beginning to soften and it wouldn't be long before the raging Pakistani sun arrived, frying lips, noses and minds.

They finished their tea, then set off down towards base camp, bidding us farewell and wishing us luck with our reconnaissance the following day.

As they drew away I turned and stared at the vast, unclimbed South Face of Gasherbrum IV, wondering how the hell we might force a way to the summit. Though slightly lower than its neighbours (at 7,985 metres) G IV looked much more menacing, the blank summit a pyramid of marble, glinting in the sun's first rays. The American expedition aimed to repeat the standard route on G II; a team of four Basques wanted to climb an established route on G I; only our team intended to establish a new route. Following the first ascent of G IV in 1958 by the Italians Walter Bonatti and Carlo Mauri, the summit had been reached only once – although the Polish–Austrian team of Voytek Kurtyka and Robert Schauer had established a seminal route up the formidable west face in 1986, climbing in a single push. Kurtyka wrote of how they ran out of gas to melt snow very high on the climb and, delirious from the effects of dehydration and high altitude, began battling across the face, forfeiting the summit and descending the north-west ridge, surviving by a cat's whisker. The virgin South Face had seen three previous attempts, two led by experienced British alpinist Dai Lampard, in 1986 and 1988, and one by an extremely strong American team the previous year.

Most climbers acknowledge that Gasherbrum IV's symmetry makes it one of the most beautiful peaks in the Himalayas, as well as one of the most difficult to climb. However, because it is not one of the famous fourteen summits of the world that reach 8,000 metres (as do G I and G II), it attracts relatively few suitors. The Americans attempting G II, camped next to us, were clearly impressed by our plans. One guy from Colorado declared us 'stud muffins', a prestigious term of endearment apparently used by his thirteen-year-old daughter.

I had first glimpsed this cirque of peaks back in 1987, when, between quitting my job at the pit and starting university, I made my first journey to the mountains of northern Pakistan. I joined Joe Simpson, John Stevenson and my landlord, Tom Richardson, on a successful expedition to the previously unclimbed Tupopdan Peak, to the north-west of the Gasherbrums. Immediately afterwards I teamed up with Simon Yates, Tom Curtis and Sean Smith in the Hushe Valley. There we made the first ascent of Laila Peak. From both these summits I had gazed towards K2 and the Gasherbrums, wondering if I would ever have the opportunity to climb them.

Andy and I spent the remainder of the day snoozing, the stove humming, continually melting snow into water for drinks. In the middle of the day, the brightness of the sun forced us to place our sleeping bags on the outside of the tent to increase the shade. Finally, by four o'clock it had begun to cool, and at six we ate our supper of mashed potato and tinned mackerel fillets.

'Another tea before beddy-byes?' I asked Andy.

'Better had,' he replied, predictably. Throughout all four of the Himalayan expeditions we had been on together he had never once refused a hot drink.

Condensation on the base of the pan in the hanging stove

sizzled then spluttered, putting out the flame for the umpteenth time. I grabbed my lighter and sparked the gas, which sent a brief, violent, blue flame out into the tent. We had just one cup each, used for both eating and drinking. I always cleaned my cup with toilet paper after meals but Andy never bothered, unfazed by pieces of mackerel and mashed potato floating in his tea. Though I acclimatised to the decrease in oxygen levels on these expeditions reasonably well, I suffered from indigestion and nausea, and the thought of 'tea à la Perkins' repulsed me. He sipped his tea, the fibres of his beard filtering out the larger bits of food which, now lodged, would freeze there overnight – nourishment to survive on in an emergency, I thought to myself. But this was not the time to be indulging in domestic tittle-tattle; simply surviving was difficult enough. I ate with my mouth open, he had strong body odour, and both of us suffered from high altitude flatulence; up here such habits and conditions were tolerated.

A slight wind buffeted the tent the next morning, but not enough to deter us. We lay in the dark, cosy, the flame of the stove casting shadows on the icy fabric of the inner tent. After an hour we had enough water for tea and ate a flapjack each before sliding into our one-piece suits, putting our warm feet into the double plastic boots and then crawling outside. The snow's crust refused to support our body weight so we strapped on snowshoes before heading slowly towards the secondary icefall beneath the South Face.

After an hour the slope had steepened and our snowshoes struggled to grip at such angles, so we took them off, our feet punching through the crust into freezing cold powder snow as we weaved through the icefall. The sun arrived at last, but still our feet froze and we forced ourselves to stop and wriggle all our toes aggressively, afraid of frostbite.

'This feels dangerous Andy,' commented Andy, referring to a band of blue-green serac ice-cliffs suspended up above us.

'I know, if it collapses we're stuffed.'

'Look over there, are they footsteps?'

'Oh yes.'

'Who the hell could that be?'

'I bet that's the Japanese guy, Bamboo Billy.'

It was hard to laugh at altitude, especially difficult to get enough air into the lungs after the long, juddering exhalation, but we couldn't control ourselves. We decided to retreat and as we did so spied a subsidiary spur emerging from the bottom of the south-east ridge, curling beneath the South Face; a potential safe campsite from which to begin climbing. Heartened, we descended a little and then traversed enthusiastically towards it, noticing that, above the spur, ice slopes ran up to join the south-east ridge above the notorious group of rock pinnacles, the obstacle that had repulsed Dai Lampard's team.

'That point must be at around 7,000 metres. From there it looks reasonable, for a bit anyhow,' I remarked, putting on more lipsalve and sunscreen.

'I agree, but check out the final 500 metres, it looks as hard as nails.'

'You never know, with good weather.'

'Well, we'll just have to go and rub our noses in it,' Andy said in a determined tone, borrowing a phrase of Tom Longstaff's, the early Himalayan explorer.

We left our loads at the base of the spur, marking the spot with a tall marker-wand, bright plastic tape attached to its tip, then set off down before the sun grew too fierce.

8th July 1993

A fortnight after our arrival at base camp, the sky darkened and it began to snow. We had carried a substantial amount of food and supplies to a camp established at 6,500 metres, at the foot of the South Face, despite the fact that each of us had suffered serious stomach complaints at some point during the preceding week. We attributed our ill health to the fact that some of the other expeditions had no strict system to their toilet arrangements, with numerous people relieving themselves above the snowfields and tiny streams used for drinking-water. This infuriated us, as we had gone to great lengths to construct a single toilet-site out of a large plastic barrel, below all water supplies. Chronic diarrhoea and vomiting are unpleasant enough at sea level but here, at 5,300 metres, dehydration cripples a person.

In the night the snow fell hard, enveloping the tent. The faint sound of Karim, our cook, shouting 'chai' woke me the next morning and Flewitt and I waded through knee-deep snow towards the kitchen tent where Brendan was chatting with Karim.

'Good sleep Karim? Warm enough?'

'Yes sir.'

'Are you sure?'

'No problem sir.'

Karim sat on his heels making porridge, wearing an eclectic mixture of our old cast-offs. Brendan never let climbing ambition cloud his vision, always keeping a watchful eye on those around him, especially the vulnerable. During the second day of the walk to base camp, under a ferocious sun, he spent hours with three local Balti porters working for a K2 expedition. They had been given barrels of kerosene to carry, which had started leaking. Brendan dressed the burnt skin on their backs, before creating makeshift seals for the fuel containers out of polythene.

The previous evening Perkins had announced that today would be his thirty-third birthday and the Americans had suggested that, after supper, all the various expeditions convene in their giant dining shelter for drinks to celebrate the occasion. We spent the morning playing bridge and drinking tea. At lunchtime we were queuing for Kate's delicious-smelling veggieburgers when the Captain appeared, his brown eyes full of sadness.

'There has been a terrible tragedy. Nine soldiers have been killed on the saddle by avalanche.'

Shocked, we comforted him awkwardly, not quite knowing what to say.

Switching to Urdu, he ordered a mug of tea from the cook and then returned to his tent. Other than the revving stove, quiet fell about the kitchen shelter. I recalled their faces again – smiling on the glacier, bright teeth, outdated glacier goggles – heading up to the saddle just four kilometres away. Young, waving, proud. Then a fresh image took its place: twisted, frozen bodies – half-buried – a brisk wind freezing their limbs black and, just audible above the sound of the wind, mothers wailing in hot, far-away city streets. And how did we feel ourselves, playing a game with such high risks? The week before flying to Pakistan Kate and Brendan had had an argument. Kate's sister, Susanne, was due to be married immediately after the G IV expedition and when discussions about Brendan being measured for a suit began, Kate jokingly mentioned that the measurements were actually for his coffin in case he didn't return. This infuriated Brendan and started a debate between the pair about accepting the risks associated with high altitude mountaineering. Brendan, it seemed, like most of us, lived mainly in denial.

All day long the snow fell, trying its utmost to crush our frail kitchen shelter, despite the extra rope we used to tension it and the ski-sticks we added as roof supports. A series of debates began about the soldiers on the col which resulted in our agreeing that they were probably ill-prepared to survive in such a hostile place, both in terms of equipment and experience. This may have been true, but, more importantly, the rhetoric comforted us, putting flesh on the naïve argument that such a thing would never happen to us.

I peed into the deep snow, my temples throbbing in time to the beat of The Pogues that resounded through the dark, night air; whisky and vodka doesn't half work well at 5,300 metres. I thought of my Swedish friends just around the corner on K2 and wondered, were they training in the same manner as the party animals on this side of the range? I turned around, a multitude of thrashing limbs silhouetted behind the brightly-lit canvas up above, dancers oblivious to the raging storm out here.

As I re-entered the tent an American climber fell from his makeshift seat and disappeared from view, appearing a few minutes later covered in snow, having rolled down the slope outside. Without hesitation, he now joined in the dancing to a thundering cheer from the crowd.

'Outrageous,' cried Brendan, as he, Andy and Chris linked arms with the Basque men, spinning each other in true Gaelic madness. In the corner, by the entrance, Mac continued to chat with the Basque girl, his matted red hair lolling more and more towards her left shoulder. I overheard them comparing their frostbite injuries, she having had toes amputated following an ascent of Daulaghiri (8,167 metres); he'd lost his toes after an epic on Mont Blanc during winter. Like a couple of war veterans, they remarked on how lucky they felt compared to the Japanese soloist's wife camped up above; she had previously lost all the fingers on one hand through frostbite. I cringed: the thought of losing even one digit from one of my fingers terrified me;

after all, my real passion was rock climbing. In fact, ever since starting mountaineering I had worried about frostbite. I had got frost-nipped (the first stages of frostbite) during a three-day winter ascent in the Polish Tatra, the year after leaving the pit. From then on I always carried at least two spare pairs of gloves, often more.

Suddenly, the young cook boy appeared asking for help.

'Member fallen in snow, maybe big problem,' he announced, wearing a cheeky grin.

Outside, one of the American climbers had failed to reach the safety of his tent, and lay face down in the soft powder, the outline of where he had broken through the surface of the snowdrift etched, cartoon-like.

'Oh fuck,' the man slurred, as Peter, a Pole and the cook boy dragged him off to the tent, stripped him and put him into his sleeping bag.

This signalled the end of the party and we staggered home, a cold wind driving snow into the erratic silver columns of our lights.

Over breakfast the following morning, Perkins agreed it had been a first-rate birthday party. We heard, via Karim, that a second American had been found paralytic outside by the cook boy and duly dragged off to his tent. Bizarrely, these two would be the first members of their team to summit Gasherbrum II. The Captain entered the shelter with a serious countenance and, following a prolonged silence, condemned us for undertaking such raucous celebrations when nine of his fellow soldiers had perished on the col up above. Attempting to subdue him, Andy mentioned the concept of the wake, but it didn't wash. Only recently, the pair had argued about the Captain's clandestine borrowing of Andy's trekking poles (confronting him about this in front of our low caste cook had led to a huge loss of face and heated arguments). And now the party.

Fortunately, after we had endured another day of blizzards, the sun appeared and the whole team began excitedly packing rucksacks, aiming to head off towards the South Face the next morning. After we'd spent two days reaching the foot of the face, however, the sky quickly wove a thick blanket of cloud and with a quiet wind, heavy snow began falling once more. It was a no-win situation: you either stayed and ate into vital food supplies that had required immense effort to carry there, or descended and risked not being in position when the weather improved. Kate and Brendan stayed, the rest of us retreated to base camp.

'Argh, argh, argh,' I banged my head on the soaking canvas of our kitchen tent and then went in.

'This bloody weather, argh, argh, bollocks.'

Karim looked at me laughing.

'Maybe Mr Andy going crazy?' He handed me some tea.

'Maybe,' I replied. The mental strain of these holidays was ridiculous. I had left the UK exactly forty days ago and still hadn't done any climbing to write home about.

'I told you, if we had brought some of that breast milk with us we'd have been set,' began Flewitt, smirking.

Allegedly, he had tasted some of his best friend's wife's breast milk before leaving home and had developed a theory that it was light as hell and contained all the nutrients required by high altitude mountaineers.

'Flew, you're a pervert. And, while we're on the subject, I've decided you've got a peculiar taste in books.'

'What's wrong Cavey, you not enjoying it?'

'No, I can't read that crap, it's too weird,' I replied, referring to a novel named *Geek Love* he had leant me. It centred around a family of circus performers, in which the mother takes poisons during pregnancy, deliberately producing freak offspring that ultimately perform in the family show. The following day, the eternal optimists Kate and Brendan returned from camp 2. So far, no one from any of the four expeditions had made serious progress on any peak.

22nd July 1993

The climbing on the lower part of the South Face was not technically difficult, but it felt serious. I had wanted to place an ice screw for the last fifteen metres, yet the ice had been full of air and grit. At last, I sighed, decent ice. First, I cut a horizontal line in the frozen wall with the pick of my ice axe, and then used the broader adze of the axe to chop, making sure I twisted the axe as I did so to prevent it from sticking – up here efficiency is critical. Wheels of ice rolled down the slope, glinting in the sun. The effort left me dizzy and then breathless, I leaned my helmet against the slope.

'Halfway,' bellowed Chris, breaking the silence, indicating that I had a further twenty-five metres to climb before I could justify stopping to belay. I knew that at the pace we were moving we would not reach the ridge today; we just had to push as hard as we could. I chopped and scraped away a layer of aerated ice at shoulder-height, then took off my mitten – shoving it down the front of my jacket – and clasped an ice screw, unclipping it from my harness. Dropping anything here was not an option. I held the screw with my left hand, angling it up slightly, and then smacked it in with the ice hammer, rather lethargically. Slowly, the decreased levels of oxygen to the brain were turning me into a punch-drunk boxer. With only the head of the ice screw showing, I clipped in the rope and relaxed.

We could see over the col on the south ridge now, towards the mighty Masherbrum and a thousand other peaks reaching into the sky. To our right, tiny specks moved up the banana-shaped ridge on the lower part of Gasherbrum II, the Americans probably. Sometimes I envied their contentment, doing the normal route on a manageable peak, as opposed to this ideal-istic game of pioneering new routes on the most difficult peaks. After balancing on my crampon points for over 1,200 feet, my legs ached unremittingly. With the sun low in the sky we began abseiling, leaving a rope fixed to enable Andy and Mac to reach our highpoint the following day and then push on towards the ridge, should the weather hold. Between our legs the zig-zagging trail we had made earlier that morning, to the foot of the face, glinted silver and black.

The pair were standing outside the tents, waiting for us as we dragged our double boots through treacle snow.

'Come and get a brew down your necks, boys,' called Perkins, holding out two mugs, seeing that we were beaten.

The two Andys made good progress the following day, nego-tiating steep ground on poor ice and then appallingly loose rock. They returned to the tent tired but hopeful: whilst approaching the south ridge they had discovered abandoned ropes from the attempt the previous year by Americans Charlie Fowler, Alex Lowe and Steve Swenson.

'We can crack this mountain given a decent break in the weather,' Andy voiced.

Kate and Brendan arrived from base camp with more supplies, but Kate had caught the sun badly and looked shattered. Still feeling strong, Mac decided to stay to support Brendan and Kate, while the rest of us headed down to base, dreaming of chips, eggs and chapattis.

Following a terrible night, Kate had remained in her sleeping bag whilst Brendan and Mac moved up the face, stopping just short of the ridge. Huge storm clouds moved up the Concordia glacier to the west. From base camp we noticed G IV's summit obscured by a cloud shaped like a giant, jumping dolphin. At times like this I worried. To be up there absorbed by the routine and the effort would be tough, but much less stressful than sitting here, mithering about what could happen to one's companions. The worry wormed its way around my mind, refusing to leave until we heard shouts late in the day as the trio appeared at the top of the icefall. At the same time fresh snow began to settle on the tents once more.

It was two days before the weather cleared and Chris, Andy, Mac and I meandered our way back up through the creaking, groaning icefall. Huge walls of ice had collapsed, snow bridges had disappeared and crevasses widened, which meant that we had to devise an alternative route. At the first camp that night Andy revealed that he felt utterly wasted. He had carried an extraordinary number of loads, fixed ropes to 7,000 metres, and organised most of the logistics of food and equipment. In fact, all of us were showing signs of wear and tear: we had been living above 5,300 metres for thirty-six days now, many of those days above 6,000 metres. Our faces were charred, lips punctuated by cold sores, and our muscles were wasting away – we were appearing more and more like victims of a famine. No matter what you eat, hard graft at high altitude and low temperatures gnaws at your muscles, revealing hips and ribs that ache at night as they cut into the frozen ground beneath the tent.

'We're all knackered, mate. You might feel better after a good night's sleep,' I encouraged.

'Honestly, Andy, I'm absolutely shagged,' Andy answered from his heart, and the following day he descended.

It reminded me of a trip to Nepal with Andy and Mal Duff a few years earlier when, having failed to secure enough sponsorship to attempt the North Face of Mount Everest, we had switched to trying a new line on the South Face of Annapurna III. Andy worked so hard at the beginning of the trip that he became severely run down, contracted conjunctivitis and spent a week on his back at base camp.

Ironically, on this occasion, Andy's return to base camp would be anything but a rest. Whilst we lay at camp 2 waiting for the weather to clear, he was helping the Americans build a rope stretcher in order to carry a badly frostbitten member of their team out into the centre of the glacier, where a rescue helicopter was due to land. The climber had become trapped high on G II during the most recent storm, and his small tent had been beaten into an icy coffin by ferocious winds. He had managed to escape during a short clear spell but with severe damage to his hands and feet.

Andy then decided to spend a day walking around to the K2 base camp to socialise with his friends Roger Payne and Julie-Ann Clyma (his neighbours back in Manchester), who were attempting the mountain with Alan Hinkes and Victor Saunders. A group of Swedes, some of whom I knew rather well, were on the same route.

He could not have imagined that he was walking into the closing stages of a huge tragedy. Hinkes and Saunders were moving from 7,300 metres to camp 4 on the Abruzzi ridge when they found Raphael Jaensen of the Swedish team, weak and hallucinating, descending from the summit. His partner, Daniel Bidner, had developed chronic cerebral oedema and, after a whole night of trying to force him down, Raphael had had to abandon him, later witnessing him fall to his death down the South Face. I had met Daniel in Chamonix, a quiet, handsome young man, who had been due to marry his fiancée on his return from K2. I had ice climbed with Raphael in the north of Sweden during one of my official reading weeks at university. Hinkes and Saunders got him to the snow cave at 7,300 metres. The following day Roger and Julie took over lowering Raphael down fixed ropes, one of which snapped on the steepest part of the climb. Miraculously, Roger had grabbed the other rope as he shot down the mountain.

The wind raged, but Roger became strangely convinced that he could smell rotting flesh. Lower down the mountain the climbers found the remains of Art Gilkey, a climber killed in a famous epic during an attempt in 1953, as well as remains from porters killed during an even earlier attempt. The smell Roger sensed was probably due to exhaustion and effects of altitude.

Meanwhile, below the South Face of G IV, I lay in the tent with Flewitt in a type of twilight zone. I watched the nylon fabric flutter noisily in the wind, but a large part of me had departed; in my mind, I was in North Wales in the Llanberis Pass below Snowdon, where sheep bleated as I fumbled the wrinkled grey rock high above with my hands, as if moving over the skin of an ancient man's face. Enjoying the summer's day, wearing just a T-shirt; enjoying the subtle exercise in balance, the grace of placing toes precisely, worried about the fall I might take if I slipped; absorbed, focused and yet already looking forward to meeting old friends in the pub for a pint, later that night. The fabric of the tent stopped moving, but still the snow fell. What if, I think . . . what if . . . we go for the summit and the weather turns? I closed my eyes.

Mac, Flewitt and I started to crack. We asked each other, why not go for G II or G I light and fast? At least we'd have a chance of reaching a summit. Brendan and Kate remained idealistic and resolute though, in a quiet way. Perhaps they were right; our permit was only for G IV anyhow.

'We're going to have a go tomorrow,' Kate called from their small bivouac tent, a few metres away.

'We're dithering,' I shouted back.

They reached 7,250 metres on the south ridge the next day and began to dither themselves. Huge clouds mushroomed down on the Boltoro glacier, frustrating them, for the next section looked okay. However, the final summit pyramid is composed of compact, marble slabs, interesting to say the least at over 25,000 feet. With the security of stable weather this might be possible, but with its current diabolical pattern it felt unjustifiable. Brendan and Kate retreated and together we declared our attempt to be over.

*

The porters arrived in shabby clothing and poor footwear and began strapping their twenty-five kilogram loads (plus sleeping blankets and food) to their home-made, wooden-framed rucksacks. These guys are the real heroes of these climbing exploits, I thought, listening to them sing together after they had run around checking the weight and security of each load. Desperate for some company, our Liaison Officer had been living at the army camp a few hours away, towards Urdukas. That morning he revealed to Brendan and Mac that he felt the reason we had failed on the peak was because we had not taken enough risks, which, either because of mother-tongue interference or perhaps a speech impediment, sounded as if he had accused us of 'not having taken enough spliffs'.

After laughing at the Captain's unfortunate pronunciation at first, his comments infuriated us, especially in view of the recent events on both K2 and G II, not to mention the soldiers perishing on the col. I brooded all day long and, the following day, decided to question the reasoning behind his assumption. Sadly, from the very beginning, my passion spilled over.

'Captain.'

'Yes.'

'Do you know what that peak is over there?'

'No, what is it?'

'That's called Trango Tower,' I continued, as he stared at the huge 5,000-foot monolith.

'Why don't we go and climb it together? We could set off this afternoon and I could show you what risk is. Come on.'

To begin with his eyes glazed over, confused by the import of my words.

'You told Brendan and Andy that we had not taken enough risks on the mountain and frankly I find it insulting.'

I had lost control now.

'What do you know about climbing risks? Have you ever climbed a mountain? I have friends and family at home and I intend to go back safely to them. Is that a failing?'

The Captain stood speechless, his lips quivering. I stormed off down the rocky path in the moraine.

'I am going to make sure Mr Cave never comes to Pakistan again,' he announced.

'I don't think he's particularly bothered,' answered Perkins.

The Captain halted the porters, telling Mac that they would not be ordered to move until Mr Cave delivered a full apology for his disrespectful behaviour.

'Captain, look, Andy has gone. He'll be in Paiju soon. I can't call him back,' pleaded Mac.

And then the team sat down and began to play a hand of bridge. This worried the porters as they knew the team were not in a hurry; indeed the team would happily play bridge for days at a time, they loved the game. They forced the Captain to continue.

Under the shade of a tree at Paiju, where we had intended to spend the night, I decided that if the others showed up I would apologize to the Captain – not for the words I had uttered but for the aggressive delivery. The gang appeared a few hours later and he accepted my apologies, but for the remainder of the trip the strain was clearly evident, each man was wary of the other and made minimal eye contact.

Four days later we reached Skardu, greeted by our good friend Mohammed Ali Chengezi.

'I have been praying for your safety every day,' he said, hugging each of us in turn.

Two days later Mohammed Ali organised jeeps and we spent a day and a half sweating and bouncing down the Karakoram Highway back to Rawalpindi. Here, we ran into the middle of celebrations: it was Pakistan's National Defence Day. We were dirty, tired, and longing for a hot shower, good food and clean sheets when the Captain spoke from the front of our minibus.

'Do you know,' he began loudly, 'I can think of no finer way to die than in battle for one's country.'

'Really,' answered Perkins, like lightning, as the driver pulled up outside of our hotel. 'Personally, I want to be shot in bed by a jealous husband.'

11

Solid rock

I had not long been back from Pakistan and still hadn't got around to cutting my hair; perhaps this, combined with a certain detached stare from having spent too long at high altitude, had led the youth to believe I might be a local drug dealer.

A customised white car pulled up, a darkened window smoothly lowered and a boy I had never seen before (thirteen, perhaps fourteen) stuck out his head.

'Excuse me Mr.'

'Yeah?'

'Do you know where I can get some good cocaine?'

I wasn't sure if I should interpret the request as a compliment on my 'cool', 'hip' appearance or as an indication that I needed to smarten myself up. Either way, I was shocked to learn of a drug culture in Royston; I thought drugs only existed in large cities.

'Sorry, no idea,' I answered, and the car sped off as fast as it could, though not nearly as fast as its spoiler and tinted windows might have suggested it would.

'Drugs are everywhere these days Andy,' yelled my brother Jonny, just turned eighteen, over a deafening stream of The Stone Roses.

All the pits in the Barnsley area had closed down now, including Grimethorpe earlier in the year. My father's best friend, Les, had witnessed the headgear being demolished, the shaft being filled in and capped. 'Andy lad, it was the saddest day of my life.' Inevitably, the local colliery closures had a huge impact on my father and many other men up our street. Having been told in their forties that their skills were no longer required, and with local job opportunities severely limited, many men began suffering from low self-esteem, lack of confidence and, sometimes, depression. Les was one of a handful of people lucky enough to get a job in the Selby coalfield. My father now worked as a security guard in Barnsley, his income reduced by two-thirds and all camaraderie lost. Many others signed on the dole. Jonny had finished college and was desperately looking for work. Unemployment in Grimethorpe was at around forty per cent; in some pockets it was up to eighty or ninety per cent. Heroin use would increase by 300 per cent over the next two years, along with recorded burglary.

'Can you clear this gear away 'cos it's doing my head in. I feel like I'm going to the bloody Himalayas mysen, every time I try and get into the kitchen,' my mother lamented. 'And turn that music down please, I'm getting a migraine.'

'Where?'

'Up in the loft with all the rest of your junk,' she pointed upstairs with her thumb, as if hitchhiking. 'Somebody called Phil phoned, by the way. He's got your CV. He wants you to ring him,' she added.

I forced the weighty bags through the small hatch into the loft, the soles of my feet quivering on an ancient stepladder. A bare light-bulb hung from a marshmallow of spiders' webs and a sea of carrier bags littered the floor along with school reports, clothes and children's toys. Lying in the corner were my crutches, covered in a film of soot; next to them sat a box full of old climbing gear, including the Chouinard Zero axe I'd bought second-hand and used to climb the North Face of the Eiger just a few weeks after leaving the pit. I propped the bags against the brickwork of the chimney breast, making sure they couldn't fall between the rafters and damage the bedroom ceiling. I moved two red nylon tubes out of the way: Pete Boardman and Joe Tasker's hammocks, the ones they had used on the west wall of Changabang. We had borrowed them from the outdoor company, Troll, for our attempt on the North Face of the Ogre, a couple of years earlier.

I was utterly broke after the Gasherbrum IV trip and desperately needed to earn some cash quickly, as I had the second part of my Guides' exams looming. It had seemed logical to try and qualify as an Alpine Guide (equivalent to a Swiss or French high mountain guide): it was good money, I'd be able to work in an environment I loved, and it would give me the flexibility to pursue my own climbing ambitions. The Guides' is the highest possible qualification in mountaineering and a mammoth task, frequently likened to completing a PhD. I had passed the summer rock climbing test before departing for Gasherbrum earlier in the year. The notoriously difficult Scottish winter section was next, followed by an Alpine climbing test the following summer. I had enjoyed working as a guide for Mal in Scotland and Nepal, and was reasonably confident about my ability to cope up to this point. However, the final exam comprises steep skiing, powder skiing and ski mountaineering. Having only skied a few times (one of those being down the local muckstack one heavy winter), I was justifiably a touch worried, but it was a long way off – two years if everything went to plan.

Meanwhile, the pay on offer for the few vacancies in the job centre at Barnsley that morning was atrocious. I picked up the phone and couldn't believe my luck.

'Start on Monday. Thurrock on the M25,' explained Phil. 'Cliff stabilization with the rock team. Seven pounds fifty an hour, ten hours a day, seven days a week – the job will last about four weeks – and you'll get twenty pounds a night for your board and food.'

Members of the rock team were infamous in the world of difficult roped-access work. They were generally big men with a reputation for hard work and hard drinking. My CV had highlighted the fact that I had worked inspecting high-rise buildings by abseil in London, prior to going to university, and also that I'd worked underground. I think the guy assumed I had worked on the coalface, for he told me that I would recognise some of the drilling machinery used on the job.

The foreman, Callum, was huge, with a large pink face, milk-white hair and a maniacal laugh. I knew him from the climbers' campsite in Chamonix back in 1986, the summer I had left my job at the pit. I had worn the 'yellow jersey' for long periods that season, gaining celebrity status as the young, audacious, retired miner who had come to tear the Alps apart. Callum was a workaholic, and I soon discovered that talking about our good old days in the Alps was the only guaranteed way of getting a rest.

My three cohorts were appropriately built for this heavy work, with thick necks and large biceps; I felt like a jockey amongst rugby players, my arms even thinner than normal, withered by life above 6,000 metres. We hung from ropes and drilled ten-metre holes into the cliff before fixing in stabilising anchors. The smallest tool on the site was the spanner used to break or tighten the metre-long sections of the drill, and this itself was incredibly heavy: a solid steel bar, four feet long and five inches thick. When the job failed to run smoothly, for example when the drill bit got stuck, Callum ran around cursing and smashing this spanner against the hydraulic drill rig. At times like these, the giant from Berwick looked and sounded very much like a ninth-century Viking in battle.

Halfway through the final week I received a message via the firm's office to phone my mother. Dave Hurry, one of my old lecturers from the university, wondered if I would be willing to teach 'A' level English Language and Literature for two days a week at Rotherham Sixth Form College, covering for the head of department who had become seriously ill. Rather reluctantly, Callum agreed to let me go home early on the final Sunday, and the next day I talked about the modernist novel to twenty teenagers. They sat there, eyeing the cuts on my hands from all the drilling, my baggy jeans and my earring. Is he a real teacher? I imagined them whispering to one another. Meanwhile, by coincidence, my mother had returned to college in Barnsley to study English Literature, thirty-three years after leaving school.

Later that week the boss, Phil, rang. 'We've got a small job in Wrexham, Thursday and Friday, if you're available. I think you'll like it.'

I walked out of a beautiful morning into a large, empty, derelict factory and found two other workmen stood staring into a shaft. Pete was a friendly climber I had met over the years on the Derbyshire crags. I had not met the bigger man, Rab, before.

'Now then Andy, long time no see,' greeted Pete. 'I hear you've been in the Himalayas again, how did it go?'

'Oh the familiar story: trying desperate new routes, bad weather, no summit – and now I'm unfit and totally skint, back living with my parents until I get sorted out.'

'Well I'm volunteering to stay up here as the safety man, you boys can get kitted up and go down and get the samples.'

'What is this place?'

'It was an underground weapons factory during the war, apparently,' answered Rab, in a north Notts. accent.

Rab and I changed into protective boilersuits, gloves and balaclavas, and strapped on breathing apparatus and then lamps. Rab passed me a bag full of test-tubes which we had to fill with waste water. He then picked up a black box that I recognised as a methanometer and began descending a set of vertical steel ladders into the gloomy hole. I regretted not having mentioned my attacks of claustrophobia, perhaps then they might have let me be the safety man who stayed on the surface.

I descended anxiously and then followed Rab through a labyrinth of tunnels, alarmed by the vivid, fluorescent-green pools of water everywhere. It's a Geiger counter we need down here not a methanometer, I muttered into the mask. Rab stopped ahead and glanced at a plan of the site, then pointed to a luminous pool and I began filling the first tube. The walls appeared solid enough, the ceilings not too low, but I still felt uncomfortable underground in a way I never did when stood on an exposed mountain face, thousands of feet above a glacier. It was a great relief to reach the surface.

'Thank God for that,' I sighed, removing the rubber face mask. 'It was like being down the pit again.'

'Oh you were a miner as well then?' queried Rab. 'A Yorkie miner?'

'Where did you work?'

'I'm a Mansfield lad,' he smirked.

'Oh right,' I faltered. His accent reminded me of Alistair. I closed down, avoiding further questions.

'Come on, let's get theses samples off to the lab and then get some dinner,' Pete called.

'I think I'll wash me hands ten times before eating today, look at the colour of the samples. It makes you wonder what the hell they were making down there,' I remarked.

The lecturing job in Rotherham ended in November. I had enjoyed it, though I was only paid for the hours spent teaching,

receiving nothing for the ceaseless form-filling or lesson preparation. The following week Barnsley Sixth Form College
contacted me, asking me to consider a seventy-five per cent
lectureship in the English department – financially much more
appealing. I visited the college, the place I might have come
myself if I had taken studying more seriously and not accepted
a job at the pit in my final year of school. I was now poised
between two distinct choices of career and lifestyle: teaching,
or becoming an official Alpine Mountain Guide. Ultimately I
reasoned that, aged just twenty-seven, I could enter teaching
at a later date, whereas guiding was a younger person's game.
I declined the job and sailed to Jersey in the Channel Islands,
joining the rock team again and determined to save enough
money for the next Guides' exam in February.

Fifteen of us disembarked in St Helier and gathered in a café,
drinking tea and waiting to hear about accommodation arrangements from our Scottish foreman, Wal.

'You can share with me Cavey, if you want,' someone called
from behind.

I turned around; it was Rab holding a key to a B&B.

'It's just a few hundred yards away, looks nice enough,' he
continued.

'Erm . . . yes, whatever, sounds good,' I said.

Rab behaved differently away from the crowd. He was less
bashful, a friendly room companion. We lay on our beds
watching the news before going out to meet the others for
dinner. I felt uncomfortable and wondered if he had been a
strike-breaker all those years ago.

In the pub, before closing time, I quizzed Callum and Lee.

'Oh aye, definitely, Andy lad,' answered Callum, a little louder
than I would have liked.

'Aye Andy, I think you're right. I'd forgotten you were a
miner like,' said Lee, clutching his pint.

'We've got a really nice flat which is much cheaper than a
B&B,' said Dicko.

The following morning after breakfast I packed up my belongings, telling Rab I'd found somewhere a bit cheaper.

'I need to save as much cash as possible,' I explained.

'No problem, youth.'

I never consciously thought about the distance I purposely kept from Rab, and I never questioned his motives for not supporting the strike; perhaps it was the simple fact that Scargill had refused to hold a national ballot. Undoubtedly, despite the passage of almost ten years since the strike, I still felt that there was a moral and political gulf between people like myself and those who had worked. Neither my father nor I had been regulars on the picket line, and we wouldn't consider ourselves hardliners, yet we had believed in the cause, that local jobs were worth fighting for. And here I was treating Rab like an alien because of his ideological and political beliefs. Understanding our differences, Callum ensured that in future we worked on separate shifts. History weighs down on one sometimes, like a heavy blanket that refuses to be thrown off.

But at home people are judged as those that stayed on strike for the duration and those that did not; there are no shades of grey, not on any terms. Like a row of piano keys, black or white. Perhaps, sometimes, such crude fundamentalism failed to understand the behaviour of some individuals. Was Alistair a better man than someone who had never even attempted to strike, I wondered? After all, he had gone on strike for eight months and been in a minority. Was there any honour in his trying? I knew that he didn't consider himself a scab. As for Rab, I knew nothing about him and his alliances, or his personal circumstances and the potential pressures on him back then. Oh, life seemed so complicated, with its determined ideals, beliefs and personal failures. How much did it matter anyhow? I thought. And then in the next moment, I stubbornly told myself, it matters more than anything.

12

Vagabonds

The strip of grey tarmac swung steeply uphill, the hairpins getting tighter as we abandoned the green pastures and occasional isolated Swiss farmhouse for the town of Leysin. The road sliced through an eclectic mixture of rustic chalets and concrete hotels until meadows appeared once more and the hillside fell away dramatically, revealing a glimpse of the lofty Alpine peaks beyond. I had just finished my first week's work as an aspirant mountain guide, and life felt good. The job was a serious one, with responsibilities and much still to learn, but to be earning a living in the high mountains felt wonderful.

'Is this the hill that Pete Boardman ran up for training?' I pressed my face against the glass.

'That's right,' Steve Monks smiled, steering with one hand, the other clutching the gear stick as he accelerated out of the bend.

'Right from the bottom?'

'I think so,' Steve grinned.

'Jesus wept, that's sick.'

I had never been fitter. Two months earlier, with a client, I had stood on the west summit of Shishapangma, 8,008 metres, in Tibet. Last month I had been free climbing in the Dolomites with my friend (and former indoor world champion rock climber) Simon Nadin, and now the guiding. On the way back from the Guides' exam in the Ecrins mountains to the south, my white diesel van had died and as a consequence I had spent the past week cycling from Argentiere to Chamonix each morning to meet my clients and the local French guide, Rémy Lecluse, my mentor. Then, after a full day at altitude, I'd cycle back up to Argentiere with big boots and rucksack. But, despite my good condition, to run up this hill from the bottom seemed ludicrous.

'That's the Vagabond Bar.' Steve steered the car sharply to the right. 'You must have heard of it.'

'Of course.' Good name for a bar frequented by itinerant mountain guides, I thought.

Though originally from Bristol, Steve now lived in Australia but returned to Switzerland each summer to work as a guide. The Vagabond was legendary, part of 1960s and 1970s British and American alpine climbing folklore.

'What's that place?'

'The American School. Sylvester Stallone studied there. Apparently it used to be a sanatorium years ago, for folk with TB.'

Steve introduced me to Pat Littlejohn, the director of the prestigious International School of Mountaineering, with whom I was lucky enough to get a job. Pat had a reputation for establishing countless audacious climbs on the sea-cliffs of south-west England, as well as first ascents in the greater ranges. Alert and charismatic, under a thinning mop of gold hair, Pat listened with eyes burning brightly as I described the climbs we had recently done in the Dolomites.

'It sounds like you're getting far too many holidays, Andy,' Pat joked, giving the impression that he desired nothing more in life than to climb, constantly to seek out adventure and uncertainty.

That evening I joined a dozen other guides at a large new chalet with sensational views overlooking the Rhône Valley.

'Hello, I'm Arianne. Who are you?' A pretty girl put more wine into the fridge.

'Andy. I'm an aspirant.'

'I haven't seen you before.'

'No, it's my first time in Leysin.'

'Well please eat some food.' She disappeared into the crowd of Swiss, Canadian and British guides and their partners, children and friends.

Big Mark Charlton leaned over. 'Arianne was a good friend of Dougal Haston's.'

'Oh right.'

John Harlin, an American former fighter pilot who had

worked at the American College, had established ISM in the early 1960s but was tragically killed when a fixed rope broke during the first ascent of a direct route on the North Face of the Eiger. Dougal Haston, a Scot, was a key figure on the Leysin climbing scene and took over the role of director in 1967. He was a phenomenal mountaineer and for ten years was a regular figure on Chris Bonington's Himalayan expeditions, making some impressive first ascents, such as Changabang in 1974 and the vast, technical, South-West Face of Everest with Doug Scott the following year – the pair famously survived an unplanned bivouac in the open at 28,000 feet during their descent.

In Chamonix, much of the alpine social scene centred around the Bar National; in Leysin, it was the Vagabond Bar, where the charismatic Haston allegedly played a central role. Sadly, in 1977, skiing off-piste one day, alone, on the slopes above Leysin, Dougal was buried and killed by an enormous avalanche.

Pete Boardman had also summited Everest via the south-west face in 1975 but, disillusioned by such large, siege-style trips, had teamed up with Joe Tasker to climb the phenomenal west wall of Changabang, a landmark of Himalayan technical difficulty. [Boardman's book *The Shining Mountain*, describing this incredible climb, still ranks as the 'must read' book for most climbers.] Boardman, who had begun by spending summers working as a guide in Leysin, now took over as director of ISM. He, along with a number of others, began to facilitate the acceptance and later affiliation of British mountain guides to the initially sensitive Swiss and European mountain guiding associations. He was elected the first President of the Association of British Mountain Guides. When Pete Boardman and Joe Tasker disappeared high up on the unclimbed north-east ridge of Everest in 1982, Pat Littlejohn accepted the job as ISM's director. Occasionally climbers joked that, statistically, the job was one of the most dangerous in the world.

I stared out of the giant window of the chalet towards the Trient Glacier that floated on the horizon and began thinking about all the different jobs I had done since leaving school: sweeping floors in butchers shops and supermarkets, shovelling coal on to conveyor belts in the pitch-black and then, just earlier in the year, twelve-hour nights drilling with Callum and the boys on the M25. Though I didn't regret a minute of it, I couldn't help feeling fortunate to be standing in that marvellous chalet, a glass of cool white wine in one hand, a piece of hot chicken in the other, being reminded of Leysin's history, peppered as it is with these legendary mountaineering figures.

Mark had gained an impressive scar across his cheek since I had last seen him in the mid-1980s, when he had regularly climbed with Callum in Chamonix.

'Oh it was an accident. A client spun round holding an ice axe, without looking, up on the mountain.'

Because Mark had a reputation for standing up for himself, many assumed that this story was a façade and that, in actual fact, he had been brawling in a dark alley.

The following day I followed Big Mark and our clients up through gorgeous lush meadows crowded with alpine flowers to the foot of the sheer limestone towers, where we spent the day climbing cracks and chimneys established by the likes of Don Whillans and Royal Robbins in the 1960s.

Leysin is located centrally in the Alps – sandwiched between the Pennine Alps and the Bernese Oberland – and affords access to a wide range of alpine resorts. We travelled to Saas Fe in the middle of that week with our clients (mine included a baker, a vet and a gynaecologist) and climbed the Weismeiss, which was a new peak for me too. Through guiding, I realised that there was more to life than the British alpinist's obsession with crowded Chamonix; I was discovering new valleys, new peaks, fresh vistas. We returned to Leysin on the Friday afternoon via a swim in a lake at Sion, then ate and, as tradition dictated, went straight to the Vag.

The place reeked of the past: a half-lit collection of basement cellars with low ceilings; two or three groups of young, long-haired American students sat on stools covered in animal skin; 1970s posters boasting Dylan and other giants playing at the fabled Leysin rock concerts; in the foreground, old-school blues moaning loudly and unashamedly from large speakers.

'Here's a challenge for you Cave.' Victor Saunders had appeared suddenly, pointing excitedly. 'Don Whillans' jamming stool.'

'What the hell are you talking about?'

'Squeeze your hand in there and try and lift the stool. It's a Vagabond classic.'

Already a few beers on, I thrust my right hand into a varnished slot in the seat of the stool. It felt desperately insecure, impossible for the hand to stick, but by now a crowd of expectant clients had arrived.

'I thought you were a gritstone jamming man, Cave.'

'Have you done it?'

'Well . . .' Victor hopped and wriggled his hands, failing to commit.

I thrust my hand in and, supporting the wrist with my left hand, slowly lifted the stool, my head about to burst with the effort, before letting the stool fall to the ground. Without further ado Victor then began pointing to a smooth beam in the ceiling, claiming that Whillans had done pull-ups by simply clamping his hands either side of it. Whillans enjoyed a noble reputation in the climbing fraternity for establishing brutally physical climbs, as well as being well known for aggressive behaviour and endless, cutting one-liners.

'You first.' I felt satisfied enough accomplishing the stool feat, and went back to the bar, the tendon in my right elbow aching like hell.

Cath Murphy and Dave Green, two mountain guides, walked in then with a guy I didn't recognise.

'Beers?'

Dave came and stood close to me, raised his eyebrows and shook his head.

'Andy you've got to check this Canadian guy out, Paul. He's just arrived from Delhi on a Royal Enfield.'

Dave and I were old friends. For years he had fantasised about doing a similar journey. I spun round with four ice-cold bottles. Paul had fine, sandy hair, skin darkened by months of travelling through deserts, and a far-away look in his eyes suggesting that a large part of his soul had been left somewhere, inadvertently leaking away during the long journey.

'Paul's a guide, he's working with us next week.' Cath took a drag on a thinly rolled cigarette.

'Yes, I just need to find a pair of boots and an axe.'

He had arrived midweek and had already been out climbing

with one of the team who reckoned he was first-class material.

'Oh we'll sort you out Paul, don't worry.' Dave reached out to light Cath's cigarette, then lit his own.

'So you came from Delhi to here on an Enfield? Good effort,' I started.

'Well. Not exactly. I went to the Isle of Skye first and then back over here to find work. I'm totally broke.' He sipped his beer.

'Actually, Scotland was pretty funny. The cops kept stopping me – not to hassle me – just out of interest I guess; the registration plate is in Sanskrit, yes? On Skye, they asked for my insurance documents. I showed them a piece of paper, cost me like 300 rupees, man, for the year.'

'Did you break down at all?'

'No, that machine is amazing, it's not super fast but the only thing I had to do was reset the tappets every couple of thousand miles.'

We moved away from the bar to hear Paul more clearly as he told of his incredible adventure: skirmishes on the Iranian borders; off-road detours; friends made and left along the way.

The following week I worked alongside Paul, Steve Monks and Big Mark on an intermediate alpine climbing course in the Bernese Oberland. Most of the clients were young, fit and able Icelanders. The opportunity to hone my guiding skills under the watchful eye of such experienced guides was superb, for I knew that the following year I could well be working alone. We walked for four hours in poor weather along moraine and then the ice of the snaking Oberaletsch Glacier, then proceeded steeply up rocks to the hut perched on the side of the Gross Fusshorn. From time to time the intricate north ridge came into view, a spectacular shark's fin of granite with rows of beautifully chaotic needles jabbing the mist.

Rain beat on the roof of the hut all the next morning as we sat drinking strong coffee and eating bread and jam. When it eased we went and practised crevasse rescue techniques on the glacier. I spent all day trying to pluck up courage to ask Paul if I could have a ride on his Enfield when we got back to Leysin, but I failed.

At 3am the following day, we woke to a sky of dazzling silver stars but a strong breeze tugged at the corners of the hut roof, making it rattle and groan. My young clients twitched with excitement, desperate to feed the desire that gnawed inside them. We picked a line through red granite boulders by torch-light. I saw the terrain steepening in the grey dawn light, and we tied-in to the rope and moved together, a few metres apart. Clouds were firing over the summit in an increasing wind, and standing on the crest of the buttress I felt its full icy blast. I was desperately unsure about taking the direct route, as orig-inally intended. I moved right, sheltering in a vague niche and urging the two boys to get a move on, gesticulating with my gloved hand like an irate traffic cop. Steve Monks was half an hour ahead with stronger clients, the rope between them arcing like the edge of a circle.

'We're going to take the slightly easier line up on the right,' I shouted into the wind, putting on my goggles and handing them sweets.

'Why?' Johan looked disappointed, hurt even.

'We still have the descent, which is not easy, and the weather is deteriorating.'

'I don't want to just walk, you know. I want to do some technical climbing.' He gazed enviously at his friends above.

'Look, I am the mountain guide and I judge this to be the correct decision. Look at the weather.' I squeezed the coils of rope in my right hand and tugged them.

'One day I will be a guide.'

'Good,' I barked. 'And then you can go where the hell you like.'

'I will,' he sulked.

Mark arrived with his clients, nodded, and, without even a glance at the direct route, moved quickly out right. As snow began sticking to our jackets my earlier feelings of uncertainty dissipated and my confidence returned; I was happy with my initial gut reaction. Just before the summit I purposefully cut left underneath a steep wall, tied the boys to a belay, and then climbed directly up, my gloved hands clearing wet snow from small, incut holds. I belayed at a horizontal crack in the rock and brought them up. They struggled, their fingers were frozen and they couldn't trust their big mountain boots on such small edges of damp, slippy rock. When they finally reached the belay, we didn't speak. I quickly tied them in before setting off

Brendan leading the bold
first pitch on the second
day of the Changabang climb

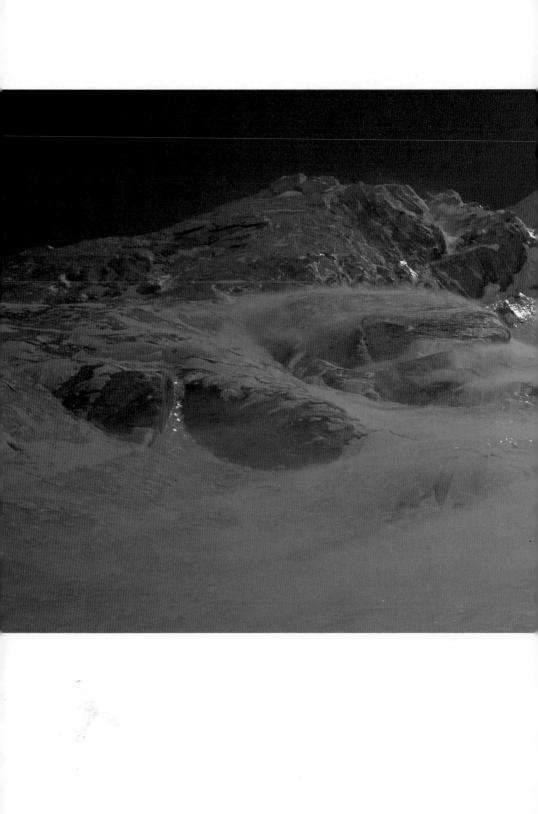

The shining mountain; a few hours before the big storm Brendan climbs towards
the top of the second icefield

Andy digs out a platform for
the bivouac tent during the
afternoon storm, day two

The day after the storm; Andy
showing the strain
of alpine-style Himalayan
exploration

Brendan on the fifth day of climbing.
Retrieving ice screws.

Andy on steep thin ice, a crucial section
that linked to the upper grooves

Brendan leads the ice tongue during day six

Andy looking jaded on the bivouac,
morning of day eight

The spray of a passing avalanche
catches the team on day twelve.
(*Left to right*) Steve Sustad, Brendan
Murphy and Mick Fowler.

Andy makes a brew just below the
Shipton Col on the fourteenth day.
Steve Sustad below.

Back at base camp
Julie-Ann tends to
Andy's frostbite

Elaine climbing Ancient Art, Fisher Towers,
Utah, USA

Arthur Cave senior

Andy climbing The Shroud, Ben Nevis

Andy on Not To Be Taken Away, Stanage, Derbyshire

once again, towards the summit. It was only a minor variation, but at least they had now sampled some technical difficulty. The blizzard was growing. On the top we shook hands
briefly, then set off down steep slopes to the left, Mark and
his clients just in front. Though not technically difficult underfoot, the route-finding was complex, with serious couloirs
lurking beyond the driving snow. Our jackets stuck to our
bodies like damp newspaper. By the time we reached the hut
the boys were looking weary.

'Bit wild up there, Andy, eh?' Steve's face was red from the
wind.

Steam swirled around the table, some of it from the silver
jug of tea, the rest from the dampness of their fleece jackets.

We drank two litres of tea between the three of us, then,
still thirsty, I went to order more from the guardian. I returned
a few minutes later and the two boys had placed their heads
on folded arms, sound asleep. I left them undisturbed for
twenty minutes and then nudged Johan.

'You're not tired are you, lads?'

They jerked their heads as if woken from a terrible dream.
'What? eh.'

'I said, you're not tired are you?'

'No!'

'Good, 'cos we've got a three-to-four-hour walk back to the
van. Let's go.'

During the walk out, I mulled over what had happened on
the climb that morning. I had been forced into making a decision – whether to climb the regular route or to try the harder
variant. If climbing with a friend of equal experience, or stronger
clients, I might well have committed to the direct finish, but not
in this case. Being quizzed by Johan had initially unnerved me;
it was an unfamiliar predicament that made me feel awkward.
Being honest, I knew that I had been a strong-willed, ambitious
youth and, in all likelihood, I would have complained in a similar
manner. His questioning had tested my resolve. Perhaps I had
become sharp a little too readily though, for as we chatted during
the walk back down the glacier that afternoon I realised that
they were smashing guys, full of fire, dreams and desires.

After a few hours in the Vag later that evening, I apologised
for my rather stern manner on that windswept ridge, almost

twenty hours earlier. But I also made a more general point, in an embarrassing, fatherly way, that ideal climbing plans must often be changed, especially when conditions deteriorate. 'Sometimes it hurts your pride, but remember ultimately staying alive is the aim.'

With that Johan nodded and went back to the bar.

I woke the next morning, desperately hoping that the Icelanders felt as hungover as I did.

At lunchtime Mark arrived with a giant cardboard box full of slightly outdated Alpine guidebooks.

'Two quid each if you want any, Andy.'

I rummaged through and got almost a complete set. Underneath lay a thick, loosely bound wad of faintly printed words.

'Someone's left their college essay behind.' I held the thing up. 'It's in French.'

'Yes, I saw that. I think it's something Pete Boardman was writing before he died on Everest.'

'What the hell's it doing here?'

'God knows, I don't think anybody's looked in these boxes for centuries.'

'How bizarre.'

'I'll pass it on. You about next week?'

'I'm working in Chamonix. I'm driving over this afternoon. Paul promised me a go on his bike last night. I'm going over now.'

I grabbed my climbing helmet and a pair of ski goggles then put on my mountaineering boots and thick gloves.

The machine was beautiful.

'Just remember it's my pride and joy. I'm very attached to her,' said Paul as he handed me the keys. I knew that he meant it, deep in his heart.

Perhaps I shouldn't tempt fate, I thought briefly, before desire got the better of me. At the second kick-start the engine purred into life, the sound and the smell of the oil bringing back fond memories. It had been several years since I had been on a bike, but I tried to act as if I rode every day. I pulled away and sped off down the viciously steep hill, out of view. The bike began accelerating towards the sharp bend by the cable car station. I remained calm at first as I stamped the sole of my left foot down on the gear pedal, but something wasn't right. Instead of decelerating, I gathered momentum until almost at the bend, feeling as if I was free-wheeling – bollocks!

It wasn't like a Japanese bike where you moved down to lower the gears; it was directly the opposite. Paul had mentioned something. Too late now! From the corner of my vision I saw a couple of tourists pull fearful faces as I hurtled towards the crash barrier. Gripped, I pumped my right foot on the rear brake pedal, but the wheel skidded violently from under me. Desperate, I threw my right heel to the ground and slid the thing around the corner, just inches from the wall. Jesus, I was alive. More importantly, miraculously, I hadn't dropped the bike. The adrenalin caused my heart to punch the inside of my ribs.

Were it not for the ridiculous helmet and goggles, I could have been mistaken for Steve McQueen in *The Great Escape* there, I romanticised.

I wanted to get off the thing as soon as possible, simply park it up and walk, but I was too embarrassed that the tourists might laugh at me, so I drifted slowly into the Co-op car park, put it on the side stand and cut out the engine. If I went back now, Paul would know I hadn't been very far and might suspect that something untoward had occurred. I leaned against the wall, feeling sick for what had nearly happened.

Eventually, I turned on the ignition and once again kicked the machine into life, setting off back up the hill. The sound from the exhaust was pure music to the ears; I took a gentle bend and felt more relaxed. When I reached the small road leading to where Paul was staying, I slowed and changed into a lower gear but, at the last minute, I pulled back the throttle and simultaneously released an almighty 'Yippee!' as I screamed off upwards and onwards, wearing the widest grin of my life.

SPACE

'. . . your mind is far better adapted to receive impressions of sublimity when you are alone, in a silent region, with a black sky above and giant cliffs all round; with a sense still in your mind, if not of actual danger, still of danger that would become real with the slightest relaxation of caution, and with the world divided from you by hours of snow and rock.'

Leslie Stephen, *The Playground of Europe*

13

Changabang

The check-in girl at the British Airways desk put the phone down, gaping at our mountain of baggage as if her eyeballs were about to explode. She looked at the five of us cowering awkwardly behind the rucksack mound, shook her head, and then stared up at Roger, clutching a letter.

'I am sorry sir but we have no record of any special baggage, I will have to charge you excess.'

'Could I speak to the manager please?' Roger requested, without ever raising his voice.

We moved to the side, allowing others passengers to advance and check in. Over the years we had developed various techniques in order to get expedition baggage accepted without being charged extortionate rates. On my first trip to Mount Kenya we had worn our big boots, duvets and salopettes and carried ropes in our hand baggage. On countless other occasions we had placed our feet under the check-in desk scales. A metal chock used for climbing had been put under the scales another time. Other friends had resorted to tying fishing line to the heaviest bag, one person pulling it up to ease the weight off the machine. Roger avoided all these techniques. He had written in advance, been promised an extra allowance for each member of the team, and now seemed hell-bent on verbal persuasion.

Another official arrived, a man this time, and took the same stance; it was impossible, we could not avoid excess baggage charges. We went through this process at least twice more until, after almost an hour, a senior member of BA Heathrow operations appeared. By now Roger had taken out a map of the Garhwal Indian Himalaya as well as a postcard-sized photograph of the unclimbed North Face of Changabang, the route we were intending to climb. Though the pair had never met before, to the disgust of the check-in girl and the other middle managers, the director and Roger seemed to be getting along rather well, chatting excitedly like a couple of old schoolfriends.

No, he had never heard of the peak, but he was impressed by its shape and size and began waving his arm, announcing that it was an honour to assist such a prestigious expedition; it was the least he could do. Roger beamed benevolently like the able politician he was – wasted perhaps, some say, as Secretary of the British Mountaineering Council.

Back in the bar Roger proudly celebrated his success by ordering a double round of drinks for the entire team. His climbing partner – and wife – Julie-Ann, seemed quite used to the behaviour, as did Nelly, Roger's mum – who lived close to Heathrow and who often came to say goodbye to the pair on their frequent trips to India and Pakistan. Roger drank his first pint in less than a minute and then, laughing at our startled expressions, wrapped his large knuckles around another full glass of London Pride.

'You look a bit thirsty mate,' I joked.

'Well the problem is,' he said in his cockney accent, preparing to use a legendary phrase of Don Whillans' and moving the glass closer towards his lips, 'I've got this morbid fear of dehydration.'

Changabang (6,864m) stands in the central part of the Himalayas, close to the Nanda Devi Sanctuary, an area associated with British mountain exploration for well over a century. It was W. W. Graham – the first person to go to the Himalayas 'more for sport and adventures', as he put it, 'than for the advancement of scientific knowledge' – who first penetrated the uninhabited interior of this region. In 1883, along with two Swiss guides, he attempted to force a route up the Rishi Ganga Gorge into the Nanda Devi Sanctuary, a route which most subsequent visitors would take. The trio were defeated by sheer walls and monsoon rains and decided instead to try from the north. Access was denied here too, though they did manage some modest climbing. Graham told the Alpine Club back in London: 'I do not hesitate to say that the peaks of these regions, with a few exceptions, present the most awful series of impossibilities that a climber can set eyes on.'

Prompted by Graham's observations, published in the Alpine Journal in 1884, the highly competent mountaineer and surveyor Dr Tom Longstaff visited the area in 1905, returning with a stronger team in 1907 with the intention of climbing Nanda Devi (7,816m). They too failed to find a way up the Rishi Ganga Gorge but they did succeed in making the remarkable first ascent of Trisul (7074m), the highest peak ever to have been ascended at that time, and accomplished it in superb style, climbing the last 6,000 feet to the summit in a single day, up and down. Earlier, the team had travelled up the Bagini Glacier directly below the North Face of Changabang and then climbed over the Bagini Col and down the Ramani Glacier. It was these views that inspired Longstaff to declare Changabang as 'the most superbly beautiful mountain I have ever seen; its north-west face, a sheer precipice of over 5,000 feet, being composed of such pale granite that it is at first taken for snow lying on the cliffs at an impossibly steep angle.'

In 1934, Bill Tilman and Eric Shipton succeeded in reaching the Nanda Devi Sanctuary after nine days of effort. Two years later, Tilman and Odell reached the summit of Nanda Devi itself. Shipton, meanwhile, surveying the area further north with Rinzing Bhutia, climbed to a notch in the south ridge of Changabang (Shipton's Col) and 'sat for an hour fascinated by the gigantic white cliffs'.

Perhaps the most lyrical of all explorers to fall under Changabang's spell was the leader of the 1950 Scottish Expedition to the Garhwal, Bill Murray: 'By day like a vast eye-tooth fang, both in shape and colour . . . for its rock was a milk-white granite . . . Changabang in the moonlight shone tenderly as though veiled in bridal lace; at ten miles' distance seemingly as fragile as an icicle; a product of liveliness unparalleled, so that unawares one's pulse leapt and the heart gave thanks that this mountain should be as it is.'

Although interest in the area continued to increase, the Chinese invasion of Tibet in 1950 lead to the Indian government imposing a set of restrictions known as the 'Inner Line' – originally a British construct – which purported that no one was allowed to venture north of a line drawn more or less parallel to the Himalayan border itself, but much further south. Changabang and its neighbours were officially off limits for over twenty years. Notable during this period were two joint Indo-American expeditions to Nanda Devi during the 1960s. The first aimed to place a large sensor close to the summit – presumably to spy on the movement of the northerly neighbours – and, after the device was lost in an avalanche, the second group tried to find the thing.

Inspired by the descriptions of these earlier mountaineers, Chris Bonington successfully applied for permission to climb Changabang in 1974. His team reached the summit by a committing but technically easy route via the Shipton Col, the Kalanka Col and then the south-east ridge. This ascent alerted the wider climbing community to the remaining possibilities on Changabang's steeper faces and ridges and the peak soon became a crucible where mountaineers could challenge themselves to the extreme, pushing the boundaries of what was physically, mentally and stylistically possible. In 1976 a Cumbrian expedition climbed the South Face, whilst Boardman and Tasker succeeded on the formidable West Face. Further impressive ascents followed until 1982, when the Indian government banned all access to the Nanda Devi Sanctuary for environmental reasons, and from thereafter Changabang remained unclimbed.

In the spring of 1996, following persistent letter-writing to the Indian Mountaineering Federation and a little luck, four friends – Julie-Ann Clyma, Roger Payne, Andy Perkins and Brendan Murphy – received a permit to attempt the awe-inspiring unclimbed North Face of Changabang, approaching via the Bagini Glacier. In stable weather, they made excellent progress up the route until the fourth day, when Andy was struck down by very serious food poisoning and the attempt was abandoned.

Before flying home Brendan sent a postcard of the mountain, inviting me to join him in another attempt the following year, but it never arrived; allegedly, in India, unless you take mail to the post office yourself and get it franked, there is always a possibility that stamps will be torn off letters and sold for cash. I finally caught up with Brendan towards the end of the summer in the Lake District and learned of the missing postcard, my heart missing a beat when he uttered the word C.h.a.n.g.a.b.a.n.g, each letter tumbling out like specks of gold dust. I had already spent seven months in the mountains that year, working as a guide. I had overdosed on mountains, and the Himalayas were the furthest thing from my mind. Yet to me, Changabang was the most beautiful, perfect peak and one I had a strong desire to climb, much more so than Mount Everest.

'Roger and Julie-Ann are keen to return. Perkins isn't bothered, he's focusing on his mountain Guides' exam. Mick Fowler and Steve Sustad are coming too.'

There were good reasons for me not to go. My girlfriend, Elaine, and I had just moved into a new house together; it was an old building and needed a lot of work to get it in shape. Elaine's father had been a good climber, a member of the Alpine Club who had visited the big mountains; she accepted and understood the risks involved. But I had introduced her to ski-touring when we had first met the previous spring (shortly after I had completed my Guides' ski test) and we had enjoyed some marvellous descents. It was something we did together. We would miss out on this if I went.

Also, encouraged by Professor John Widdowson, I had just begun research for a PhD into language variety and social identity among former coal miners in the community where I used to live – a project driven by a desire to capture something of a rapidly vanishing world. I wasn't sure how much leave I could take. For a fortnight I couldn't stop thinking about Changabang. Eventually I rang him. 'I'm up for it,' I said.

We climbed out of a taxi in Lapjat Nagar Market and the mid-morning heat of Delhi smacked us like a fireball from an exploding oil-tanker, as we merged with a rushing stream of people. We pushed on up a street dedicated to the sale of hardware, past chaotic, over-stocked shops, competing signs and groaning beggars with missing limbs. I pointed at one shop, shrugged, and the four of us squeezed in between brightly coloured plastic buckets of every size and a tall stack of silver-coloured pans and plates, ducking our heads as we did so to avoid headbutting iron contraptions that hung from the ceiling. I smiled at the shopkeeper, who was dressed in an immaculately clean white shalwar kameez, then stared down at the list Julie-Ann had given us – halfway-down it read 'Milk-whisk'. Roger and Julie-Ann's level of organisation was anathema to the rest of us.

Mick and Steve took a portion of the list and disappeared into another shop to speed things up. After half an hour of scouring the place, Brendan and I were served sweet chai in fine cups whilst the shopkeeper's young assistant hurried around, weighing our pans, clearing dust out of plastic bowls and wrapping stoves until an impressive pile of items, packed into boxes and sacks, blocked the shop's entrance. Brendan took a wad of rupee notes from his bumbag and paid the man.

'So where are you going, gentlemen?'

'To the mountains in the north,' replied Brendan.

'Trekking, sir?'

'Yes, kind of trekking,' said Brendan, as if relishing the understatement.

We shook hands and thanked the man, explaining that we would return later with a taxi to collect the stuff.

Outside, Steve and Mick were being hounded by young street vendors, one selling multi-coloured umbrellas designed to sit on top of the head, another selling small blackboards. Mick looked exhausted from the heat, like the rest of us, and eventually he succumbed to the incessant hawking, buying one of the peculiar hats and wearing it immediately.

'Excellent,' he smiled. 'I needed a sun hat for the walk to base camp.'

The boy selling blackboards looked envious at his colleague's sale, even a little annoyed, and decided to target Steve, repeating his sales chants louder and faster. But after a couple of minutes Steve cracked, spinning around and lowering his spectacles to the eye level of the small fellow.

'No! Go away!' he roared, most of the street turning to look.

Understandably, the ferocity in his voice shocked the boy and, though I too was glad to hear an end to the whining, I reminded myself never to get into an argument with Steve. I would later learn that Steve was a superb guy, but he did not suffer fools gladly. A cabinet maker, originally from Seattle, he was probably the most experienced Himalayan climber in our group, with over fifteen years of incredible achievements and tales of hardship notched up, though he virtually never gave public lectures or wrote about any of his adventures. 'Never write anything. You'll only regret it,' he claimed Don Whillans had told him during their 1981 expedition to Shivling.

On the second day in Delhi, Mick and Steve went to clear our freight through customs. Roger and Julie-Ann met with our Liaison Officer, Narinder Singh, and attended a briefing with officials of the Indian Mountaineering Federation. Meanwhile, Brendan and I took a taxi to Saddar Bazaar to complete some of the shopping. During this trip Brendan became obsessed with trying to locate a small shop selling a particular type of plastic box that had proved particularly useful for transporting things up to base camp the previous year.

After a full hour of traipsing after Brendan, up and down identical-looking, crowded streets, I demanded we stop for a cold drink. It began to rain, the water lubricating the filth on the ground so that it oozed into the thin gap between the soles of my feet and my sandals. The street had an intense aroma of sweat, dead meat and over-ripe fruit. Down at one end a cow with garlands of flowers around its neck stood chewing a cardboard box.

We set off again, Brendan pausing at an intersection of tiny back streets, a determined look in his eyes.

'What's wrong with those boxes over there?' I asked, pointing at a nearby shop.

He wagged a raised finger.

'We're close, very close,' he assured me.

Slightly perturbed by the distance we had journeyed into this maze I checked my pocket, reassured to find a scrap of paper with the name of our hotel written on it – just in case we became separated, I thought. We passed a man sitting by a red cloth covered in rows of second-hand teeth. Bored with this interminable search for boxes, I gesticulated that Brendan was missing a front tooth and when I asked if he could help, the man forced Brendan to sit on a small stool, enthusiastically trying a number of yellow, stained teeth until he was determined he had the perfect match.

'I'll think about it,' said Brendan, laughing, standing up and edging away from the stall. 'Not today.'

'Tomorrow?'

'Maybe tomorrow.'

Miraculously, around the next corner, Brendan found his boxes. We stacked them into a small, motorised rickshaw and then began weaving through the never-ending streets, rain bouncing off the plastic roof, the driver somehow steering the handlebars with one hand and the stump of a withered, disfigured arm. The scenes of everyday life we passed in Delhi were difficult to comprehend: swathes of people rushing in all directions, many, it appeared, living on the streets; tiny, frail men pushing huge loads of fruit, others sat in the rain selling watches or waiting for shoes to polish; exhausted bicycle rickshaw boys curled up, sleeping; a beggar with no legs dragging herself along on a wooden trolley. I thought of what Vikram Seth had written concerning his country, that despite the extreme poverty and hardship there was a spirit and a vitality in the Indian people that enabled them to continue carving out niches of existence. What I saw there that day was a will to survive, to keep on living despite the odds. It shocked and mesmerised me simultaneously, and it was impossible not to feel guilty at the frivolity of our own aims; we had come all this way simply to climb a mountain, to try and impregnate our own lives with some significance.

We left Delhi in the dark, climbing out of the plains and into the cool, past the colonial hill stations and on up towards the mountains. We had to wait for an hour to change buses at Rishikesh and began wandering the streets aimlessly, until we noticed the word TEMPLE painted on the side of a very ordinary-looking building, an arrow alongside it pointing to a set of steep stairs.

'Let's check it out,' enthused Mick, and we all followed – all except Julie-Ann who felt uncomfortable entering a Hindu place of worship just for a look around. Mick, the taxman from Derby, was held to be one of the world's finest Himalayan alpinists but you would never know it to meet him; he refused to take himself seriously and was a great master of understatement. Beneath this veneer, however, there was a hard-nosed determination that I had witnessed a few years earlier in Scotland, where we had pioneered a couple of difficult, new, winter routes.

'Can I help you?' asked a low voice from the darkness.

Startled, we turned around, a little embarrassed; even Roger looked lost for words. A big man dressed entirely in white and with long silver hair was sitting cross-legged on a raised plat-form. It was Mick who broke the silence.

'I'm not sure you can, actually,' he answered.

'Please, sit down.'

We gathered beneath the man, our backs against the chill of the wall. To the left hung a large photograph of a gentleman with short hair, dressed in a military uniform peppered with medals; it was an old photograph of the same man.

'Well I know this might sound daft but I've got a terrible crick in my neck.' It was a hell of a long shot, I thought, but perhaps Hindu holy men had osteopathic powers.

'Please, come, sit. Take off your shirt.'

Briefly, giggles rippled through the room and then died away as the babu dipped his thumb into a white powder, before pushing it firmly into the centre of my forehead. I closed my eyes. After ten minutes he released his thumb and, as I stood up, Steve Sustad started up.

'My shoulder gives me a lot of trouble.'

'Come here please,' he called.

He asked Steve if he meditated regularly, and when Steve answered no he informed him that he must have done in a previous life, as his third eye was open. Steve shrugged his shoulders, unconvinced by the rhetoric.

Ten minutes later Roger raised his hand, not wanting to miss out on any healing. 'I've got a really bad back,' he told the man.

Perhaps it's an old guiding injury, I thought. Both Roger and Julie-Ann were mountain guides, though neither of them did this full time; Roger worked for the BMC and Julie-Ann had an academic career in genetics. Only the stoic Brendan, it appeared, was truly fit and well.

We exited this peculiarly biblical scene into the intense bright sun and continued our journey northwards, the road climbing alongside the holy River Ganges, through countless gaudily painted villages, places even more colourful than the English seaside resorts of my childhood holidays. The bus lurched around an increasing number of bends, accompanied by a never ending chorus of screeching horns from buses and ornately decorated trucks that zipped past us, seemingly out of control. As we approached Srinagar, the air in the bus cooled as the sun dipped and then disappeared.

That night, from the guest house window, I tried to photograph a spectacular electrical storm but, by the time I had consulted the manual on my new, electronic, slow-release cable and set up the tripod, the sky had turned a quiet, still black and the only sound was of rain pouring from the roof of the hotel on to the street below.

In the bus the next day, the crick in my neck was stiffer than ever as we rattled up towards Joshimath, where we intended to organise porters, find a cook and buy most of our food. Occasionally, wonderful white blossom trees clung to the edge of the road; behind them a sheer 1,000-foot drop to the foaming river below. It was a little too early in the year for the hordes of pilgrims to be making their spiritual journey along the Ganges up into the snowy abode of the Gods. However, as we entered Joshimath we did pass a couple of scantily dressed men, one in bright orange another in yellow, walking barefoot and holding tiny parcels of belongings and outstretched brass begging bowls.

We rushed around the following day, shopping and packing thirty-six porter loads of twenty kilograms each, whilst snatching glances up at the surrounding hills, each of us commenting in turn on how worryingly low the snowline looked for the time of year.

In the afternoon I had a haircut and, afterwards, persuaded the man to un-crick my neck. He held my head as if gripping a rugby ball, twisting it violently until an almighty crack reverberated around the wooden shack. He charged fifty rupees for the privilege. The neighbouring wooden shack was a public telephone service and I decided to phone home. 'I'll be out of contact now for about a month, so don't worry love if you don't hear anything,' I reassured Elaine on a crystal clear line.

On the way back to the hotel I met Mick, returning from the post office. He had failed to post home his son's toy man, 'Woody', which he had brought by mistake. Apparently, the item was too big to be a letter, and yet too small to be a parcel and so the clerk had refused to accept it. Mick revelled in collecting yet another anecdote of ludicrous, unpredictable Indian bureaucracy.

CHANGABANG

A local bus dropped us at Jumma the next morning and it felt such a relief to be finally walking into the heart of the mountains after nine days of travelling, shopping and frustration. It was a beautiful landscape, totally devoid of other westerners, and peaceful, except for occasional birdsong and the tumbling river below. I enjoyed walking at the back, breathing the scent of pine trees, trying to capture something of the place on film. At a small summer hamlet half a dozen locals sat around, and Brendan surprised them all by handing out photographs he had taken of them the previous year, keeping a promise I often made but rarely honoured. We passed a couple of male goats, horns locked, vying for supremacy, then followed a large moraine bank up towards Dunagiri, a deserted village perched at 4,000 metres; people would come with their animals soon for the summer season, said one of the porters.

Dramatic peaks soared in every direction as we continued our climb early the next morning. The porters bent forwards, straining under the weight of the loads, each footstep placed precisely on the boulders that led up past the snout of the glacier. Most wore leaking, cheap, plastic training-shoes, having decided to pocket the cash Roger and Julie-Ann had given them for boots. We climbed to almost 4,400 metres along a patchwork of snow.

At base camp, in thickening snow, Roger and Julie-Ann handed out bundles of rupees to each man in turn; they shook our hands and then hurried back towards the valley in clusters. We spent the remainder of the day putting up our tents and improving a shepherd's stone hut, covering the roof with a nylon tarpaulin brought from home. Originally from New Zealand, Julie-Ann was smaller than Roger but had a lithe, muscular frame. Watching the zeal with which she carried rocks over to the shelter helped me to understand her success in the high mountains. The effort of lifting just moderate-sized rocks made my head pound like a bass drum and my lungs burn, but I consoled myself with the thought that we were almost at the height of Mont Blanc.

Brendan and I were anxious to start acclimatising our bodies to the thin air immediately so early on the second morning we headed out across the east Bagini Glacier. Up ahead Brendan was crouching down, the cone of gold light from his headtorch scouring the silk whiteness.

'What's up?' I panted.

'Look here, I think this is the track of a snow leopard.'

Awestruck, we stared down at the cat's pawprints in the thin layer of snow, the tracks meandering towards us from the far bank as if the animal had come to weigh up the new visitors camping opposite. It was my tenth year of exploring the Himalayas, but I had never seen even a hint of a snow leopard before. We needed to keep moving in order to get up onto the main glacier before the sun rose too high and softened the snow, and we carried on over the peaks and troughs of the glacier, our hearts filled with childlike wonder, honoured to be travelling through such a remote and unspoilt land.

As we cornered the moraine slopes of Purbi Dunagiri up towards the Bagini Glacier proper, the sun lit the sky behind the enormous North Faces of Saf Minal and Kalanka. Other than a Czech route up Kalanka's North Face, this entire cirque of walls was untouched.

A little further and there, at last, was Changabang: lonely, cold; shrouded in eerie, cerulean light. I dropped my rucksack into the rocks and stared, mesmerised by the sun's first rays slowly sweeping from the summit towards the glacier 5,000 feet below. Adrenalin pumped through my chest, as I suddenly realised the enormity of what we had come to climb.

'Jesus wept. It's outrageous.'

'I thought you'd be impressed.' Brendan chuckled at my excited reaction.

Changabang did not look real and as we got closer the sun etched out its steep flanks more aggressively, making it look more and more like something a child might draw rather than an actual mountain.

Though I had been ski-guiding in the Alps during most of April, Brendan was the one who powered ahead, breaking trail through deep snow like a man possessed. After seven hours of effort, we reached the advanced base camp-site next to a small glacial melt pool directly across from the North Face at around 5,100 metres. We erected the tent and collapsed into it, feeling all the effects of altitude – lack of appetite, headaches, dehydration. We knew that in order to adjust to the reduced oxygen levels we had to push our bodies even higher, and so we climbed to 5,700 metres on Purbi Dunagiri.

'It looks like a different mountain this year,' said Brendan, gazing up at our route.

The main difference was that the groove of ice they had climbed to reach the second icefield the year before no longer existed; in fact, there looked to be less ice on the face generally, and what there was looked green and hard. There was a lot of unconsolidated snow on the glacier, as if the snowy winter we had heard about had been accompanied by extremely high winds and low temperatures, never giving the snow a chance to rest on the face and transform into ice.

Back down at base camp we taught Vikram how to make chips and egg and then set about constructing a hanging stove. Unfortunately all I had managed to find at home was a normal gas stove, which would be useless on a climb as steep as this, with nowhere to rest it. Rather than being annoyed, Brendan relished the challenge, and watched as I wrapped wire and plumbing tape around metal strapping. He suggested using a piece of thick rubber to cradle the gas canister; it worked a treat.

'Metal Mickey,' I called, parading the Heath Robinson invention around to show the rest of the team.

Unimpressed, Steve pointed to a pair of crampons.

'Hey whose are those?'

'Mine,' I announced. 'They're brand new. I've never used them before. Why?'

'They're death. They're always clogging up with snow.'

'Oh, so what sort have you got?'

'I've got the same ones.'

For the next seven days the three independent teams reconnoitred the face, prepared equipment and acclimatised. Narinder was physically strong and helped us to ferry loads up to the higher camp – he worked at a mountaineering centre in Daram Sala but he knew the technical difficulty of the route was beyond him. On our final acclimatising foray we tried to reach the Bagini Col and leave a cache of food and gas there to use during our descent of the southern side of the mountain. Conditions were so treacherous underfoot, with the snow crust refusing to support our weight, that we aborted the attempt and spent the afternoon camped next to Steve and Mick, entertained by their eccentric banter.

'Enjoying you holidays, Steven?'

'Yes Michael, and you?'

'Oh, absolutely wonderful. Steve you couldn't pass me another headache pill could you?'

Mick admitted he was always slow to acclimatise.

We talked about tactics and it appeared we were preparing to climb the same line. Roger and Julie-Ann were thinking of climbing a parallel line to the left, initially, but then the same upper-groove system. One more day of rest and then we would set off, followed by Mick and Steve, two days behind, and then Roger and Julie-Ann, a day after them. We didn't want to end up fighting for limited bivouac space.

We went to bed reasonably early the night before leaving base camp. I decided to write a few words to Elaine, I was missing her badly.

Wednesday 21st May 1997, Base camp.

Dear Love,

I won't be able to write for a week or so as we are setting off towards Changabang in a few hours. We will hopefully spend 6–8 days climbing and descending it. I will think of you every day and miss you every night as I sit on some ledge – ah well, at least I have my new super sleeping bag.

The weather turns crap every afternoon but each morning it is glorious. The moon is full at the moment, perhaps full properly tomorrow.

I feel our love here so strong but nevertheless I'll rush back for the material substance as soon as poss.

Love you always.

A long kiss Andy X

PS Hope you haven't had to worry too much. Take care dear.

Brendan was listening to Oasis on his walkman again, he seemed obsessed with it. I turned off my light, took a sip of water and then slumped onto the pillow, closing my eyes. The day after tomorrow we would be on the route and dreaming of such comfortable sleeping arrangements as this, I thought. It never occurred to me that I might never see Elaine again.

14

Lift off

I felt calm in the night. I was lost in private thought, following on behind Brendan, the pool of light from his headtorch gliding purposefully across the frozen glacier. The nightmare arrived as night seeped away. Seeing the mountain again brought a tightness in my stomach, a fear of what we were hoping to achieve; the sheer enormity of the wall, the commitment, all the things that could go wrong. Perhaps Brendan's experience of climbing partway up the face the previous year enabled him to remain more optimistic, to rationalise the task ahead, breaking it down into achievable units.

I felt hot and agitated and the weight of the rucksack crushed my shoulders.

'Oh God this is useless,' I muttered under my breath. 'Waste. Of. Bloody. Time,' I announced, more emphatically, as if it would soothe my anger. For a moment I considered that my rucksack might be heavier than Brendan's and then, feeling guilty, dismissed the idea.

I stopped, wrestled the pack to the ground, tore off a layer of clothing and decided to say something.

'My rucksack feels too heavy for a route like this,' I called, pitifully.

He paused and turned around, his red suit vivid in the early morning light, behind him the stupendous ice-streaked North Face of Changabang, the mountain we had always dreamed of climbing. It looked surreal just then; ghostly, a smoky-blue gem turning pale-golden from the summit down as the sun's rays climbed over neighbouring peaks.

'Maybe I'm carrying too many clothes? I might ditch something.'

'It could be chilly up on the route,' Brendan warned.

'I could always leave the bivvy bag. My sleeping bag's got a waterproof coating.'

'If you like,' he said in a supportive tone.

'Oh bugger it, I'll take it all. I'll probably never find it again if I leave it here anyway.'

I knew that once we reached the bottom of the face we would put on our harnesses, uncoil the ropes and don crampons and ice axes; our rucksacks would feel lighter then. I also knew that I would be calmer once we were established on the route itself, absorbed by the act of climbing. However, this rationale did nothing to lessen the intimidation I felt as I manhandled the rucksack back on to my shoulders and we edged once more towards the wall, two tiny red specks on that enormous, brilliant-white glacier.

As the angle of the snow steepened my legs suddenly collapsed into a hole – the Bergschrund – my waist jamming at ground level. We should have been roped together so that, if one person did fall in, the other could hoist them to safety. But it was too late now. I glanced down at the sucking void then up, towards Brendan, who was disappearing from sight. I tensed my forearms, pushing them into the snow, desperate not to sink any deeper. I scissor-kicked my legs, my boots swinging in space until they found something solid to push on. I reached as high as I could with a gloved hand, clawing at the soft snow. I half wriggled and half scrabbled, heaving my chest and then gradually my hip on to the snow above. I clambered away from the gaping hole and slumped against the slope, my lungs struggling to deliver enough oxygen. A hundred feet higher, I joined Brendan; he had stamped out a platform and was busy putting on his crampons.

'I fell in the Bergschrund down there,' I sighed, my chest burning. 'It was nearly over before we'd started. We should have had the rope on. That was really stupid,' I said tersely, not meaning to be critical of him but instead furious with myself (a mountain guide); normally I never travelled on such glaciers unroped.

We climbed through tedious, steep snow for 500 feet, carving out bucket seats at the end of each rope length where we could sit and belay. As the hours passed, I kept a nervous watch over the hanging serac up to our left, a five-storey tower block of blue ice, constantly deliberating over whether or not we were in the direct line of fire. At least if we were and it decided to shed an apartment-sized chunk or two, we would be obliterated instantly. We teetered across unpredictable snow that was loosely attached to dirty brittle ice, ice so hard that it broke two of our six ice screws. I took a postcard-sized photo of the mountain from the top pocket of my windsuit and squinted at it. The sky had clouded over and I started to puzzle about where we would spend the night. Beforehand, we had marked all the obvious potential sites for bivouacking on the face with tiny black crosses and, by my reckoning, we were still a long way from the first decent place. As Brendan moved up into much steeper terrain the sun – which had so recently warmed our fingers and toes – became a useless pale disc, hanging behind a veil of cloud before disappearing altogether. I climbed as fast as I could towards Brendan, enjoying the security of a rope above my head, saving energy by hooking my ice axes into the holes in the ice that he had made earlier.

'Anywhere to sleep around here?' I asked rhetorically when I arrived. It was much worse than I had imagined. Brendan passed me the pegs and the slings.

'Well it doesn't look very promising.'

Just above, powder snow hissed down either side of a square granite shield.

'I'll try the left hand gully, there might be somewhere to bivvy up there.'

'Okay, good one Andy.'

The tone of the exchange belied the seriousness of our situation: we needed somewhere to sleep very soon. I traversed gingerly leftwards, the blades of my ice axes jabbing the two-inch carpet of ice that unfurled down the wall. Fortunately, as the ice reared up, it became thicker and I managed to place a reasonable ice screw. After a hundred feet I entered a shallow groove and manufactured an awkward rest by bridging out my cramponed feet and leaning my torso towards the ice.

If I fall from here, I'll probably end up somewhere below Brendan, I thought, deciding to place another screw. I slipped my hands out of my gloves, leaving them threaded through the wrist loops attached to my axes; speed was essential now. I twisted the reluctant teeth of the screw into the wall of ice until satisfied that it was sufficiently buried and then reached down for the rope. Out of nowhere came a muffled drumbeat followed by an icy rush of snow. In a flash I dropped the rope and grabbed the shaft of the axe with my bare hand. Snow thumped my face and chest ceaselessly, accumulating at an alarming rate, slowly burying me. I tensed my legs, trying to hold steady. I dared to lean out a little, allowing the build-up of snow to exit between my legs. My cheeks stung, then went numb as if bitten by a seething serpent. During a lull I grabbed the rope and clipped it into the screw. It was impossible to get my hands back into the gloves, the damn things were packed full of freezing snow. I pushed them hard, forcing them in, and climbed nervously up and out right onto a sloping ledge below a steep sweep of granite. It was poor but it would have to do for tonight.

Brendan arrived, a positive air about him, his suit covered in snow.

'Character-building stuff Andy, good lead mate.'

'Thanks,' I said, starting to shiver. 'I think we should stay here, it's getting late.'

'Yes. I'm sure we can hack it out a bit,' he suggested confidently.

There was no chance of putting up our small tent but at least we could sit in our sleeping-bags, perhaps half-lie down even. I changed my gloves and we put on our duvet jackets; the temperature was plummeting. Brendan's jacket was an ancient blue thing. He could have had a new one like mine free of charge, but to his mind there was nothing wrong with the one he had, so why change? This was the philosophy he applied to motoring too, choosing to drive an ancient pale-blue Cavalier, rebuilding the engine and patching up the body-work rather than buying a new one. It was the engineer in him, the love of solving problems rather than walking away from them. This is why he had warmed to the idea of creating Metal Mickey rather than become upset by my incompetence at leaving the stove back in the UK.

We hung Metal Mickey from the belay, filled the pan with compacted snow and sparked him into life – the inaugural mug of tea. My throat burned with thirst as we set about chipping and scraping the ice away with our axes and our feet, trying to fashion something large enough to crouch on. We had drunk a litre of liquid each during the day and eaten some cereal bars, but we had been on the move for over twelve hours. It took almost forty minutes for the snow to melt and then heat up. We drank the first pan of lukewarm liquid in gulps, passing it between us then adding more snow, desperate now for food. We had been hacking at the ground for almost two hours when we reached the freckled granite beneath. Brendan got into his sleeping bag while I prepared the evening meal – mashed potato with a packet soup thrown in – which I made in our mugs, attempting to keep our one pan clean. We ate quickly and afterwards, though I wanted to sleep, I filled the pan with more snow and chunks of ice by torchlight. We knew we had to drink more liquid.

'This stove is bloody awesome. Better than the one I was supposed to bring,' I enthused.

'Metal Mickey!' cried Brendan loudly, as if unveiling a new circus act, obviously delighted by our ingenuity. 'We should market these when we get back mate.'

'The best thing is that it's getting plenty of air. Mind you it might be tricky in really high winds,' I commented.

As the blue flame danced beneath the pan I began organising my sleeping arrangements. Just before leaving home a friend and fellow mountain guide, Twid, had given me a top tip for preventing a bivvy bag sliding off meagre, sloping ledges. I passed a sock on the inner side of the fabric and then tied a lark's foot knot on the outside, using a thin piece of prussick cord, and attached it to the belay. Lower down the fabric, I did the same. I passed Brendan the two mugs of tea, turned off the stove and packed it away. I took off my plastic outer boots, zipped up the integral gaiters, and then stashed them up above inside my rucksack.

I shuffled into the sleeping bag.

'Comfy mate?' asked Brendan, passing me my mug.

'I'll tell you in the morning.'

All night long spindrift as fine as silt found its way into my bed, chiefly through the tiny gap I had left in the zip of my bivvy bag where the rope tied to my waist-harness exited. Being suspended by a couple of tied-off socks was uncomfortable, but perhaps the best system given the scarcity of space. Repeatedly though, I slipped from the ledge and began to wonder if Twid was playing a terrible joke – revenge for the time in Chamonix (we had just met) when I told him that I was a fully qualified hairdresser and set about chopping at his mop with a pair of scissors on a Swiss Army knife.

'Good morning sir,' greeted Brendan when I finally poked my head out into the morning sun.

I felt rough, like a casualty from some wild, all-night party. Brendan took a photo of me squinting in the bright sun then handed me a mug of tea. I got the impression he'd been up for ages, politely waiting for me to emerge. Slouching there with my eyes closed, I luxuriated in the warmth, sipping through dry lips, while Brendan began organising the climbing gear. My gloves, which were down near my feet, were still extremely damp on the insides and, though I had spares, I would feel vulnerable until I got them dry. I clipped them into the rope above, hoping the sun might dry them out. As part of my nightly routine I had slept with a damp pair of socks between my thighs, a reliable spot for drying things. Inevitably, during the day's climbing, your feet sweat inside the double boots. Ideally, you remove the outer boots. Once inside the sleeping bag you take off the insulated inner boot too and replace the damp socks with dry ones (placing the damp socks between the thighs).

Up above, the climbing looked difficult and I felt relieved that it was Brendan's turn to lead. A smear of ice, a narrow, crisp sheet of linen, soared up into a line of jutting granite overhangs. Thirty feet above me, without a single piece of protection, Brendan looked totally in control, concentrating yet relaxed. He had been climbing well this year, soloing many bold winter routes, such as Galactic Hitchhiker and Minus One Gully, both in one afternoon, on Ben Nevis; he was, without question, clearly focused on his climbing. He disappeared out of view and, as I continued to pay out the rope, I peered around this magnificent arena. The elegant unclimbed Purbi Dunagiri sat behind and, out to the right of us, the spectacular crenellated ridge from where Pete Boardman and Joe Tasker had begun their legendary ascent on the audacious west wall, twenty one years earlier. In front of me sat a small patch of black lichen hoping to feed from any melting ice above; a rare sign of life in this hostile, vertical world.

'Safe Andy,' hollered Brendan.

I quickly smothered my face in sunscreen, and then battled through four layers of clothing in order to go to the loo. Life feels good, I thought, as I started up. I forgot the negative aspects of the previous day as gradually the climbing became steeper and technically more interesting. At the belay, I congratulated Brendan on a superfluous lead and craned my head back. A steep, soaring corner lined with a five-foot strip of ice, like lemon sorbet scalloped out here and there by an imaginary ice cream scoop.

'Andy, turn around, look at the camera, it's a stunning shot,' Brendan called, hanging from the belay.

I glanced down, grinned and then turned back, seeing clouds firing over the summit from the south. I climbed up for another ten metres and then stopped, my lungs working overtime in the thin air. I'll place an ice screw, I thought; that's always a good excuse to stop. Out left, the granite looked impeccably smooth, as if sliced by the blade of a butcher's cleaver, reminding me of the tremendous El Capitan in Yosemite Valley, California. The icy groove ended abruptly at a roof, and I took a hanging belay from a couple of aluminium chocks that I beat into a vertical crack. The clouds had descended now and our only option looked to be out rightwards, along a mixed ramp of rock and ice that would, hopefully, lead us to the foot of the first icefield.

By the time Brendan had climbed up to me and then out to a triangular snow patch on the edge of the icefield, the weather had gone from reasonable to berserk, a strong wind driving snow into our faces and freezing our eyelashes together. We had no choice but to stop; if anything the storm was intensifying. I traversed over to Brendan and, desperate not to spend another night out in the open, we began cutting a platform for the tent immediately.

'It really is a different mountain this year,' reflected Brendan, once we were inside the tent. 'It's way colder for starters, and this weather crapping out every day at two o'clock . . . We had clear blue skies on the climb last year.'

'It's snowed every day since we've been here, even down at base camp.'

'I know. It's crazy.'

The wind buffeted the tent, billowing the fabric up against Brendan's face like a full sail.

'Outrageous behaviour,' he chortled, displaying his absent front tooth.

The outside edge of the groundsheet, about a third of the floor, dangled in space. We hung Metal Mickey from a karabiner clipped to a loop of tape in the apex of the tent roof and began melting snow. When I unzipped the door to collect more snow I was transfixed by the scene on the giant icefield above. A sea of snow danced down the vast, steep sheet of ice, collecting and breaking like surf on either side of our tent before cascading down towards the glacier. It reminded me of film footage I had seen of storms in the Arctic, of weak sunlight filtering through great flowing swathes of dry, crystalline snow. It was a sublime sight, both electrifying and terrifying. Thank God for our little tent, I thought, retreating inside and zipping out the world.

We had only been on the climb for two days, yet already it was beginning to feel normal, our actions becoming efficient and our conversations routine. It was the most unsociable form of companionship, separated by a rope most of the day and then too cold and exhausted to chat in the evenings. However, our deep trust of each other and commitment to a shared goal provided an intense, enduring bond. We also drew strength from loved ones at home. I wore two watches, one on each wrist. On the left wrist was a watch with an altimeter and an alarm; on the other, a fancier dress-watch with a leather strap that Elaine had bought me for my thirtieth birthday. I had left this on UK time so that I could try and imagine what she might be doing at that point in time back home. I noticed that Brendan wore a purple silk scarf around his neck, given to him by his girlfriend Kate. I wasn't sure whether or not they were still going out together – they had had their share of ups and downs over the last few months. Still, it was telling that he was wearing the scarf on the route.

The third day dawned beautifully. Down below, Mick and Steve, who had been watching our slow progress, started up the same route, moving at a similar pace. We now embarked on the first icefield, a giant skating rink, tilted at fifty-five degrees, with an almost impenetrable skin of steel that shattered and splintered until the sun softened it a little. The constant avalanches had acted like giant polishing rags on the surface of the ice, making it much tougher than we had bargained for. We had just three out of the original six ice screws functioning properly now, with one other that could be used if beaten sufficiently with the ice hammer. They were a mixture of 1987 vintage Polish titanium screws and marginally superior Ukraine ones. We placed just one ice screw for a belay (often only halfway, as the damn things were so exhausting) and tied ourselves into the axes as well. In the Alps during the 1980s climbers from Eastern Europe and the Soviet Union would regularly barter with these ice screws, exchanging them for money or climbing equipment and clothing not available in their own countries. The screws were made by climbing engineers working on the Russian space programme or in armament factories.

With relief, I exited the icefield at the top left-hand corner and, out of rope, took a stance. I glanced up. The climbing ahead looked technical but more satisfying. Our photo of the face boasted a potential bivvy site about four or five hundred feet higher, directly beneath the second icefield. Brendan tiptoed across to me, collected the protection and then moved up, his crampons scratching blank rock, searching for tiny edges to balance on. He looked composed as he heaved himself up, jammed his feet into a crack and started placing a chock for protection. Suddenly, a rattling sound echoed and we watched in horror as one of his ice axes tumbled down the wall, bouncing off the ice and then out of sight.

'Shit!' Brendan was furious. He had devoted himself to this mountain, committing himself financially and emotionally, not to mention the time element. 'Shit!' He spat.

He climbed back down and peered into the increasing cloud bubbling below. We would have to go down now. I was furious too. Why hadn't he tied his ice axes onto his rucksack for God's sake, like me?

'Okay, watch me here, I'm going to climb down.'

'Alright, watching you.'

My system made things fiddly, yet I wanted to be certain I couldn't lose an axe.

'Thank God for that,' he sighed. Somehow the axe had miraculously stuck in the snow, just a few feet lower.

Climbing stylishly, as if compensating for his mistake, Brendan scratched up the wonderful, clean granite wall, twisting his axe blades into cracks, hooking his crampon points over small nubbins, occasionally piercing a fist of ice. I followed and then punched my way up a narrow, exhilarating, vertical gully.

'Okay climb!' I screamed into the abyss once secured, the adrenalin still pumping through my veins.

Half a rope-length away from the second icefield the sky had turned a heavy grey. It was almost two o'clock and, as I stood belaying Brendan, small snow flakes began falling. Before long I was being bombarded by gushes of powder. By the time it came for me to climb I was buried in snow up to my knees. We spent over an hour chopping into the snow and ice before erecting the tent and escaping the blizzard. We drank tea and soup and ate spicy noodles, trying to relax as we knew we couldn't climb any more that particular day. We joked, lamenting all the classic long rock climbs we could have been enjoying back in Britain instead of sitting here, 2,500 feet above a glacier somewhere in the Indian Himalaya.

Like every other morning, the weather on the fourth day began perfectly and, psychologically, the day represented a triumph for Brendan as we climbed beyond the high point of his team's attempt the previous year. The second icefield was bigger and steeper than the first and its skin was tougher still. Although we began the day feeling fresh and vigorous, after five hundred feet of balancing on blunt crampon points, we started to lose momentum. I sat astride my rucksack (which was tied to an ice screw a little higher), the sun bouncing from the slope, burning my cheeks. A long, low veil of spindrift descended the icefield, first enveloping Brendan, then the two strands of rope, before racing towards me. I took a couple of snaps with my camera and then quickly pulled my hood over my helmet, turning away as the gentle shower swept by.

There were two distinct routes leading towards the third icefield, both of them looked desperate. I preferred the look of a series of steep ice-bulges on the right as I knew, from studying the face through binoculars, that they definitely linked up. However, the lack of sufficient ice screws meant I chose the line further left – a ribbon of ice running up to a steep, snow-covered granite buttress. After eighty feet I had a crisis of confidence; the climbing above looked too difficult and frightening. I hung from the wrist loops of my ice axes with leaden arms, my calves quivering as the crampon points strained to maintain contact. I was a tiny, fumbling figure atop a thousand-foot high, dirty, frozen windscreen. I reversed back down to where Brendan stood, feeling slightly embarrassed at having wasted so much time achieving nothing. With hindsight perhaps I might have persevered, as now the sun had gone and banners of spindrift started hissing past. The biggest storm either of us had ever experienced was about to unleash its fury.

'I'm sorry Brendan, it just doesn't feel right up there,' I said.

'No worries, I'll try out right if you like.'

Four days of climbing was beginning to show. I felt shattered and was immensely grateful for Brendan's offer, as the route looked savagely steep and the sky had turned ominously black. I clipped back into the belay and handed him the protection.

'I think I'll leave my sack here and pull it up later,' he suggested.

'No problem, go for it.'

His foot slipped, sounding like a sharp stone being dragged across glass, and I felt a hand squeeze my innards. Oh, how I hated watching. Because of the scarcity of functioning ice screws he stopped after just a hundred feet, yelling for me to start. Forbidding clouds now shrouded us and the ominous sound of thunder approached, like the cry of a hunting dog. A storm here could be fatal, I thought.

Brendan was tied to one ice screw, hanging on vertical ice and, by the time I reached him, the afternoon storm machine had reached fever pitch. We desperately needed to escape; time was striding on and spindrift crashed down incessantly. We both knew that we would be very lucky to survive a night in the open in such conditions. I took the two functioning ice screws plus the half-damaged one and traversed nervously rightwards in a sensational position until, beneath, I saw a vertical smear of ice stuck to the rock, which offered my only escape route. I tried to relax but as the thunder increased so did the wind, threatening to tear me from the wall. I climbed on, full of fear. Snow continued to cascade down, pummelling me. The wind suddenly increased tenfold and a violent thunderbolt struck just above. I had climbed beyond the point of return.

Seventy feet above the belay I tried to place a screw. It refused to bite. Tiring rapidly, I clipped into one of my ice tools. It held for a few seconds, then ripped. Both crampons ripped simultaneously, all my weight falling onto the remaining ice tool. Fuck . . . I'm going to die! Struggling under the weight of the pack I bowed my head – the wind blew from below now, with a terrifying force – trying to lift out the axe, my only point of contact with this world. I was trapped in some evil vortex. A mad experiment gone awry. I was a flea in a web, waiting for the deadly spider to deliver the killer blow. There was not enough time to think of loved ones, people left behind. Deep inside, an instinctive desire to fight rose in my chest and I started hurling my exhausted arm at the ice. After a few blows the blade bit tenuously and I regained position. Slowly I turned the screw into the ice. At the halfway mark I tied it off and slumped on to it.

We were in the eye of a furious storm. Neck, nostrils, ears, gloves packed with snow. When Brendan arrived he was retching with pain. I had never before seen him show his suffering so openly. Seeing this hard little bastard wince and groan only served to underline the seriousness of our predicament. Somehow he climbed on, gladiatorially, up a thinly iced corner.

I flapped my arms to stay warm, but it was a losing battle. I babbled, swore, screamed and shrieked, believing I might be going insane. I seconded the pitch shouting that I needed something to eat. I was verging on hypothermia. Brendan held out a food bar and I snapped at it like a starving dog, the wrapper still on. I spat out some of the wrapper then climbed up into the night.

I traversed leftwards as the angle relented towards a prominent snow arête that was just visible; at least we could attempt to sleep there. When I reached the arête the storm had dissipated. I had already used the decent ice screws and spent twenty minutes beating the partially damaged one into the ice before tying it off; but only a third of it had gone in. I also tied myself to the two ice tools, just in case.

'The belay is shit!' I yelled into the night. 'Be careful.'

Normally Brendan was the most super-meticulous, steady climber but, within minutes of his starting, I was yanked tight onto the belay and realised that something had gone seriously wrong. It was completely dark except for a tiny light flickering a long way below me. He had nose-dived sixty feet diagonally leftwards, taking a huge swing. Now he started climbing a more direct route up to the belay.

'That was lucky,' he commented when he arrived. 'I could have lost my headtorch.'

At 11pm we crawled into our tent, mentally and physically shattered. During fifteen years in the mountains I had never experienced such a harrowing few hours. I was flabbergasted and angry. Had he not realised how appalling my belay was? But it wasn't the time for argument. We had survived, that was the main thing.

15

Committed

Ten thousand tiny silver stalactites – our breath in the night caught and frozen – lined the inside of our cramped tent; like the fur of a snow leopard sparkling in the morning sun. I lay still, for even the slightest movement encouraged the icy slivers to leap down onto your face and melt. What day is it? I wondered. Not which day of the week, like Monday or Friday, that's meaningless up here. I mean, how many days have we been climbing this thing? I circled my lips with my tongue, halting sharply and wincing as I hit a patch of new cold sores. The skin on my face felt tight and burnt, as if I'd been standing too long next to a blazing fire. I closed my eyes. It was day five, I suddenly remembered, and we'd started with food for eight days.

Desperate for a pee, I grabbed my plastic bottle, unzipped my sleeping bag and then wriggled out of it a little, ice falling onto my cheeks. I felt exhausted and decided on the lying-down method; a bold manoeuvre, for the slightest mistake meant a wet sleeping-bag. I didn't manage much, I was so dehydrated, and what I did manage was the colour of malt whiskey and smelt putrid. I screwed the lid of the bottle tight, noticing that my finger ends were completely numb on the right hand; I must have been frost-nipped during the storm the previous afternoon. Despite lying on a foam mat in a huge, down sleeping-bag and wearing every layer of clothing I possessed, I could still feel the cold knifing my back and shoulders. I reached for my spectacles, which were coated by filigrees of ice, and started breathing on them forcefully, trying to defrost them.

'Good morning sir,' welcomed Brendan, his throat sounding a little gruff.

'Morning,' I said, sitting up slightly and moving my legs so that he had more room to hang the stove. A good proportion of the tent floor was simply hanging in the air, daylight glaring straight up through it and, in the corner, my heavy outer boots and a couple of gas canisters sagged, testing the skills of the seamstress who had stitched our nylon home together. Both of us remained tied to a rope, attached to an ice screw outside, just in case the snow we were perched on collapsed.

As we drank our first tea there was a silence, as if neither of us could face discussing what our plans should be. I found the quiet harder than Brendan; he seldom spoke for long anyhow and probably thought me a chatterbox. I decided not to mention his fall. Ten years earlier, in 1987, when I'd cashed in my miner's pension of £1,500 and set off on a five-month quest through the Himalayas, I'd been utterly convinced that I wanted to spend the rest of my life climbing hard new routes on the earth's big mountains. I'd begun organising major aspects of life – work, relationships – around expeditions. But that morning, perhaps for the very first time, I was starting to have serious doubts about this pursuit. The storm had terrified me. Could I put the fear behind me?

'Brendan, there's something I need to tell you.'

'Oh yes,' he replied inquisitively.

'Elaine was going to phone and tell you anyway.'

'Go on then.'

'I hate the cold.'

'What do you mean?'

'Well, we had this big argument at home, about whether or not we should open our bedroom window at night. Elaine likes it open, but I find it too cold. So, she threatened to phone you the week before we left to tell you that I'm a fake, a lightweight, not the hardy mountaineer people think I am.'

'Excellent,' Brendan giggled.

'Brendan, by the way, I don't feel up to climbing today. I feel utterly wasted.' I felt relieved that I'd said something.

'No worries mate.' Brendan pushed his head outside. 'The weather is perfect again now, like every morning.'

'It'll be rubbish again by two o'clock. You can set your watch by it.'

'You're probably right.' He came back into the tent, holding his fingers up. 'I think I got frost-nipped a bit yesterday.'

'Me too.'

'Really? Jesus, it's so different to last year.' Brendan paused for a while, then said: 'I tell you what, why don't I go and retrieve the screws I left behind yesterday?'

'Good idea.'

Brendan had climbed directly up to the final belay after his fall the night before and this meant that the ice screws I had placed for protection were still stuck out on the icefield. I passed the ropes through the belay device, standing by the tent in my duvet jacket and big mitten gloves, soaking up all the warmth the sun could offer, as he traversed horizontally out across the steep, emerald-green ice. Wisps of spindrift spiralled and tumbled head over heels from the summit, flowing over the great vertical screen of pale granite and brushing patches of ice that clung to the rock like frozen tears. A few hours earlier I had almost died on that very slope, but now the scenery began to woo me with its inescapable beauty; it was like the spell of a cruel lover. I felt torn. I was too scared to carry on and yet the thought of descending immediately filled me with anguish. Even though I was hungry, even though I felt cold and weak and wanted to say enough is enough, the splendid, opulent architecture charmed me.

I knew that the lure of Changabang was much more than physical beauty, it was a fusion of so many things. This was a mythical mountain, a treasure trove of tales of man's successes and failures, scenes acted out on the many sides of this gigantic prism. And there I stood, paralysed, halfway up the North Face.

'Okay, take in. I'm coming back,' Brendan yelled, piercing the deep silence.

I squeezed the ropes firmly in the palm of my gloved hand and glanced up at the next section of the climb, a 200-foot tapering vertical highway of rippled ice. I looked away sharply, full of dread. Wallowing in the sumptuous mountain scenery had not diminished my fear.

'Good effort Brendan. Did the screws come out okay?'

'Yes, not too bad actually. God it's nice to climb without a rucksack. How are you doing?'

'I feel absolutely knackered to be honest. I need to rest today.'

'You might feel better after a few brews and a good night's kip mate.'

'I hope so,' I said, sounding uncertain.

He could see that I was struggling and I appreciated his relaxed, gentle manner; had he tried to coerce me into going up that day, I would almost certainly have rebelled. I had hated everything about the previous day: my going the wrong way at the top of the icefield, the storm, Brendan's fall. But I internalised my deeper fears for the sake of team harmony. I remembered Pete Boardman writing about the need to avoid personal conflict during major undertakings such as this.

Boardman had exploded when Joe Tasker kept taking photos of him in an exhausted state, yelling 'If you take another picture like that, I'll thump you.' The pair were stressed and tired, high on the West Face, and soon after they decided to descend their fixed ropes, retreating to base camp for a rest and more supplies. Unfortunately, we did not have the option of descending and leaving 2,000 feet of fixed rope in place; we were climbing in alpine style, not capsule style. We had just two thin ropes, each one 200 feet long. If we descended now, we would have to climb back up the entire route. Boardman and Tasker's route had been incredibly bold at that time and we knew only too well that our own ideas had been shaped and inspired by their startling vision; however, alpine style is a purer and more committing form of ascent.

'Fancy some spicy noodles before we move the tent?' asked Brendan, the sun bouncing off the black of his sunglasses.

'That sounds a good idea.'

'Okay, I'll tidy the ropes out if you want to get the stove going.'

After moving the tent we drank more tea and ate chocolate biscuits and fruitcake, then snoozed and managed to dry out our sleeping-bags and gloves. The biggest disruption to our plans during this particular ascent had not been the technical difficulty of the climbing but rather the weather, which had consistently reduced our actual climbing time. Brendan suggested that he could lead up the ice tongue with me bringing up the rear. 'It might not be as bad as we think,' he encouraged.

The first four days had been extremely intense and I certainly felt better for the rest day, probably due in part to the mental space it afforded, along with a good night's sleep and the break from physical exertion. As we discussed tactics I knew in my heart that, if I pushed the case for descending, Brendan would support me. But I also knew that to descend was to abandon any hope of reaching the summit. Perhaps I was conscious, too, of the fact that we had both recently failed on our projects: I had run out of time after becoming stormbound just one day's climbing away from the summit of Trango Tower in the Karakoram in 1995, while over the last few years Brendan had failed twice on the neighbouring north ridge of Latok I, not to mention his attempt on Changabang the previous year.

Hours of gazing through binoculars whilst acclimatising had convinced us that the next section of the climb, from the top of the ice tongue to the upper groove, would probably be the steepest and most demanding of the entire route. We stared at our damp, dishevelled postcard of the face, struggling to see any potential bivvy sites.

'Okay,' I said. 'Let's have a look at the ice tongue tomorrow.'

The following morning the spiked soles of Brendan's boots disappeared up into a perfect, sapphire-blue sky, the occasional frisbee of ice chinking past. The ice tongue was a thin ribbon of toughened, rippled glass glued to vertical rock. The ripples reminded me of the Artex plastering with which my mother had insisted we decorate the inside of our entire house in the early 1980s. Brendan had been keen to try out my ice axes and so we'd swapped. His were lighter and required much more force to get a placement and I felt drained after climbing just thirty feet of the tongue. I climbed up to join Brendan, passing two curious, gigantic chunks of granite – shaped like battered old coins – that sat on the smooth wall of rock, seemingly unjoined.

Brendan's belay looked good, a collection of wired chocks in sound granite, precisely where the ice tongue terminated. Pulling up my rucksack was much more exhausting than the actual climbing and when I had finally hauled it to the belay I clipped it into a sling. Unfortunately, however, the sling wasn't properly attached and the rucksack screamed out of sight towards the glacier until, after a hundred feet or so, it slowed, bounced and then stopped as the rope came tight.

'Bloody hell Andy, what's going on?' It was the first time I had heard Brendan sound angry.

I apologised, feeling a little guilty about how annoyed I had felt with him after he had dropped his axe on the third day. I hauled the rucksack up; fortunately it was still intact.

Brendan set off again, climbing straight above the belay, a look of determination in his face. He paused in a dramatic position, scanning the overhanging wall above for holds. I knew that if we cracked the next three or four hundred feet we might find a ledge where we could pass the night. But Brendan couldn't find anywhere to place protection and after half an hour of trying he started down climbing towards me, rebuffed. I suggested climbing out left and then traversing back right; it looked hopeful as there was a fracture line splitting the granite. After a brief rest Brendan was off to investigate, his crampons scraping at the rock, elbows locked at ninety degrees as he hooked the blades of his ice axe over a series of small edges on the wall before finally twisting them into the base of the crack. He fiddled with some wires until they bit in the crack and then clipped in the ropes, refusing to use them for aid, determined to free climb the pitch despite the weight of the rucksack. My hands were covered in sweat watching him; it was an inspired performance which invigorated me. Go on lad, give it some, I willed secretly. After an hour of solid effort he shouted that he'd found a belay and I punched the air and clenched my teeth. The negative energy that had surrounded me the previous day vanished. I felt alive again.

The climbing above looked equally difficult, Brendan reported, and there was nowhere to spend the night. It was also late. We decided to fix a rope to our high point and return to the snow arête below. That way we would get another night lying horizontally and could leave a lot of climbing equipment up here. Down below I could make out the other two teams: Mick and Steve doing battle with the second icefield and, a day behind them, Roger and Julie-Ann. I waved, shaking an arm in the air, and the two belayers, a thousand feet apart, waved back.

Undoubtedly, the downside of having a rest day was that we were using up a significant proportion of our limited food supply. We had only brought food for eight days, nine at a push, and this was our sixth day. The summit was still 3,000 feet away and the terrain now looked dauntingly steep. Later that afternoon Mick and Steve appeared at the snow arête looking justifiably tired, but positive.

'Why have you spent two nights here?' asked Mick.

'Thought we'd hang around a bit and enjoy the view,' explained Brendan, playfully.

It was the first social contact we had experienced for almost seven days. Though we had plenty of gas and tea bags remaining we only had two more evening meals and breakfasts, so we were delighted by the news that they thought they might have a little spare mashed potato powder that they could give us if necessary, once up on the ridge. It was a vague arrangement, but one which boosted our confidence. We spoke about tactics too and contemplated teaming up as a four, though we worried that this might complicate things such as finding enough space for us all to bivvy on.

The next day I felt much stronger physically, and tried to push the thoughts of the ferocious storm to the back of my mind. We climbed up the two ropes we had fixed, leaving them in place for Mick and Steve and taking their ropes to climb the rest of the route with. It took much longer than anticipated to reach our high point and this prompted Mick and Steve to take a rest day; they would follow on a day behind.

The headwall stretched away spectacularly, smattered here and there with splashes of clear water-ice and cut by a groove. I felt as if I had been a mere passenger the day before and I desperately needed to get my teeth stuck into something to regain my confidence. For the first time on the climb, I decided to leave my rucksack behind. I teetered out left, along an intimidating ramp below a blank bulge of rock. I placed a poor wire behind a small flake and clipped the rope. I threw my right foot onto a square edge and rocked up, cupping my left hand on the axe and extending until, with a straight arm, I could reach with the other axe. I tried to stay calm, breathing regularly as the tip of the axe rallied up and down and side to side, searching for anything to catch on. Nothing. My left shoulder began to shake with the strain. I reversed the moves and looked over at Brendan, disappointed.

'Maybe out here on the right, mate. It's steep at the bottom, but if you could get into that groove . . .'

'I'll have a look.'

The base of the groove was severely undercut. I couldn't reach the first decent hold. Conscious of the time, I smashed a piton in above Brendan, clipped in the rope and then started swinging until I had enough momentum to stab a veneer of ice with my axe and pull up. I swept my left arm over my right, forming an X, then flicked the blade into another piece of ice the thickness of a small shaving mirror. My right boot skidded into space. I jumped it up onto a matchstick edge and stood up.

The next hundred and fifty feet were the most enjoyable of the route so far. After all the worry and fear of the last two days I at last had conviction flowing through my veins. I felt invincible. I paused at two-thirds height, my arms stretched over a three-foot overhang, my lungs on fire. I stared down, 3,000 feet of air beneath my boots, and began to laugh. 'We've cracked the bastard.' I was in the middle of the beautiful head-wall at over 20,000 feet, the first person ever to navigate through this barrier. Technically, it was one of the hardest pitches I had ever led at such an altitude and yet, oddly, it felt reasonable. At the belay I could see that the upper groove had intermittent seams of ice, it didn't look impossible. 'We can do this, I know we can,' I told myself. 'If only the weather holds.' Brendan arrived, equally enthusiastic about the quality of the climbing, carrying on into the base of the soaring groove system. Just then I heard someone yelling from below. The wind had strengthened and snow began sliding over the ice. I strained to hear what was being said. 'Have you got a needle and thread?' I thought I heard. Being tired, my immediate reaction to this query was, what the hell are they doing down there? Have they brought needlework with them to stave off the boredom?

Above, Brendan tackled mixed ground. Moments earlier he had unintentionally dislodged a rock. I had consoled myself that Julie and Roger were out to the left and Mick and Steve were on a ridge crest, so surely any debris would bounce either side of them. I was painfully wrong. The shouting started again; clearly someone was distressed. It sounded like Steve. I began to panic.

Down below, Mick and Steve had cowered in their tiny tent as a horrific screeching sound drew ever closer. They hadn't had time to reach their helmets and had pressed themselves against the inner wall of the tent, rigid with fear. Seconds later a large rock had ripped through the fabric. It had missed Steve's head by just two inches.

They screamed up abuse and we shouted apologies, full of guilt. Meanwhile, two more rocks struck their tent and spin-drift began pouring in. Steve had a large needle with him, and a spare pink boot lace, and he set about stitching the tent back together. There was nowhere else to hang the tent; instead they put on their helmets and lay still, praying. It was anything but a rest day for the duo.

Just before nightfall I crawled onto a pitiful sloping ledge. Up above was a similar-looking, ice-covered ramp. I could find nowhere better to spend the night. I climbed to the higher place, tied off the ropes, and brought Brendan up to the lower ledge. The smell of steel on granite lingered in the fast-dying light as I swung the blade of the axe again and again, trying to carve a bed for the night. To believe I am going to transform this tiny, sloping, ice-covered ledge into a reasonable place to sleep is really quite absurd, I thought. One person sitting on one (not too large) buttock, perhaps. Two people? Absolutely no chance.

'You're going to have to find somewhere to sleep down there mate,' I shouted to Brendan, poised on a similar protuberance forty feet below.

This will be . . . I tried to remember . . . night number seven. Before long it was completely dark, but we continued in the beam of the headlamps, chipping and scratching away at the iron-like ice welded to our respective bits of the mountainside. My arms were heavy with the effort and I decided to stop briefly and start cooking. Taking the stove out of the rucksack was like handling a new born baby. Drop this and no drink. Up here, at this altitude, no drink means you eventually die. Placing three or four dense chunks of granite-peppered ice into the pan I turned on the gas and then, as I lit it – oomph – a small blue shadow danced on the wall.

Slowly the ice turned to liquid.

'Food's nearly ready Bren,' I called into the gloom, my throat sore from the lack of drink. Since breakfast we had drunk less than a litre each and had been climbing continuously for over fourteen hours. The effort of shouting brought a bout of light-headedness and so I bowed my head, leaning forward so that my helmet rested against the wall; a gesture interpreted by mountaineers the world over as 'I am totally fucked'.

The temperature plunged now, anything metal glinting with early frost. When Brendan arrived he was wearing his down jacket over the top of his one-piece waterproof suit. We stood huddled together, our cramponed feet biting in to the rock and ice, clutching our plastic mugs full of noodles and relaxing for the first time all day. We had climbed a key section of the route and briefly congratulated each other, hardly noticing the small chunks of stone trying to rip out the fillings in our teeth. There was still a way to go to get off this damn face. Then there was the summit ridge to climb, followed by the descent. And we only had one night's food left. Right then none of these things entered my head.

Brendan retreated to his spot below and got ready for bed.

My place was so poor that I decided to try the clove-hitch-around-the-sock technique again. I clipped the bottom of the bag into a wire-nut jammed in a crack and the top into a tied-off piton. It took an eternity to take off my crampons, sort out the climbing equipment and squeeze into the suspended sleeping bag.

Then came the spindrift. Gathering momentum up above, it thundered down onto the bivvy bag. I zipped myself in, but was too late. Laced around my neck, the snow began to melt, running down my chest. All zips closed from now on, I decided, but still, with each successive attack, it found me. Snow always finds a way.

Hanging like this meant the inside leg, pressing on the rock, went dead. Shuffling and squirming facilitated a semi-turn allowing circulation to return to my right leg as concurrently it ceased in the left leg. I had always maintained that the night spent hanging below the White Spider on the North Face of the Eiger had been my worst bivvy, but this would take some beating. I cursed. The elation earlier in the day following that magnificent piece of climbing had long since gone.

The sky on the eighth day was a perfect blue. We had to get off the face soon if we were to have any chance of reaching the summit. Brendan re-entered the gigantic, icy, open-book corner, his lungs sucking at the thin air, straining like over-filled balloons. The dull thud of his axes smashing the ice bounced out across the sea of featureless granite like a slow, erratic church bell.

By mid-morning we were established on the right wall of the groove, standing beneath an imposing overhang – fortunately, as the daily storm had landed early and masses of snow careered down the groove. Periodically the muffled voices of Mick and Steve floated up through the increasing storm. It was both good and bad that they hadn't decided to retreat. It was good, I thought, because hopefully they still had some of that potato powder left. It was bad because the rock on the over-hang I had now started to climb was extremely loose; stacked chunks moved, big enough to decapitate a man in a flash. Desperate not to disturb the rocks I decided to use a couple of aid points. My heart was in my mouth as I turned the final bulge, my whole body weight suspended by a blob of brass, half the size of a baked bean, wedged into a hairline crack.

The ground above looked deceptively easy but Brendan discovered powder overlaying smooth granite slabs, which were difficult to protect. Don't fall, I begged quietly, thick snowflakes starting to stick to my sunglasses.

'Okay safe,' yelled Brendan eventually, no more than a rope's length from the south-east ridge. We needed all our concen-tration for this final section of the route. It was surprisingly sustained and this was no place to slip. I praised Brendan for his bold effort and then climbed up steep, mixed ground until poised below the large, undisturbed cornice. I wielded my axe repeatedly at the giant meringue feature before crawling over onto the south side of the mountain, night almost upon us.

I woke with a start, the alarm bleeping in the pitch-black. I unzipped the tent, filled the pan with snow, sparked Metal Mickey into life and then, to the lullaby of the gurgling flame, glided back into sleep. An hour later we peered out into the world whilst drinking our first tea: thick mist, a brisk breeze and intermittent snow showers; not a good summit day.

We were horrified to learn that late the previous night, in the darkness, we had managed to erect our tent rather close to a cornice that overhung the 5,000 foot North Face; indeed, part of the tent was in space. We moved the tent and then settled back into our sleeping bags and put the stove back on.

'Dr Stuart's Tea?' asked Brendan.

'Sounds good.'

Over the past nine days we had grown close, becoming like a couple aware of each other's likes and dislikes, tolerant of each other's eccentricities. Initially, I had detested this Dr Stuart's Tea that Brendan had insisted we bring, but it was growing on me and, more importantly, there was little else left. We had gas for three more days, a few tea bags, one meal of noodles, a couple of small packets of soup and a few cereal bars. We prayed that this bad weather wouldn't deter Mick and Steve from climbing up onto the ridge, for by now we had begun fantasising about their mashed potato as if we had been invited to lunch at Buckingham Palace.

'Bloody hell, I've just remembered it's my birthday today!' I glanced at my watch to confirm the fact.

'Happy Birthday mate,' said Brendan sitting up and rustling around in his navy blue stuff-sack.

'Thirty-one years old, Jesus, I feel like a hundred and seven.'

'Here you go.' Brendan passed over a handful of chocolate bars.

'Where are these from?'

'Oh just a few extras I threw in, there's three each.'

I couldn't believe his generosity. We had spent a long time at base camp weighing our rucksacks to ensure they were equal in weight and then he had put in six of these and never once complained. I unwrapped a bar and slowly nibbled at the chocolate, terrified of losing a crumb; it was like a scene from *Charlie and the Chocolate Factory*.

We spent the remainder of the afternoon inside the tent, philosophising, which seemed like a luxury after the daily grind of the North Face. Brendan rarely spoke about his work as a scientist in a research laboratory in Cambridge. If asked about his occupation his normal response was 'I sort of work in computers', a rather vague statement that painted a dreary picture and tended to stop people probing any further. But he explained a little more that afternoon. He was involved in multi-service networking for Olivetti; one of the projects was hoping to facilitate online sharing of surgical procedures among doctors throughout Europe. He spoke about the difficulty of working nine-to-five when in 'blue sky' research and the fact that sometimes he would work late into the evening if the creative juices started flowing. I knew from Kate, however, that he was addicted to the TV soap *Neighbours* and, certainly as a post-doctoral researcher in Buckingham, he would rush home for each new instalment and then return to work. He wondered how I had managed to get funding for my own PhD that I had started six months previously at Sheffield University. I explained that the scholarship had traditionally aimed to support researchers trying to solve geo-engineering problems associated with coal mining but that, more recently, following the anni-hilation of the coal industry, the remit had been widened to include sociolinguists like myself who were interested in recording and analysing the speech patterns of these communities.

At one point our conversation veered into literature as I asked Brendan what he thought of the Arundhati Roy novel he had been reading at base camp.

'Yes, *The God of Small Things*, well to be honest I didn't reckon much to it.'

'What do you mean?'

'Well . . .' He paused. 'It was really tedious. Nothing happens. Anyway what about your book?'

'*The Golden Gate* by Vikram Seth, I enjoyed it. It's extremely clever, the whole thing's written in verse.'

'What's it about?'

'It's set in San Francisco and it's about folk who are unlucky in love I guess.'

I shut my eyes, trying to forget about tomorrow and the fact that by then our food would be completely finished. I thought about Elaine, where she was and what she was up to. It seemed like a lifetime ago that I had seen her and I missed her terribly. I knew she was planning on taking a holiday with friends to the Isle of Lewis in the Outer Hebrides. I had never been myself, but I had heard about its wonderful, unspoilt white beaches and turquoise sea.

Outside, silence, except for the wind sharpening itself on the corner of the tent.

16

Checkmate

I felt strong the following morning, arrogantly so. I leant my knees against the snow, waiting for Brendan to emerge from the tent, tingling with excitement, eager to reach the summit. To the south, Nanda Devi soared into a cloudless, still, metallic-blue sky. To the north and east the earlier orange tidemark of dawn had receded to reveal row after row of unknown peaks stretching towards Tibet, like empty white seats in a vast concert hall.

Unroped, and with relatively light packs, we cramponed across a sheet of névé towards where we had smashed through the cornice two days earlier. Our summit looked deceptively close.

'I feel like I'm out for a trot in the park,' I said, regretting the haughty tone straight away.

Brendan appeared to be moving more slowly today.

'Do you want me to take a bit of your gear?' I asked.

'If you like.' He handed me the two water bottles and I stuffed them into my pack.

After an hour we were forced from the increasingly steep southern slope and back up towards the ridge itself where, because of the sensational exposure, we decided to tie-in to the rope. As Brendan climbed up I scanned down to the right, unable to see any trace of Mick and Steve. Where the hell were they? Brendan signalled for me to start and I took a few paces immediately below the ridge, then plunged my axes into the snow trying to reach the crest. Unexpectedly, a two-metre long section of the ridge snapped off at chest height, diving down the North Face and then smashing into smaller fragments before disappearing out of view. I froze rigid, a surge of adrenalin stabbing my chest. Sixty metres away, Brendan sat in a bucket seat, looking relaxed, a leg on either side of the ridge.

We moved at a snail's pace, delicately weaving our way up the fragile, twisting arête and disappearing into a thick, still mist. 1,000 feet higher, at the south summit, my initial enthusiasm had all but vanished and the earlier feeling of hunger had been replaced with a deeper, aching emptiness, as if my stomach were trying to wring itself out, desperate for nourishment.

'That's where Pete and Joe's route must come up,' I said, breathing heavily, pointing down the west face. Brendan nodded slowly.

I set off down towards the gap, known colloquially as 'the Horns of Changabang', where two, smooth, overhanging rock walls curved towards each other. I had to drag my legs through snow as heavy as flour to cross the gap. At its deepest, I sank up to my waist. As Brendan climbed down towards me I began visualising a great sequence of moves up the edge of the right-hand horn. The rock looked impeccable; at home, I thought, we would spend hours on summer evenings puzzling out different ways to the top of wonderfully shaped boulders like these.

We battled through deep snow up to an easier-angled arête that lead up to the corniced summit.

'Don't go any further,' I shouted to Brendan in the mist, framing him in the viewfinder of my tiny camera.

We've done it, I thought, and with tears of relief wetting my eyes I climbed up to join him.

'I'm really chuffed,' said Brendan as we shook hands.

Thick cloud cruelly denied us a view. 'We could be anywhere, we could be in Scotland,' I commented. 'We could be in the bloody Cairngorms.'

A moment later giant neighbours towered out of the sinking cloud.

'Wow, look at Nanda Devi. What a summit,' began Brendan.

'Amazing. That must be Dunagiri behind us.'

'Yes and look on the horizon, that's Kamet.'

We stood there for a few slow minutes, trying to digest the raw beauty of the scene, both of us silently acknowledging that in those precious moments we were somewhere very close to the inexplicable kernel of all our desires and ambitions. Now a veil of mist obscured the view and we set off down.

Once back up on the north summit, I started down the twisting arête we had to descend back to our tent 2,000 feet below.

'I've got to eat something,' I announced. I frantically searched the lid of my rucksack and, thank God, I found a small chocolate biscuit to share.

'Fantastic,' I cried, each crumb slowly melting on my tongue. 'What have we got left to eat down in the tent?'

'Not a lot. Two chocolate bars each and a packet of soup.'

'At least we've got plenty of gas for melting snow.'

I descended first, though going first or second hardly seemed to matter on such a steep, crenellated ridge. One mistake and it was all over. I stared to the left, down the North Face, and felt light-headed.

'Who in their right minds would want to climb up there?' I joked.

'There are some crazy people around, hey?' smiled Brendan.

'If I slip, remember to jump down the other side,' I remarked, hiding my fear. The South Face, although less steep, looked equally menacing; it was covered in overhanging ice-cliffs and gaping crevasses.

The long day was taking its toll. I found the concentration of having to perfectly place each foot mentally exhausting. Our progress was slowing. Place the axes once, then kick the left foot and then the right foot. Axes – left foot, right foot. Axes – left foot, right foot. When the rope came tight, I stamped out a small platform in the snow.

'It goes on a bit doesn't it,' said Brendan on arrival.

'Too fucking right,' I muttered through painful, cracked lips. I wanted this climb finished now.

Suddenly I heard voices. I looked around but nothing, only Brendan climbing steadily down below. I searched the lower part of the ridge. There. I could see something moving. A lone dot 1,000 feet below. Mick and Steve had followed us all the way up the North Face.

'Is that you Steve?' I bellowed. 'Steve is that you?'

'Yes.' Then after a pause, 'How are you?'

'Good. And you?'

'Fine.'

Yes, Yes, Yes. I knew they had surplus food.

'The boys have made it up.' I told Brendan when I arrived, quick of breath.

'Excellent news,' he beamed.

We threaded our way down the ridge, through a curtain of cloud, to the point where I had spotted Steve. Nobody. We glanced through the gash in the cornice where they had obviously emerged from the North Face.

'Hey, Andy, Brendan! Down here.' It was Mick, about 200 feet directly below us on the South Face. He sounded distressed.

They had exited the North Face at a slightly higher point than us and were traversing on the South Face when Steve lost his footing. Wet afternoon snow had collected between the points of his crampons and his feet shot from beneath him. He fell onto his side, sliding. Instinctively, he went to jab his ice axe into the slope, desperate to arrest the fall, but his enormous rucksack prevented him from rolling onto his chest and instead dragged him backwards. Steve zipped down the steepening face. Mick looked on in horror. He was too far below the ridge to jump down the opposite side and save them. Instead, he plunged his axe into the snow, braced himself, held the rope around his waist. He felt the spikes of his crampons begin to strain in the ice, his final point of contact. He saw a vision of his family.

'Ultimately, I crumpled to one side and came on to the axe. I felt just a token resistance as I was dragged down. My feelings were of total despair. All those promises to my wife and children.'

Mick catapulted through the air. He landed with a violent thud, tangled in ropes and unable to move, with blood running down his face. It was 5pm and the weather was deteriorating. Miraculously, Mick didn't seem to have broken any bones. He called out to Steve, who also lay in a web of ropes a few feet away. There was a silence and then Steve croaked, 'My ribs hurt, I don't feel too good.'

Personally, I couldn't help feeling envious of the spacious snow platform they had inadvertently landed on below us, so much grander than the one we had had to chop out for own tent. God knows what might have happened had they not landed on the ledge; the icy South Face disappeared below them for a further 5,000 feet. I also worried that, being out of reach, we wouldn't be able to scrounge some of their legendary mashed potato powder. But these very selfish thoughts were cut short by Steve, who was lying in the tent.

'I want a helicopter,' he demanded.

'I'm not sure they fly this high, Steve,' I called down.

'Venables got one to rescue him off Panch Chuli,' he shouted.

Mick looked forlorn standing outside the tent, but he assured us we could do nothing to help until the morning – Steve was not deteriorating – and so we returned to our tent for the last of the instant soup. Once inside, despite our fatigue, our minds were in a whirlwind. Exploring every avenue of escape, we concluded that everything hinged on the extent of Steve's injuries.

The following morning we traversed back to the crest until directly above the others then lowered a rope; the weather was worsening and we needed to move as fast as possible. Steve was suffering intense pain as he clawed his way up the fifty-five degree ice slope. Once reunited on the ridge we discussed the possible descent options. A helicopter was out of the question for, even if a pilot existed who was willing to fly to such a height, how would we contact them? We had no radio or telephone and if we left Steve here and descended what would he eat? It was an absurd suggestion that we dismissed at once. There were only two options available: the North Face or the South Face. Steve was eager to abseil back down the route we had just ascended; he wasn't sure he could walk and climb for a further three days, plus there was a lot of snow around. The rest of us were keener to descend the longer but much easier South Face – the descent we had considered during our acclimatising and reconnaissance – chiefly to avoid the relentless, debilitating spindrift avalanches and violent storms. Finally, we chose the South Face and rationalized our equipment so that we were an efficient four-man team. We discarded two of the ropes and a lot of the technical rock protection, such as friends and chocks, and convinced Steve to lighten his pack considerably. Much of this equipment had been given to us free of charge by sponsors anyhow. Brendan and I insisted that our stove was superior to the manufactured one that Mick and Steve had brought from the UK and so we left theirs behind. It started snowing now and the visibility disappeared. We deduced that Roger and Julie-Ann must have chosen to retreat because of the consistently poor weather.

Gaining the flat col between Changabang and Kalanka involved a couple of diagonal abseils and then some impressive churning through thigh-deep snow by Brendan, the rest of us following on. Food was the only word I thought of now, it bounced around my skull like a rubber ball, driving me insane. Steve was clearly suffering, but at least he was moving. At the col we agreed that it was too late to continue any further and pitched our tents. It was a large, relatively flat area and for the first time in a very long while we were able to untie from the ropes and sleep without a harness around our waists. Brendan and I lay in our tent, exhausted.

'Do you two want to come over for dinner?' hollered Mick.

We sat up with a start, frantically pulling on our boots and gloves, and then crunched across the snow. It was incredibly cramped in the tent, but warm enough and the thought of eating made me shake with anticipation. I had never felt hungry like this before. I let the first small spoonful of potato sit in my mouth a while; this was an unforgettable meal. When the food was finally finished the others suggested that I lick out the pan; now that was a birthday present!

If the climb had drawn Brendan and me closer, now the descent would draw the rest of us together, more than we could ever have imagined. In many respects intense relationships on a climb such as this are out of time and place and, despite the fact that we spent limited time together in Britain and knew each other in relatively superficial terms, an indefatigable trust thrived.

The next morning brought a biting wind. The simplest task took an eternity as I had to constantly stop and unfreeze my fingers; eventually I was forced to crawl inside the tent to pack my rucksack. The serious lack of calories over the preceding few days meant that my body had started to prioritise, principally looking after the major organs rather than pumping enough blood to the ends of my fingers and toes. Also, Brendan and I had spent the last four nights sleeping above 21,000 feet and we had the common symptoms of mild altitude sickness: pulses much faster than at sea level and intermittent headaches due to fluid retention on the brain.

We roped up and began our descent down an easy-angled glacial ramp, but before long the visibility vanished and it started snowing again. As we descended we had reason to feel confident; our bodies were drawing in the thicker air and Mick reckoned we had enough food to last another three days. I had memorised this side of the mountain from a photograph and knew that ultimately we needed to reach the edge of a lower, subsidiary glacial ramp below the South Face of Kalanka, from where a prominent spur between two couloirs led down to the Changabang Glacier. Afterwards, we would have to climb over two high cols, each over 6,000 metres, to reach our starting point below the North Face. Exiting via the serious Rishi Ganga Gorge was not a viable option as there would be no bridges across the river and the route had probably been washed away by the monsoon rains; to our knowledge, no one had been in there for twenty-five years. Brendan and I took it in turns to go out in front, wading through the snow; Mick and Steve were tied-in to the middle of the rope. I concentrated on navigating, using a compass to fix on points during slight clearings, and felt sure that we were on the correct route. My main concern was the relatively warm temperature as we descended into the mist, especially considering the copious quantities of snow lying everywhere, but we didn't have very far to go before exiting this shelf and heading down towards the Changabang Glacier.

Lines of blue-green seracs and crevasses restricted our route choice and we were channelled towards an abrupt, hundred-foot chimney of ice that dropped down to the lower glacial ramp. Despite the appalling visibility, we had negotiated the upper glacier successfully – no mean feat considering its complexity and extraordinary size. I placed an ice screw and abseiled down, the other three growing smaller above as I slid down the rope. In the distance I could hear snow slides rumbling; the sun was beginning to heat up the slopes above us, slopes that we couldn't actually see because of the dense layer of cloud enveloping us. I unclipped from the rope and yelled up for the next one to descend, deciding to move down the slope to a safer zone under a wall of ice to the right. I walked as if stepping over waist-high fences, lifting each leg out from the deep snow and punching it forward, balancing with my forearms. After just a few minutes I paused, exhausted. Suddenly, I was moving. The slope had turned into a smooth-flowing river. I felt weary after so many gruelling days, unable to fight the sensation. Wow, I'm being taken down hill. This is easy. This is like surfing. Abruptly, I snapped out of the daydream, feeling sick with fear. I tried to resist but the snow simply tugged harder at my legs. Soon I would be buried and the game over.

I knew a lot about avalanches, though I had never actually been struck by one before. I had spent a week in Chamonix the previous winter on an avalanche course specifically aimed at mountain guides working on skis. I could identify different layers in the snow-pack, recognise different snow-crystal structures and the strength of the bonds between the various layers. I remembered the graph the tutor projected on to the wall concerning the survival rates of victims buried in avalanches: the chances of survival diminish rapidly to fifty per cent in the first half-hour; after that the plotted line curved aggressively down towards zero.

I wanted to turn around to see if the others were still afloat but I couldn't, my thighs gripped solid by the snow. My heart thumped against my chest and my face blazed. Slowly the flow stopped and I scurried sideways as fast as I could, cowering under the ice-cliff. Steve, Mick and Brendan arrived and we sat on our rucksacks, shaken, in a quandary about what to do next.

'We could always spend a night here under this ice-cliff, we're reasonably well sheltered.' Mick had a valid point.

'I'm just worried that if the weather craps out we're going to be stuck up here with no food,' I offered.

'I must admit, it would be nice to get down,' Brendan said.

A small snow slide hissed past above, spraying us all with a fine white coating. Steve sat lopsided trying to alleviate the searing pain in his ribs. We decided to descend. We tied back in to the rope and Brendan set off, climbing horizontally at first, eager to pick out a good line.

'He reminds me of Dick Renshaw,' said Steve. From what I had heard about Dick Renshaw there were similarities: quiet, determined and tough, yet selfless, with a gentle manner and a disturbing modesty.

The weather lifted momentarily and we could see that the best way was actually straight down. Brendan climbed back towards us and then we all set off towards a more modestly angled snow slope. I went out into the front, thick snowflakes blowing in a freshening wind. I knew we couldn't be far away from the point where we needed to abseil down to the spur and couloirs that led to the Changabang Glacier. We reached a long, wide crevasse blocking our route; I skirted around it to the right. We furrowed through the snow, a group of physical wrecks. Suddenly I realised that we had dropped too far; it was imperative that we locate the precise spot from which to descend and avoid the enormous ice cliffs that we had identified in the photos of this face back at base camp.

Demoralising as it was, we turned around and crawled painfully back uphill. We passed the crevasse and this time turned to the right. After a further twenty minutes we were there. Thank God! With a bit of luck we had found the place, in spite of the foul weather; a flat area on the edge of a vast icefield. From here an abseil, perhaps two, would see us into an easy gully and then down onto the Changabang Glacier. Mick abseiled first and I followed.

'It's too steep,' Mick shouted just as I began. 'Too steep for Steve.'

Mick was right. Suddenly it became undercut, and a free-hanging abseil with broken ribs would have been dangerous. I climbed back out and Brendan volunteered to set up another anchor out to the right. He left his sack with us and declined our offer of a rope, preferring to solo as the angle was modest enough. We were all utterly exhausted by now. Brendan spent at least twenty minutes trying to get a screw in. There was a lot of névé but not much ice.

'I've got a solid one now,' he eventually shouted across to us.

'He does remind me of Dick Renshaw,' said Steve once again. 'We used to call him "the little angel". Always ready to do the job others didn't want to do.'

Seconds later a quiet noise came from above. Way up, an avalanche was released and then another and another. Three or four silent slides joining forces and rushing towards us. Time stood still. In a panic I began screaming and yelling.

'Brendan. Brendan. Brendan!'

For fuck's sake! I started to beat my axe into the slope up to the hilt and then clipped in. The whiteness took an eternity. Brendan saw it but had nothing with which to clip into the ice screw. No rope. No sling or karabiner. No second ice tool. Absolutely nothing. I turned away terrified. Eventually it came. So quietly and so softly it took Brendan away first, like a waterfall. But it did not stop. It raced towards us forcefully, unstoppable, like molten magma. Steve had an air of calm about him, no creases of anguish in his face; perhaps he knew that things of such magnitude were way beyond our control. I folded my shoulders together, like wings, open-mouthed in horror. It slowed as it hit the flat ground just in front of us, halting less than twenty feet away. I was paralysed. I started rocking my head, trying to control my breathing.

'Is Brendan okay?' I yelled down.

'It's fine down here,' I thought I heard Mick shout. I felt hopeful.

'Is Brendan with you?' I shouted again into the mist, desperate.

There was a long silence and then a roar, 'No!'

'Oh . . . Fucking hell, he's gone.' I screamed.

Darkness was not far away. I felt helpless, as if standing at the gates of hell. What if another avalanche struck? We would have to abseil from here now. I placed another ice screw, shaking with fear. Steve clipped in the rope and then I abseiled down towards Mick, the exposure was sensational. I was stunned at the size and steepness of the cliff we were descending down. It stretched for a further 300–400 feet below and then ran into steep snow slopes and rock steps for a further 2,000 feet down towards the glacier. There was no sign of Brendan.

Mick had been terrified by the tons of snow pouring over his head; it seemed to have lasted an eternity. Part of it had pummelled his shoulders and helmet; he had no idea that Brendan had been among it. As Steve abseiled towards us, Mick put his hand on my shoulder. Like me, Mick had never lost a friend during a climb. I was too shocked and too exhausted to cry. Brendan and I had been such a great team and we had overcome so many obstacles. I felt lost now. Mick took over the rest of the descent, organising the abseils. We stumbled down a steep snow slope on to a safe-looking rock ridge between the two giant couloirs and began erecting the tents using our headtorches. Steve offered to share my tent to comfort me, and I gladly accepted. All the while we shouted Brendan's name into the night, desperate to hear a reply. I knew he was dead.

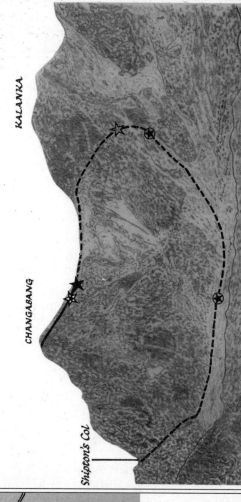

CHANGABANG South Face

— Andy Cave and Brendan Murphy reach the summit ridge from the North Face on the other side, go to the top and return to their camp

— - — Line of descent in 1997 by all four showing bivouacs ✪ and return over Shipton's Col

☆ Fowler and Sustad reach the ridge and have a 60m fall down the South Face camping where they stopped.

☆ Where Brendan was swept to his death by an avalanche

KALANKA

CHANGABANG

Shipton's Col

CHANGABANG North Face

Clyma Payne Variation

Camp locations: B6, B5, B4, A5, C3, A4, B3, A3, R2, C2, A2, B2, A1, B1, C1

1996

1997

A   J-A Clyma, R Payne, 26 May to upper icefield on 30 May 1997

B   A Cave, B Murphy 23 May to summit on 1 June 1997

M Fowler, S Sustad 25 May to NE Ridge on 1 June 1997

C   J-A Clyma, B Murphy, R Payne, J Perkins 9 June to central icefield on 11 June 1996

17

The long march

It had been a bitterly cold night and the soft early sun made the crystals flash like minute mirrors in the snow. We stood on the ridge by the tents, scanning the gigantic slopes below. Nothing. Above us a long line of deadly blue ice-cliffs hung, and above those the South Face of Kalanka, sagging with the weight of the recent snowfalls. We were all stunned by what had happened to our friend and we shouted his name until our throats rasped, our words echoing like the songs of small birds trapped in a huge glass cathedral.

My hand had started pounding in the night, as if being walloped by a blacksmith's hammer; its only consolation had been that it distracted me from constantly replaying the vision of Brendan being swept away. At first light I lifted the hand from my sleeping bag, shocked to see a black, swollen, blistered thumb.

'Have you had frostbite before?' Steve had asked softly, adjusting himself into a peculiar crouching position trying to minimise the pain.

'No, what about you?'

'Yes, a few times. I lost some toes,' he sighed, trying to sit up.

I presumed this was a result of his horrific Aconcagua epic, but didn't probe any further. 'What do you think to this? How bad do you reckon it is?'

'It doesn't look too bad. Try not to get it infected, though, and whatever you do, don't let it get cold again.'

Before heading down, Mick taped a cardboard box from a photographic film over the damaged thumb in order to protect it from excruciating and harmful knocks and then gave me a large pair of warm, soft mittens to use. I would have to rely on my left hand as much as possible. Inside Brendan's rucksack I found five exposed films, some gas and some tea bags. I put them into my rucksack and left the rest on the rock crest.

We chose to descend via the right-hand couloir because it appeared more certain of connecting to the glacier without any impasse; to make an error and have to climb back up such a huge face was not an option in our current physical state. Every so often Steve stopped and screwed up his face, a testimony to the agony he was suffering. I held my ice axe in my left hand whenever possible, desperate not to burst the black blister on my right thumb. Gazing down the Changabang Glacier towards the fabled Nanda Devi Sanctuary, I fantasised about a group of trekkers being camped there, people who could offer us food. But I knew that it was pointless and painful to allow my imagination to wander like that, as the whole area was out of bounds to any visitors. There was nobody down there, there never would be. So forget it.

On the glacier the sun had softened the snow to thick soup and we all agreed that trying to climb over Shipton Col that afternoon would be too exhausting. Instead we stopped by a small glacial pool, lit the stove and collapsed into the tents, searching for shade. Out of earshot, Steve told Mick he thought I would probably have to have my thumb amputated at the second joint.

Frostbite attacks fingers and toes first, which is what makes it so terrifying. We need our toes for balance when walking, our fingers for almost everything else we do. As a climber, and a climber passionate about rock climbing, frostbite is the stuff of nightmares. My first encounter with frostbite was in late July of 1987, at the Hunza Inn, a Hotel in Gilgit, northern Pakistan. It was my first time in the Himalayas and I was feeling quite proud of myself. I had quit my job at the pit a year earlier and, along with John Stevenson, had made the first ascent of a mountain named Tupopdan at the head of the Hunza Valley, close to the Tibetan border. Joe Simpson had been forced to turn back halfway to the summit because of the pain in his leg – damaged during his famous epic in Peru.[*] A

[*] As described in his book *Touching the Void* (Vintage, many editions, most recently 2004)

strongly built man entered the hotel, carrying and dragging an impressive array of bags and rucksacks which he duly dropped in front of the reception.

'I'm Andy,' I called, walking towards him, introducing myself.

'Dick,' he said, holding out his hand.

As we shook I quickly guessed who was standing opposite. The hand was big but parts of fingers were missing. I flinched but he just squeezed firmly. This was the formidable Dick Renshaw, the man who had suffered terrible frostbite during his ascent of Dunagiri with Joe Tasker.

We now sat not far from the giant South Face of Dunagiri, huddled around a crumpled, damp map, staring at the faded contour lines and trying to ascertain which of the various notches in the western skyline, thousands of feet above us, was the Shipton Col. Despite our exhausted state it was imperative that we maintained momentum and crossed over to the Rhamani Glacier tomorrow, and choosing the wrong route might lead to a dead end – in more ways than one – given our fragile condition and lack of food. As the day began to cool, we ate the last of the mashed potato and tried to sleep, praying that the weather remained settled for the next two days, and knowing that it meant the difference between living and dying.

I stared at my watch: 1 am. It was now precisely fourteen days after starting the climb. I eased my fleshless shoulders into the straps of the heavy rucksack and set off with the others across the glacier, thousands of gems sparkling in a fathomless black sky above. Underfoot, the crust refused to bear our weight and the jarring as each foot punched through into freezing deep snow made Steve wince and groan. But I found myself ignoring the sound of his pain. We had to get to that damn col before the sun destroyed the fabric of the snow altogether; otherwise we would be wallowing up to our waists. A huge painful boil had developed on my neck now, vying for attention with the cold sores and the dying thumb. We had just one gas canister left, one small packet of noodles and a couple of tea bags, yet our packs were still heavy as we had to carry enough ropes and hardware to abseil down the 800-foot vertical rock walls on the other side of the col. Mick had sprouted one too on the side of his face. Joking and laughter had long since ended, now it was simply us and the mountain.

The snow slope increased in angle and for a while it appeared more frozen, likely to support my body weight. After just a few paces, however, I disappeared up to my knees, the unexpected jolt forcing me to stop and fight for air. Battling in the dark I felt myself become less and less human; more animal-like. I faded into a peculiar trance, a mixture of total calm underpinned by aggressive determination, driving me on. Down below, Mick rested his head in the snow, utterly spent, then suddenly burst into life – as if afraid of never waking – taking ten more steps before bowing his head against the slope once again. Further below still, Steve swallowed his agony and dragged himself upwards. We had spent our whole lives searching out obstacles to overcome in the mountains, always pushing the boundaries of what we thought possible, and it had led to this scene of devastation. As dawn broke Nanda Devi slowly turned gold, but it was lost on me; beauty was a luxury I could no longer afford. It could have been a scene from *King Oedipus*:

> Where is there any beauty
> For me to see? Where loveliness
> Of sight or sound? Away!
> Lead me quickly away
> Out of this land. I am lost,
> Hated of Gods, no man so damned.*

To my left a featureless grey wall of granite appeared. Above, on the col itself, I saw a small tooth of rock burning in the sun. I climbed up, my heart quickening with anticipation. Is it the right place? I felt myself pull away from the others now, desperate to stare down the opposite side, to know if we had a viable escape route. Rhythmically I smashed my feet into the

*Sophocles, *King Oedipus*, in *The Theban Plays*, translated by E.F. Watling, London: Penguin, 1947, p. 63.

slope but was forced to stop every few paces, gasping at the freezing air, devouring it. I scoured the rock by the col for signs of previous explorers. Suddenly, I saw something flash and set off towards it. Once there my shoulders ached, begging to be free of the rucksack, but I couldn't wait and started smashing my left axe against the wall, slicing through mushrooms of snow and ice. It was an old line of fixed rope attached to pitons. I laughed aloud, dropping my rucksack into the softening snow and peering over, the huge Rhamani Glacier snaking out of view to the left. Straight ahead was the Bagini Col which we still had to cross to escape, although not before a lot of abseiling down ice-streaked walls and another night out somewhere. I wanted to yell my excitement to the others, but instead I slumped in the snow feeling desperately tired, hungry and dehydrated. Chips and egg, that's what I will have at base camp, I promised myself.

'We're sorted Mick, there's a bunch of pegs here. Doug Scott, Martin Boysen and co. must have put these in during the first ascent.'

'Brilliant.' He forced a weak smile of relief. 'Steve must be in a bad way, I've never seen him move so slowly.'

'He's a tough bastard,' I said, my throat croaking. I filled the pan with snow and lit Metal Mickey. Mick started organising the first abseil. When Steve arrived I noticed he had the two tiny teddy bears that his daughter had given to him stuffed into the pocket of his jacket. Mick had the wooden figure with him – 'Woody' – the toy he'd failed to post back to his young son. The protective powers of these talismans were being tested to the full. We drank tea quietly, too exhausted to speak.

I heard a yell. Steve had abseiled down to Mick and now it was my turn to go. I thought of Brendan, soothing myself, thinking how he would rest in one of the most remote and beautiful mountain valleys I had ever been in. Soon the tiny spring flowers would be pushing their way through the thinning snow, carpeting the edges of the Changabang Glacier. Before disappearing over the col, I turned around one last time and said goodbye.

I glided down, holding the rope in my left hand until I reached a steep step where I needed both hands to control my speed, the glacier gently swinging below. Somehow I knocked my thumb and an agonising pain burst up through my wrist into my forearm. I squeezed my eyes shut until the pulsing eased. We pulled the ropes slowly, careful to extract any twists. Between us we must have abseiled down thousands of metres of mountainside, but we could not become complacent; getting a rope stuck up here was not worth contemplating. Mick led the way, slithering down the intermittent stripe of ice stuck to the wall and reinforcing the old anchors that he found, ensuring that our abseil points were good before calling us down.

On the fifth and final abseil the frozen ropes stuttered through the belay device and my feet punctured the surface of the snow that led out to the glacier. Regrouping on the snow-covered moraine, we coiled the ropes and then stumbled towards a giant artery of glacial ice that stretched up towards the base of the Bagini Col. Bonington's first ascent crew must have camped somewhere around here; Tasker and Boardman had begun their legendary climb from this glacier too. Below, not too far away, was the sacred Nanda Devi Sanctuary. But we were too weak to ponder for long on the historical and spiritual importance of the place.

Delirious from the lack of food and liquid, I felt that I had become dislocated from reality; I was in an outdoor theatre, one part of me acting out this nightmare, another part voyeuristically watching. I threw my rucksack down on to the vast sheet of ice and sat down, my back in spasm from days of carrying the burdensome load. This would do for a campsite.

We put up the tents, flecks of yellow and blue in an icy wasteland, hemmed in by a formidable horseshoe of steep peaks. I tensed, slowly pulling off the mitten, not sure if the thumb had been refrozen during the long cold climb up to the col earlier in the day. A keen, rotting-fish smell drifted from the tattered cardboard. It felt squelchy.

'My thumb might be infected.'

'Start taking antibiotics as soon as you get back to base camp,' instructed Steve.

'You never appreciate how much you need a thumb until you lose use of it.'

I felt guilty, selfishly talking about my thumb and wondering about how it might affect my ability to rock climb in future. Brendan was dead and Steve was in horrific pain.

The flame of the stove burned brightly but it was approaching the end of its life. We drank tea and then lay in the tents snoozing, waiting silently for evening to approach so that we could justify eating our last meagre meal. I tried to install a new film into my camera but the battery had been drained by the persistently low temperatures. I contemplated throwing it away to save weight.

I wasn't aware of it, but Steve was quietly pleading with Mick to be left here, rather than follow us over the Bagini Col down towards our advanced base camp below the North Face. Once there we would have the gas and the food we had stashed before departing. Mick interpreted Steve's request as wanting to be left to die, for he could not survive here alone until a rescue team returned. Perhaps his condition was affecting his judgement. We were still one full day – probably two – away from base camp. There was the distinct possibility too that Roger and Julie had abandoned us, fearing the worst. But we would not leave Steve here, even if we had to drag him over the final pass.

On the fifteenth day breakfast was the simplest imaginable: one tea bag shared between three. Now everything was finished. I stuffed my sleeping-bag into my rucksack with my good hand, rolled up my Karrimat and then put on my harness, crampons and helmet. I took a few steps from the tent and tried to pee. An eggcupful of bright urine spluttered onto the ice before a horrid burning sensation flashed into my groin. Impatient, I put on the rucksack and turned around, staring at the final col. A cold breeze filled the tent, which I hadn't bothered to zip shut.

'Andy haven't you forgotten something?' It was funny, despite all the years living in Britain, Steve still sounded like an American, like a boy from Seattle.

'What do you mean?'

'Erm . . . your tent, yes?'

'I'm leaving it.'

'What?'

'It weighs too much. Anyhow if we don't make it over this col today we're all finished. We won't be needing tents.'

I turned away and started. After just a few yards I stopped to tighten my hip belt on the rucksack and turned around.

Mick and Steve had set off too; behind them the yellow tent rolled down the glacier, like a large balloon with too little helium. Brendan and I had first used the tent on Gasherbrum IV; who knows, maybe someday future explorers would find it wrapped around a rock on the banks of the gushing Rishi Ganga.

Mick seemed to find fresh new vigour on this final slope, moving determinedly between bouts of pushing his head into the snow slope and closing his eyes, as if he were saying to the Gods: 'I am not finished yet!' The sun heated up the snow so we sank in further, our boots as heavy as concrete. Yet we willed our bodies on and on.

A hundred feet below the col we hit a band of rock. I was desperately tired. Enough is enough, I begged. I dreamed of meeting Roger and Julie-Ann at the col, sat waiting for us with food and drink, offering to take our packs. But this was fanciful; they didn't know where we were and might even still be on the North Face.

We decided to tie-in to the rope, even though it looked relatively straightforward. I moved up, balancing my crampons on flakes of rock sprouting from the snow, belayed by Mick. It was comforting to have the rope: this was not a time for rushing; we had moved beyond exhaustion and were so close to surviving. At the col I leaned over my ice axe, lungs heaving, relieved to be finally finished with the uphill. I stared at the slope on the other side, disappointed that it wasn't gentler. The others arrived and we traversed to the right before entering a smooth furrow of hard snow-ice that rushed down to the Bagini Glacier. Fifteen days of effort, of total concentration, must have taken its toll because my crampons balled-up and suddenly I lost my footing. I shot off, careering on my chest down the steep icy runnel, towards the glacier. Pouncing onto my ice axe I pulled it to my shoulder, driving the blade into the ground, my arms shaking with the strain. I lay on the slope smouldering with adrenalin. I opened my eyes, I had stopped. I cursed the crampons. Steve was right, these damn things are lethal for this sort of climbing. My confidence shaken, I stood up and gingerly reversed down the remainder of the slope.

We lurched down over snow-covered moraine humps, delirious, dwarfed by the North Face that we had spent so long climbing up. Changabang had always had an air of unreality about it. Even in photographs it looked fake, as if it was part of a stage set, a ludicrous blade of granite and ice, a monolith; perhaps a bit too over the top for a real mountain, though nice to look at. And that's how it appeared now, its outline thickly delineated, contrasting against a dark blue sky, offering itself in 2-D only. The summit looked so ridiculously unattainable; I might as well have been staring at the moon.

Steve and Mick started arguing about the best route down and decided to split. Steve twisted his leg coming down a slope of soft snow masking hard ice; out of view, Mick slipped on a steep icy section and cut his hands. I followed first Steve and then Mick, grateful for their footsteps, pausing just above advanced base camp. Steve and Mick seemed to have recovered their temper and shook hands, congratulating each other and pointing up at the North Face. I looked away, my chest full of pain; for me there were no such feelings. All I could think of was how I would desperately miss Brendan and the opportunity to relive our achievement together over the coming years. Feeling deeply hollow I made my way down to the stash of food, alone.

Roger and Julie-Ann's tent had gone but I spotted some bags of food and gas. I grabbed a flapjack and started on it immediately, large dry lumps sticking in my throat. Mick and Steve arrived. We drank tea then boiled water to heat some vacuum-packed prepared meals; mine was beef stew and dumplings, pure ecstasy. A rush of energy surged to my temples, forcing me to close my eyes. We drank more tea, filled our bottles with juice and then started on fruitcake, the tank was bottomless.

'I'm going to carry on down to base camp,' I managed between mouthfuls, feeling bilious. The sun was still high in the sky.

'What, today?' Mick sounded surprised. 'I reckon it's best to sleep here and then descend in the morning.'

'I'm worried about my thumb, it really stinks. I could start the antibiotics tonight. I'm also anxious that Roger and Julie-Ann might leave, if they haven't already.'

'Are you not tired?'

'I feel better now I've eaten something.'

'You sure you'll be okay?' Steve sounded concerned.

'Yes honestly I feel fine, I know the route.'

After just two hours I was drained empty again. Every fifty yards I rested the base of my rucksack on rocks, trying to relieve my sore, stiff shoulders and neck, wondering how much bloody further it could be. I believed I was close to the junction of the two glaciers but as I passed a small glacial pool I realised I was nowhere near it. Demoralised, I slowed to a crawl. I felt dizzy, finding it hard to keep my balance, and eventually fell over. Damn. I should have stayed with the others.

When I finally reached the junction it was late, the light fading. As if hallucinating, I could picture myself walking, watching my other self stumble down the rubble-covered glacier. I watched my exhausted legs trying to move quickly, my feet trying to hold steady on the snow-covered moraine. I stopped at a huge slab of granite, resting my rucksack against a tall cairn that Brendan had built the previous year. I took a sip of water. Minutes later, when I tried to lift the rucksack back onto my shoulders, a pain shot across my chest. I put the rucksack back down. Across the peaks and troughs of the glacier I could make out base camp, normally about an hour away.

I jettisoned the rucksack and in slow motion, using the ski poles to stabilise my jellied limbs, edged over the first moraine peak. By the time I had reached the top, the chest pain had returned and I was scared. The rotting-fish smell of the festering frostbite forced me on; I had to get some medicine. I had to get there before they abandoned camp. I had to tell them what had happened.

After a full half-hour I had travelled a pitiful distance from the rucksack. I yelled into the approaching mist. There was no reply. It looked like it was about to snow. The thought of only making it halfway and sleeping out without a sleeping-bag, refreezing my hands and feet, frightened me enough to turn back. I crawled into my sleeping-bag on a slightly sloping, giant granite rock.

After almost twelve hours of wonderful sleep I shuffled out of the snow-covered sleeping-bag. I took a short piss, which turned the snow bright orange, and then stuffed the sleeping-bag into the rucksack with my good hand. I felt refreshed inside, but still I walked like a delirious junkie. In my head I rehearsed the words I would say to the others. I was convinced they would see me a long way off in my conspicuous red suit and would become suspicious at the sight of just one person.

As I wobbled down the final stretch to base camp I felt intoxicated by the spring air. A small red bird that had arrived with the new sunny temperatures sang and hopped at my side, guiding me back to the camp. The overnight ice had not yet melted from the edge of the stream and I stamped straight across, crunching it under my staggering, lead-heavy boots. I was so glad of the ski poles: they gave me dignity by allowing me to walk in a reasonably straight line. Once close enough I shouted a small hello and immediately Narinder and Vikram came out of the kitchen shelter, holding out their hands warmly but nervously. It had been eighteen long days. Narinder waited for my words, water welling in his eyes.

'Mick and Steve are coming,' I said. 'Brendan is dead.'

Roger and Julie-Ann had been close to Brendan, I walked over to their tent and sat down, my heart audibly drumming against my chest. They had just woken up and were still lying in their sleeping-bags.

'Brendan is dead,' I said, holding Roger's hand and then hugging Julie.

Listening to my words the pair looked shocked, their eyes full of sorrow, even though they had suspected something had gone seriously wrong after such delay. I sat on my rucksack and recounted our epic descent. Roger and Julie had only returned from an eventful eleven days on the face the previous morning, and it transpired that we had probably missed each other on the glacier by just a couple of hours. They had left food for us on the outside chance that we might descend that particular way. They themselves had reached the upper icefield, below the tongue, before becoming trapped in horrific weather for three days. Their tent had almost been destroyed by powder avalanches thundering down and they had had to abort one attempt to descend as the weather was simply too atrocious. Julie was suffering from a bronchial infection and their stove had stopped functioning properly. Finally they had escaped by abseiling back down over a further two days. The duo had lost weight; their cheeks were sunken and their faces had been whipped by the wind. They had planned to leave the following day, believing we might have attempted to descend via the Rishi Ganga Gorge, therefore exiting via Lata into an entirely different valley. Either that or we had perished on the mountain.

'Go and get a drink, sort yourself out a bit then we'll have a look at your finger.' Julie's voice was soft, gentle. I fought back the tears.

'Sahib.' Vikram held out a mug of chai and a bowl of porridge.

'Thanks Vikram.' I ate quickly and then stuck my head into the shelter. 'Maybe chips and egg for lunch?' I needed comfort food, and desperately desired a fragment of normality following the emotional whirlwind of the past few days.

'No problem sahib.'

I finished the tea then walked over to the tent sitting next to the prayer wall and took off my boots, discovering that the front halves of both my feet were numb in spite of looking perfectly fine: mild frostbite or a reaction to kicking my toes into bullet-hard ice day after day. Inside the tent I lay down. On top of Brendan's clothes was his Walkman. I reached for the headphones and flicked the play button. Oasis. I should have guessed, he seemed obsessed with this album. I turned on to my side and started to sob uncontrollably.

Later that evening, after supper, Mick, Steve and I opened a bottle of vodka. The others had retired to their tents; the porters would arrive in the morning and we would start the journey home. I had a birthday present from Elaine too, which I opened; it was a beautiful silver hip flask that had originally belonged to her father. It was full of sloe gin, which I passed around. Steve and Mick were insistent that we should pose with our tops off the following day and get some shots of our emaciated bodies; I didn't fancy it much, but couldn't particularly explain why.

I finished the last of the sloe gin and then sloshed another generous measure of vodka into my plastic mug before passing the bottle. We discussed Brendan's death and the fact that, if he had taken the rope or, indeed, a sling to clip in with, he may well have survived. It was human error, we concluded, even though deep down each of us knew that if the avalanche had struck just a few minutes earlier and travelled further to the right, we would all have been lost.

Despite the serious injury to his ribs, Steve talked enthusiastically about his trip in the autumn to the North Face of Jannu in Nepal, another great last problem of the Himalaya. He began bemoaning the fact that there are relatively few people in Britain who are actively pursuing difficult new Himalayan routes in alpine style. Mick and Steve mentioned a list of about a half-dozen people who they would be happy climbing with on such big committing ventures.

'You're on the list,' claimed Steve, looking straight at me from the other side of the kerosene lamp.

I tipped back my head, downing the entire mug of vodka.

'Take me off the list, I've finished.' I said standing up.

I said goodnight and then ducked under the tarpaulin sheet into the still, black night.

ASH

But the coals were murmuring of their mine,
   And moans down there
Of boys that slept wry sleep, and men
   Writhing for air.

And I saw white bones in the cinder-shard,
   Bones without number;
For many hearts with coal are charred
   And few remember.

Wilfred Owen, *The Miners*

18

The cost

The coal spluttered before settling back to a gentle sigh and
the yellow flames stretched up the chimney, blessing the room
with a generous glow. I was sat listening to eighty-one-year-
old Bill Wilkinson speak in short bursts about his remarkable
life as a coal miner.

'In 1959 the first mobile X-ray came to Monckton pit and
they sent for me,' he continued, his lungs working extra hard
with the effort. 'Afterwards they sent me to Sheffield for a
second opinion and when I got there they said "you haven't
got pneumoconiosis you've got bronchitis".

'Three years later the same thing happened, they said "you
haven't got pneumoconiosis you've got bronchitis". This
happened four times and then, when bronchitis became payable
(worthy of compensation), they said I "had" got pneumoconiosis. And I am twenty per cent pneumoconiosis, mind you,
that's if they tell you the truth, because there are some days I
can hardly breathe.'

I thanked Bill for sharing his tales with me and switched off
my tape recorder, pondering on what twenty per cent pneumoconiosis meant. I had only ever climbed above 8,000 metres
once, but it had been a humbling experience and even my
companion, the legendary Babu Sherpa, had been forced to let
his face rest in the snow, his lungs burning. Was every day like
that for Bill, or was it worse? I left him sat in his armchair by
the fire and walked the short distance back to my parents'
house, wondering if he would live long enough to see any
compensation for the industrial disease he was suffering.

A few weeks later my father and I went out for a drink in
the village, planning to meet up with my mother and her friends

in the local working men's club at the end of the night to celebrate her birthday. We started in The Ship, which hadn't changed
much over the years, apart from a fall in trade.

'How are you cock, alright?' asked the landlord.

'Fine Keith and you?' I replied.

'Not too bad love, I'm still taking the tablets, but I'm down
to forty a day now.' Keith said this with a straight face as he
pulled the pints, harking back to the sort of banter he would
have enjoyed every day when he worked at the pit.

We sat at a table and sipped our beer, the taproom almost
in darkness, just a few customers stood huddled against the
bar. In its heyday the whole place would have been rocking,
certainly on a Friday night. Perhaps it was a bit early. We
finished our drinks and walked up Midland Road to the snooker
club.

Despite his arthritic knees and poor eyesight my father annoyingly won the first two frames, easily. I bought another round
of drinks. He wasn't much of a drinker and I thought the effect
of the beer might give me the edge in the third frame. In
between shots we reminisced about the long evenings we had
spent with his step-father, Harry, playing on the small uneven
table years ago as Edith, my grandma, watched on, fag in hand.

My father was born two months after his own father was
killed underground in an accident. I told him that I'd recently
been talking to an old miner named Fred who had worked
with his father, who witnessed the accident and who took his
jacket after his death, continuing to wear it underground as a
reminder of their friendship. As children we were told that our
heavily pregnant grandma, Edith, first learnt of the tragedy via
a young police constable who arrived at the doorstep clutching
the pit-boots of her young husband, whereupon she fainted.
We knew little else of the accident. That night, halfway through
the third frame, my father began to open up, speaking about
the circumstances surrounding the death.

'They say my dad was a great snooker player you know.
That was his passion. In fact the day he was killed he'd actually swapped a shift with his brother Albert so that he could
attend an important match at The Bush to qualify for a regional
team.'

'I didn't know that.'

'Yes, he'd worked a double shift down in the Gloucesters' seam and was travelling back to the pit bottom when it happened. Do you want another pint?'

'Go on, yes.'

When my father returned from the bar another man had joined us, a short wiry fellow in his seventies.

'I was there love, when he was killed,' the man began. 'Arthur got in a tub to travel outbye and somebody had done a shit in it and so he got out and sat in the next tub, that was the front tub. It was illegal to ride in the front tub.'

'The steel rails we were travelling on must have been faulty because we derailed. One of the rails smashed through the front tub. It speared young Arthur through the thigh and stomach.' My father listened without flinching as the man described the details.

'He stood up and then passed out,' he explained. 'We got him out of the pit but he died later in hospital. It happened on a Monday and my dad wouldn't let us go to work for the rest of the week.'

I was shocked by the frankness of his description but maybe I had forgotten the openness, the straight-talking nature that this mining community can sometimes display towards subjects others might consider taboo; the account was certainly not meant to be in any way gratuitous.

'And my Uncle Albert, he was the union representative at Monckton, he never went down the pit no more. Did you know that?' my father asked, looking straight at me.

'No.' I said

'He never set foot down the pit again.'

My father had not lost his magic touch and cleared up from the blue to win the third frame. I couldn't use my frostbitten thumb as an excuse either, as it had now fully healed. As we left to walk down and meet my mother down in the club my father nodded towards another man.

'He was a Monckton man,' he said, once outside. 'But I can never remember his name. He got caught in the coalface cutting machine, I think. They reckon he was very lucky.'

It seemed everyone had a name suffixed with 'man' identifying either the particular pit they worked at or the job they performed: 'Monckton man', 'Grimey man', 'Houghton Main man'; 'machine man', 'winder man', 'belt man' – he knew this despite not always knowing their given names.

We walked past a row of boarded-up shops, then down the hill past where we used to wait for the pit paddy, opposite Les Parkes' butchers shop, which was also boarded-up. It was a beautifully clear night, and straight ahead stars shone brightly above the outline of the muckstack.

We entered the club just as the bingo was finishing, the smoke hanging under the low roof, a rush to the bar and a buzz about the place; so this is where people come on a Friday night.

'Hey up Andy lad, or rait Arth,' called my uncle Philip, acknowledging us with a wink and a slight nod of the head. He was only a small man but he had a deep thumping voice and a brashness of manner that could be intimidating to strangers. I got served and took a drink over to my mother, who was sat with her girlfriends; she had recently finished a degree in sociology and was hoping to find a job. I went and sat down next to Phil, from whom I had bought a slide projector. We had used it at the memorial slide show we organised for Brendan's friends and family a few months after we returned from Changabang.

'It works a treat Phil,' I said.

'It will do, it's nearly new. They're one of the best sort tha can get, them,' he said irrefutably.

He hadn't been using it much anyhow; since being made redundant from the pit he couldn't afford to pursue his passion for photography. He had used the money I had given him to pay for a year's insurance on his three-wheel car.

The turn tonight was a middle-aged man in a black silk shirt who had a decent voice; it appeared to be going down well.

'How long before tha gets thy pension then Phil?' my dad asked him.

'Bloody pension?' He pushed his chin towards his neck. 'My ashes will blowing about up on the muck-stack long before I get my pension, I'm telling thee.' He spoke as if it were the only true thing he knew.

My mother often mentioned her brother's wish for our Auntie Emma to scatter his ashes up on our local mountain.

*

Drinking a cup of tea the following morning, before leaving my parents' house, I gazed out towards the trees where the great climbing adventure had begun all those years ago. I was thirty-one now. Where had all the years gone? I said goodbye and drove home.

As I left the village I glanced back across the flat farmland towards the muckstack. The stack was the single physical reminder of the world of mining in the village now, and even that had been covered in grass and levelled so that it resembled a modest walker's peak rather than the big, blue, angular mountain of my childhood. The final bit of headgear – the giant number 2 winder – had been blown up a few years earlier. Many locals walked up to witness it, a few caught the occasion on video. Coal mining now only existed in stories and a few brief forms of speech: two former workmates chatting on Midland Road use the leave-taking 'Right then I'll see you on the tailgate', an acknowledgement of their shared past and shared fate; women reminiscing, wondering how they 'managed' during the strike; drunken men under tables in the pub pretending to pull the chocks in on the coalface.

The following year I was driving up the Llanberis Pass in North Wales, heading for the small rocks that nestle in the base of the valley. It was a beautiful clear day but cold – a touch of frost on the corner of the windscreen – and so before venturing out I sat inside the car with my rock-shoes above the dashboard, the heaters turned on full blast. Straight ahead was the magnificent Dinas Mot where Alistair and I had climbed during the strike. We had spoken recently, the first time for almost eighteen years; we had fallen out and then lost touch. He had married Deidre; they had two kids and lived in Canada. He worked in an office for a mining company. He remembered how hard I had been on him, that day in Edale, when he told me that he had decided to return to work before the end of the strike, mainly to save their relationship. I said, looking back, I realised that I was just a kid and hadn't suffered the pressures he had suffered. We laughed about that trip to Wales, The Diagonal, the night we became legends on the pool table in the Padarn. He had always hated the pit, he said, and spent every minute down there dreaming of climbing.

Out on the boulders the friction was superb, my fingers sticking to the textured stone like the lips of slow-kissing lovers. From the top of the highest boulder I could see the young mountain ash that Brendan's friends and family had planted in his memory, just the other side of the river.

I had returned from Changabang bewildered, my ultimate climb marred by the death of a good friend; a dream-turned-nightmare at a single stroke. Not only were my feet and hands damaged but I was emotionally cold, unable to love those around me in the way they deserved. Incapable of concentrating on my academic work I was forced to stop for six months. I became withdrawn and self-obsessed, despite being surrounded by the love and support of friends and family. Some climbers criticised us, said we had pushed ourselves too far and that we should have retreated in view of the appalling weather. Others understood better, arguing that taking risks is the very bedrock of true adventure.

Close friends asked me if I thought I would return to the mountains in light of this awful ordeal. I didn't have much choice, I had to return to the Alps to earn a living, to bolster the welcome but modest university scholarship I had been awarded. And this particular return to the mountains became a definite turning point. I showed my clients the natural splendour of the high mountains, taught them how to travel safely, took them to high and remote mountain refuges and climbed uncrowded peaks. Through the joyful eyes of my clients I learned the true meaning of adventure again, returning home with something of my former self restored, exorcised in part from some of the horror of those final days in India.

The sun was sinking and, for a moment, on the slopes of Snowdon, up behind Brendan's tree, countless rocks glinted like treasure. It didn't seem so long ago that we were climbing together on these cliffs, the weekend before departing for our attempt on Gasherbrum IV. I lamented the fact that we would never hear his voice again, but knew that in the crowded climbers' bars, in the gullies and along the ridges, the spirit of the man would never leave.

The sun had almost gone now and the skin on my fingertips felt sore but I didn't want to stop. I cherished this feeling of movement, of puzzling out sequences by placing the feet just right. For a moment I realised that it was the exact same feeling that I had experienced as a boy climbing trees. It was like gymnastics, chess and dance all tangled together. Somehow it seemed so quintessential, so perfect.

Acknowledgements

Many people have helped bring this book into being. Firstly, I must thank the men and women who generously shared their mining experiences with me; those roaring coal fires and endless cups of tea will always be remembered. In the recent past Bill Wilkinson, Tony Martin and my uncle Phil Eaton have all sadly passed away. I need to thank those I worked with at Grimethorpe Colliery in particular, for teaching me that humour and self-respect can triumph over adversity.

Over the years I have been fortunate enough to climb with many excellent companions, from the wind scoured summits of Patagonia to the quiet, magical forest of Fontainebleau. Some of these friends are mentioned in these pages, many are not; I hope the words I have chosen capture something of the essence of our memorable adventures together. Of course, I am indebted to Skip for introducing me to the Barnsley Mountaineering Club back in 1983 and to Mal Duff for introducing me to the Scottish winter experience. Sadly, in 1997, Mal suffered a heart attack on Mount Everest and died.

Lowe Alpine has supported me for many years now, and I owe special thanks to David Udberg, Clive Allen and Paula Davies. The British Mountaineering Council and the Mount Everest Foundation need a special mention for their generous financial support of many of our expeditions.

I am also indebted to Kate Morris, Joe Simpson and Ed Douglas for encouraging me to pick up the pen and write in the first place, and to my agent Euan Thorneycroft for his conviction in the project. My family have been extremely supportive of me writing the book too. I must thank all the people who have checked details in the text, in particular Andy Walker and Sally Zigmund who offered invaluable comments on an early draft of the book. Numerous people have kindly supplied photographs for the book, for which I am very grateful. My editor Tony Whittome has given precious advice and his enduring enthusiasm has helped lift my spirits on more than one occasion. James Nightingale has done a marvellous job in tracking down archival photographic material.

Finally, I would like to thank Elaine, my wife and best friend. She has provided invaluable comments on every chapter and shown unwavering support from start to finish.